CULTURAL COMPETENCE IN FORENSIC MENTAL HEALTH

CULTURAL COMPETENCE IN FORENSIC MENTAL HEALTH

A GUIDE FOR PSYCHIATRISTS, PSYCHOLOGISTS, AND ATTORNEYS

WEN-SHING TSENG, M.D.

DARYL MATTHEWS, M.D., PH.D.

TODD S. ELWYN, J.D., M.D.

Routledge
Taylor & Francis Group

NEW YORK AND LONDON

First published by Brunner-Routledge
This edition published 2012 by Routledge
711 Third Avenue, New York, NY 10017, USA
2 Park Square, Milton Park, Abingdon, Oxfordshire OX14 4RN

First issued in paperback 2016

Routledge is an imprint of the Taylor and Francis Group, an informa business

Library of Congress Cataloging-in-Publication Data

Tseng, Wen-Shing, 1935–
    Cultural competence in forensic mental health: a guide for psychiatrists, psychologists, and attorneys / Wen-Shing Tseng, Daryl Matthews, Todd S. Elwyn.
        p. ; cm.
    Includes bibliographical references and index.
    ISBN 0-415-94789-8 (alk. paper : hardback)
    1. Forensic psychiatry.   2. Cultural psychiatry.   3. Psychiatry, Transcultural.
I. Matthews, Daryl B.   II. Elwyn, Todd S.   III. Title.
    [DNLM: 1. Forensic Psychiatry.   2. Cultural Diversity.   3. Mental Disorders—ethnology.   W 740 T8815c 2004]
RA1151.T84 2004
614'. 15—dc22
                                                                                                    2003027253

ISBN 13: 978-1-138-96706-9 (pbk)
ISBN 13: 978-0-415-94789-3 (hbk)

CONTENTS

PREFACE

The idea that mental health services should be provided in a culturally competent manner is commonly accepted nowadays among scholars and clinicians in contemporary multiethnic societies around the world. An awareness of the importance of culturally competent forensic psychiatry has developed and is increasingly viewed as a requirement in a modern society emphasizing the basic human rights of people of diverse ethnic and cultural backgrounds. Despite this, few books address it in detail or at all. This book, *Cultural Competence in Forensic Mental Health*, intends to fill this vacuum for forensic psychiatrists, psychologists, and other mental health workers, as well as attorneys and judges.

This book is a joint collaboration of three authors—one of us (Tseng) is a specialist in cultural psychiatry, another (Matthews) is a specialist in forensic psychiatry, and the third (Elwyn) is a specialist in the law. By combining our expertise in these areas, we attempt to develop and create a new body of knowledge and experience addressing the cultural aspects of mental health. We have the advantage of sharing our clinical, forensic, and teaching work in the same department, and we have worked closely together to seek integration of the book as a whole.

The book comprises 10 chapters. In chapter 1 we provide an introduction to culture and mental health, define "culture," discuss how cultural factors influence legal systems and procedures, and list various ways culture will affect the practice of mental health. In chapter 2 we elaborate in detail the general aspects of performing culturally relevant forensic assessments. In chapter 3 we examine cultural considerations in the use of psychological measurement in forensic evaluation. In chapters 4 and 5 we review cultural aspects of various psychiatric disorders, crimes, and behavioral problems in a forensic context. In chapter 6 we examine the spectrum of forensic practice areas and discuss how to carry out culturally competent forensic evaluations in various types of criminal cases, civil matters, and family-court issues. We also address general aspects of working with clients, attorneys, and judges on cultural issues as well as the specialized subjects of assessment of competency, insanity, risk of violence, disability, determination, and child custody. In chapter 7 we focus on the legal regulation of mental health, addressing cultural aspects of civil commitment, maintenance of professional boundaries, and ethical issues. In chapter 8 we discuss cultural competence in the correctional setting. Then, in chapter 9 we undertake cultural analyses of several veral significantly interesting forensic cases including forensic cases in which we participated. Finally, in chapter 10 we provide a review, comments, and suggestions for future directions.

We aimed this book broadly at various disciplines involved in mental health and the law. This group includes forensic psychiatrists, forensic psychologists, and attorneys, as well as general psychiatrists, clinical psychologists, and social workers who work with persons accused of criminal charges or facing other legal encumbrances. Readers of different disciplines may find different degrees of interest in various chapters, but we organized the book as whole in such a way as to cover forensic mental health as widely as possible for comprehensiveness.

We balanced the subject matter between forensic application and cultural theory, and we derived the material primarily from the medicolegal situation in the United States, but, as much as possible, we also refer to various cultural settings around the world. We attempt to examine the subjects broadly from a more universal as well as a cross-cultural perspective. We hope the book will be useful not only for readers from the United States but also for international forensic psychiatrists and scholars.

In many chapters we inserted several case vignettes for illustration of the issues elaborated in the text. Although some of the vignettes are hypothetical, most are based on actual cases with some modification for purposes of confidentiality. In the cases, honorific terms such as "Mr." or "Mrs." are used for humanistic as well cultural purposes. The opinions or suggestions we present throughout this book reflect our professional opinions that we hold at the present time. We surely have no claims to absolute accuracy or thoroughness. We expect our views will differ from other experienced writers in our disciplines. We express our views with the hope that they will stimulate the readers to explore their own.

Cultural forensic psychiatry is a newly developing field. Because of this, many questions may be raised that as yet can be answered only in a limited way. Even where empirical evidence is not strong, we attempt to provide guidance and advice based on our experience. Our main goal is to stimulate the awareness that there is a great need to be culturally concerned in practicing forensic psychiatry, psychology, or law.

We would like to express our thanks to many persons who assisted us in working on this book project. Dr. Keisuke Ebata, former director of the Tokyo Metropolitan Comprehensive Mental Health Center, helped us search for forensic publications from Japan and understand the pattern of forensic psychiatric practice in Japan. Professors Li Congpei and Fang Ming-Zhao from the Institute of Mental Health, Peking University, provided us the forensic psychiatric publication from China and clarified for us the questions regarding the practice of forensic psychiatry in China. From our department, psychiatric residents Shae Lock, MD, Tina R. Melendrez-Chu, MD, and Walid Pedro Eweis, MD, contributed case vignettes for illustration in the book; Malina Kaulukukui, LSW, an expert on Hawaiian culture, provided her opinion on a Hawaiian case. Lisa Anne Matsumoto, MLIS, and Cheryl K. C. Andaya, MA, assisted us in literature search, and Christine Yoshida assisted us in checking the list of references and index. Ms. Kathy Luter Reimers, through her dedication, provided helpful English editing. Everyone's valuable contributions to this book are greatly appreciated. We also would like to express our gratitude to our wives Jing Hsu, MD, Esther Solomon, and Kim Tran Elwyn for their unconditional support and encouragement to us while we worked on this book.

Finally, we are grateful to the publisher, Brunner-Routledge, for its commitment in undertaking the timely and needed publication of this book, and we are particularly thankful to executive editor George P. Zimmar, Ph.D., for his vision and assistance in supporting the work and to associate editor Ms. Shannon Vargo for her helpful guidance in improving the manuscript. We hope that this book will promote cultural competence in forensic mental health and relevant cultural consideration in the practice of law.

Wen-Shing Tseng, M.D.
Daryl Matthews, M.D., Ph.D.
Todd S. Elwyn, J.D., M.D.
Honolulu, Hawaii

ABOUT THE AUTHORS

Wen-Shing Tseng, M.D., Daryl Matthews, M.D., Ph.D., and Todd S. Elwyn, J.D., M.D.

Wen-Shing Tseng, M.D., is a professor of psychiatry at the University of Hawaii School of Medicine. Born in Taiwan in 1935, he was trained in psychiatry at the National Taiwan University in Taipei and later at the Massachusetts Mental Health Center of Harvard Medical School in Boston. He was a research fellow in culture and mental health at the East-West Center from 1970 to 1971, before being recruited as a faculty member of the University of Hawaii School of Medicine, where he became a professor in 1976, and served as training director for the psychiatric residency training program between 1975 and 1982.

As a consultant to the World Health Organization and for teaching and research projects, he has traveled extensively to many countries in Asia and the Pacific, including China, Japan, Singapore, Malaysia, Fiji, and Micronesia. He served as chairman of the Transcultural Psychiatry Section of the World Psychiatric Association for two terms, from 1983 to 1993. In that capacity, he developed a wide network of colleagues around the world in the field of cultural psychiatry. Relating to the subject of culture and mental health, he has coordinated numerous international conferences in Honolulu, Beijing, Tokyo, and Budapest. He has held the position of guest professor of the Institute of Mental Health, Peking University, since 1987.

He has conducted numerous research projects, mainly relating to the cultural aspects of assessment of psychopathology, child development, family relations, epidemic mental disorders, culture-related specific psychiatric syndromes, folk healing, and psychotherapy. The studies resulted in the publication of more than 80 articles in scientific journals and book chapters.

He has edited/coedited the books: *People and Cultures of Hawaii: A Psychocultural Profile* (University Press of Hawaii, 1980), *Chinese Culture and Mental Health* (Academic Press, 1985), *Suicidal Behaviour in the Asia-Pacific Region* (Singapore University Press, 1992), *Chinese Societies and Mental Health* (Oxford University Press, 1995), *Migration and Adjustment* (in Japanese) (Nihon Hyoronsha, 1996), *Chinese Mind and Psychotherapy* (in Chinese) (Beijing Medical University Press, 1997), *Culture and Psychopathology* (Brunner/Mazel, 1997), *Culture and Psychotherapy* (American Psychiatric Press, 2001), *Asian Culture and Psychotherapy: Implication for East and West* (University of Hawaii Press, 2004) and *Cultural Competence in Clinical Psychiatry* (American Psychiatric Publishing Inc, 2004).

He has authored the books: *Culture, Mind and Therapy: Introduction to Cultural Psychiatry* (Brunner/Mazel, 1981), *Culture and Family: Problems and Therapy* (Haworth Press, 1991), *Psychotherapy: Theory and Analysis* (in Chinese) (Beijing Medical University Press, 1994), *Handbook of Cultural Psychiatry* (Academic Press, 2001), *Clinician's Guide to Cultural Psychiatry* (Academic Press, 2003), and *Modern Psychiatry, 2nd Edition* (in Chinese) (Buffalo Book Co., 2003). For the *Handbook of Cultural Psychiatry*, he has received "Creative Scholarship Award" of 2003 from the Society of the Study of Psychiatry and Culture.

He is a distinguished life fellow of the American Psychiatric Association (APA) and the member of the American Academy of Psychiatry and the Law (APPL). He organized a course on "Clinical Application of Cultural Psychiatry" for the APA meeting (2003, 2004) and a panel on "Cultural Competence in the Practice of Forensic Psychiatry" for the APPL meeting (2003).

Presently, he is a member of the Board of Directors of the Society for the Study of Psychiatry and Culture and honorable advisor of the Transcultural Psychiatry Section of the World Psychiatric Association. Because of his research, publications, and experience, he has gained a reputation as an expert in cultural psychiatry, at both the national and international levels.

Daryl Matthews, M.D., Ph.D. is a professor of psychiatry and Director of the Forensic Psychiatry Program at the University of Hawaii School of Medicine.

He earned his M.D. degree and Ph.D. degree in sociology from Johns Hopkins University. He completed his residency training in psychiatry at the Johns Hopkins Hospital, a fellowship in forensic psychiatry at the University of Virginia, and is board-certified in general and forensic psychiatry. He has served on the faculties of Johns Hopkins, Boston University, the University of Virginia, and was formerly Professor and Director of Education in the Department of Psychiatry at the University of Arkansas for Medical Sciences.

He has been Visiting Professor of Psychiatry at the University of Madrid and an instructor at the U. S. Department of Justice National Advocacy Center. He maintains a small nationwide consulting practice in forensic psychiatry as a member of Park Dietz and Associates.

An award-winning psychiatric educator, Dr. Matthews is a member of the American Board of Psychiatry and Neurology, Forensic Certification Committee and serves on the editorial board of the PRITE Exam, the world's most widely-used standardized test of professional competence in psychiatry. He has chaired both the Education Committee and the Ethics Committee of the American Academy of Psychiatry and the Law (AAPL). He also has been a Councilor of AAPL and serves as AAPL liaison with the Spanish Society of Legal Psychiatry. He is Past President of the Arkansas Psychiatric Society, a Distinguished Fellow of the American Psychiatric Association, and a Member of the American College of Psychiatrists. He serves on the APA Judicial Action Committee and he has consulted and testified nationwide in scores of major civil and criminal cases, the majority of which involve violent behavior and/or sex offenses.

Todd S. Elwyn, J.D., M.D. is a Clinical Instructor and Fellow in Forensic Psychiatry at the University of Hawaii School of Medicine. He completed law school at the University of Washington and practiced law at a large firm in Ohio before attending medical school at the University of Michigan. He completed general psychiatry residency training and a fellowship in child and adolescent psychiatry at the University of Hawaii. As a Fulbright Graduate Research Fellow and as a Japanese Ministry of Education Scholar he has conducted cross-cultural research in Japan, and published in the areas of cultural psychiatry and cross-cultural medical ethics and law. During residency training he was awarded several national honors, including the Rappeport Fellowship by the American Academy of Psychiatry and the Law, the Laughlin Fellowship by the American College of Psychiatrists, and the Ginsberg Fellowship by the Group for the Advancement of Psychiatry.

LIST OF CASES

1

Introduction: Culture and Forensic Psychiatry

Forensic psychiatry has only recently developed insight into the importance of providing culturally competent forensic mental health services. Cultural competence has become a requirement of our modern society, as it is in any advanced society that emphasizes basic human rights and gears itself toward meeting the needs of an ethnically and culturally diverse people. The United States, like many other nations, is becoming increasingly multiethnic and polycultural. Providing culturally relevant and effective forensic services has become a fundamental expectation and an essential professional task. Examining the cultural dimensions of the mind and behavior will enable us to understand the nature of actions and the motives for them in a more comprehensive way. This, in turn, will assist us in providing more suitable and meaningful opinions to be used in the making of legal decisions.

One accessible source of information concerning how culture interacts with law comes from the various world legal systems. However, as astutely pointed out by Appelbaum (2002, p. 462), forensic psychiatry to date has been sadly bereft of cross-cultural perspectives. In part, this neglect may relate to a perception that the differences among legal systems make the study of forensic issues in other countries—much less other cultures—unlikely to yield practical benefits. Such

1

solipsism tends to blind us to the reality that there are other, different, and sometimes better ways of responding to the issues that form the core of forensic practice from what we use every day. Expanding forensic psychiatric practice to include such cultural considerations is a new professional challenge.

WHAT IS CULTURE?

Culture, Race, Ethnicity, and Minority

To explore the subject of cultural competency in forensic psychiatry, we must first clarify the concept of *culture*. Also, we must distinguish several related terms that are used to describe sociocultural issues, such as *race, ethnicity*, and *minority*.

Culture. The term *culture* (kultur, in German) was originally coined by a German scholar in the late 18th century to refer to the achievements of civilization. Later, British scholars used the English word *culture* to define it as the complex whole that includes knowledge, beliefs, art, laws, morals, customs, and any other capabilities and habits acquired by man as a member of society.

Since then, scholars of behavioral science have defined culture in various ways (Kottak, 1999). After analyzing several hundred definitions and statements about culture made by anthropologists and others, U.S. anthropologists Kroeber and Kluckhohn (1952) summarized the formulated concept often used by contemporary behavioral scientists as follows: "Culture consists of patterns, explicit and implicit, of and for behavior acquired and transmitted by symbols, constituting the distinctive achievement of human groups, including their embodiments in artifacts; the essential core of culture consists of traditional ideas and especially their attached values; culture systems may, on the one hand, be considered as products of action, on the other as conditioning elements of further action."

In simpler words, Barnouw (1963) stated, "A culture is the way of life of a group of people, the configuration of all of the more or less stereotyped patterns of learned behavior which are handed down from one generation to the next through the means of language and imitation."

Race. The term *race* means something quite different from *culture.* In the past, *race* has been used to refer to a group of people that is characterized by certain common physical features, such as color of skin, eyes, and hair; facial or body features; or physical size. On the basis of these attributes researchers distinguish one group from other groups. Anthropologists have used the term *geographic race* to indicate a human population that has inhabited a continental landmass or an island chain sufficiently long enough to have developed its own distinctive genetic composition as compared with those of other geographic populations (Hoebel, 1972). However, with improvements in genetic study, analysis of DNA among members of different races has shown that there are greater variations within racial groups than between them. Thus, races are socially and culturally constructed categories that may have little to do with actual biological differences. They are the products of historical and contemporary social, economic, educational, and political circumstances (American Anthropological Association, 1999).

Ethnicity. Ethnicity refers to social groups that distinguish themselves from other groups by a common historical path, their behavior norms, and their own group identities. The members of an ethnic group are affiliated and may share a common language, religion, culture, racial background, or other characteristics that make them identifiable within their own group. Thus, culture refers to manifested characteristic behavior patterns and value systems whereas ethnicity refers to a group of people that shares a common cultural feature or root culture.

Minority. A minority is a relatively smaller group that is identified against the majority group in the society. Strictly speaking, minority groups may not necessarily suffer from social disadvantages. In fact, some minorities have more privileges and enjoy more social achievements than the majority. However, in most cases, minority peoples encounter mistreatment by the majority and suffer from discrimination and social disadvantage. Thus, minority peoples often hold resentment toward the majority, whether openly expressed or unspoken. As we already mentioned, the concept of "minority" is a social one, often related to economic or occupational factors that may or may not be related to matters of ethnicity or culture. The term should be used differently and precisely and not be confused with the term or concept of culture.

Implications of Culture in the Legal System

Moving beyond conceptual clarification, we must next recognize the significant clinical implications and applications of culture (Tseng, 2001, p. 26). Several issues in the practice of forensic psychiatry require special attention with regard to culture. They are as follows:

1. Culture refers to the unique behavioral patterns and lifestyles shared by a group of people, which distinguishes that group from others.
2. Culture is characterized by a set of views, beliefs, values, and attitudes toward things in life. Culture may be expressed in various ways that regulate life—through rituals, customs, etiquette, taboos, or laws. It is manifested in daily life and reflected in cultural products, such as common sayings, legends, drama, art, philosophical thought, religions, and political and legal systems.
3. In practice the identification and determination of the cultural background of an individual can be problematic, because the impact of culture can be conscious or unconscious (in other words the person or his or her family may or may not be aware of it) culture is abstract and can be amorphous, culture is not static over time and is often in flux (i.e., subject to cultural change over time and through different generations), and culture's impact on subgroups of people (even those living within the same society) may vary greatly with subcultures.
4. Conceptually, the anthropological term *culture* is different from the socially defined terms *race, ethnicity,* and *minority.* However, for the sake of convenience, a cultural system is often identified by socially related terms (nation, ethnic or racial group, or geographic area), referring to an identified cultural group (such as Japanese culture, Latino culture, European culture, etc.).
5. Language is one of the instruments through which culture is transmitted and expressed. Through language, culture communicates not only semantic meanings but also underlying conceptions, values, and attitudes, which can be very **different** among different cultural systems. Comprehending another person's culture through his or

her language can therefore be quite challenging, particularly when that language is very different from our own.

6. Culture exists as a recognizable social or institutional pattern at the macroscopic level and as individual behavior and reactions at the microscopic level. The individual may be consciously aware of it, or it may be operating at an unconscious level. Culture includes concepts, attitudes, and judgments related to right or wrong.

7. Although an individual may have trouble explicitly recognizing and identifying his or her own cultural system, most people do identify with their own ethnic or racial groups. Ethnic or racial identity refers to the psychological way in which a person identifies with his or her own ethnic or racial background, as well as how one feels about his or her own ethnicity or race. People tend to develop certain views and attitudes about the ethnicity or race of other people. This is called "ethnic or racial transference" because it is derived from a projected view about others, which may be stereotyped or biased.

8. Culture is an organized system of knowledge and beliefs that allows a group to structure its experiences and choose among alternatives. Culture guides and motivates behavior and largely determines the course of our lives. As an extension of this, culture defines good or bad and the punishment that is deserved for wrong behavior.

9. Each society, based on its history, social background, and cultural system, develops certain regulations, including particular etiquette, customs, ethics, rules, and a political administration to regulate people's lives. A legal system is among these social regulatory systems and is developed primarily to judge wrong from right and to decide the nature and severity of punishment for wrongful doings. In other words the legal system is a part of the larger sociocultural system.

10. All the persons involved in the legal process, including the judge, prosecutor, attorney, experts and other witnesses, jury, and parties in the case, as human beings, will be influenced by their own perceptions, attitudes, beliefs, and value systems (the elements of culture) in their thinking, interacting with others, and making decisions. This includes the transcultural understanding of others, the phenomena of

ethnic or racial bias and transference (i.e., the displacement of projected cognitive and emotional bias or ignorance of other people's ethnic or racial backgrounds). The legal process operates within a legal culture as a whole. The legal culture is based on certain assumptions and beliefs about how legal procedures should proceed, with particular rules and a distinctive spirit. At the same time, the legal process is significantly, whether explicitly or inexplicitly, influenced by the cultural backgrounds of the parties involved.

LAW IN VARIOUS CULTURES

Differences in Roles and Functions of Law in Society

Law as the Major Force for Social Regulation

From the social and anthropological perspectives, there are various ways by which a society can enforce and maintain social regulation. Customs, etiquette, taboos, and moral principles that define socially emphasized and culturally valued conceptions and practices about "proper human relationships" are some examples; religion, ethics, and law are others. Society may be regulated on a practical level through political power and administrative force. The extent to which different cultures regard law as the major force for maintaining order varies greatly. In many developing societies, particularly in agriculture-oriented ones, collectivism is emphasized. Etiquette, customs, taboos, unspoken social rules, or recognized custom-based laws may be more important than a formal (written) legal system. Societal members share a common background so informal mechanisms can be relied on for resolving disputes. Making explicit through law such things as, for example, at what point an agreement constitutes a binding contract may be viewed as less important. In contrast, in most developed urban societies, particularly industrialized societies that emphasize the individual, explicitly defined social rules and laws are the key forces for keeping order. Individuals in such societies often come from different backgrounds with widely varied customs. The law provides a set of rules that persons from various cultures can look to for guidance on how to behave.

Cultural Concepts of "Wrongness"

Perhaps it is human nature to want to believe that right and wrong are apparent, explicit, and easily defined. However, in real life they are not always so easy to distinguish, and there are many gray areas in between. This is true even in the legal system because right and wrong are subject to social and cultural definitions and concepts. Some illustrative examples of topics for which right and wrong are currently debated in society include whether it is wrong to artificially terminate the life of a fetus, to have physician-assisted suicide, or to punish severely wrong behavior with death.

A nation's legal position on such issues may shift over time and vary in association with changes in culture. For example, in some societies, an intimate relationship between persons of the same gender is still considered wrongful behavior deserving of punishment. In the United States sexual intercourse between homosexual partners was viewed as wrong and criminal in some states but not in others, until recently, when the U.S. Supreme Court ruled that such private matters should not be subject to and punished by law (*Lawrence v. Texas*, 2003).

Differences in Punishment Practices

The customs and practices of a society that define right from wrong may be codified into law and enforced by legal sanctions or may be handled by informal extralegal methods. Although our primary concern here is the various legal punishments, we should note that the informal means a society uses are also very important and revealing of cultural attitudes and beliefs. Societal changes are often marked by these two approaches coming into conflict. For example, in India we can observe the extralegal practice of "bride burning," where women with a dowry deemed insufficient by the groom's family are at risk of being burned by in-laws, persisting despite legal prohibitions against it. At times, social practices and the thinking behind them may change at a slower rate than legal changes, although sometimes the society changes and the law struggles to catch up.

Legal systems establish, in a public way, how wrongful behavior will be penalized. However, legal systems differ in their operating procedures, in how they define right and wrong, and in the choice of punishments that may be administered. The flouting of public morality in Iran, for example, has been punished under Islamic law by public floggings ("Row Over Public Floggings," 2001). In the case of murder, Islamic jurisprudence offers the interesting solution of allowing the families of victims to decide whether to accept monetary compensation from the perpetrator for the death of a loved one or to demand the perpetrator's execution (Chaleby, 2001). In the United States the contours of punishment have been shaped by the prohibition against "cruel and unusual punishments" in the Eighth Amendment to the Constitution. Such punishments as emboweling while alive, beheading, public dissecting, burning alive, or drawing and quartering were proscribed from early on (Radin, 1978; *Wilkerson v. Utah*, 1878, p. 135).

The death penalty illustrates how the severity of punishment for wrongful behavior varies greatly both within and among cultures. In the United States federal law provides for the death penalty, but state laws vary. At present, 12 of the 50 states do not have a death penalty. At the international level Neapolitan (2001) examined and cross-tabulated statistics on the application of capital punishment by geographic region. In Arab regions 94.4% of societies have capital punishment, 86.7% in northern Europe (formerly the USSR), 65.4% in Asian regions, 61.9% in sub-Saharan Africa, 37.9% in Latin America, and 0% in eastern and western European regions.

Among Western societies it is well-known that the legal system of Portugal takes a relatively lenient attitude toward punishment. Indeed, Portugal was one of the first countries in the world to abolish capital punishment, doing so in the 1870s. As a result, Portugal developed one of the highest rates of imprisonment among European countries. Moreover, the longest prison sentence that can be applied is 25 years, and, in many cases, it is possible for the inmate to be released conditionally after serving half of the sentence (Gonçalves, 1997). In other countries without capital punishment, life in prison without parole is a common alternative to a death sentence. In contrast, in some societies that practice capital punishment, any severe criminal offense, rather than just murder, may result in a sentence of death.

Kury and Ferdinand (1999) pointed out that the punitive nature of punishment is subject to public opinion and changes over time, particularly when there is a change in social conditions. In recent years there has been growing support for punitivity among broad segments of the population, not only in

European societies but also in the United States, where capital punishment is being used more and more frequently. At the same time, critics of the death penalty continue to publicize its systemic problems and argue that its use constitutes "cruel and unusual" punishment. Recent court victories, such as the limiting of capital punishment to defendants who are not mentally retarded (*Atkins v. Virginia*, 2002), may signal a momentum away from its use, but this remains to be seen.

Variations in Legal Systems

Historical Evolution

Legal systems, as they are currently conceptualized and recognized, represent a gradual evolution through the course of human civilization. In ancient Egypt, for example, there was no separate code of law governing the people's behavior. Law and government were provided by the Egyptian religion. Religion was conceived and translated into life by human beings, inspired to exercise their highest spiritual capacities. The human conscience was thought to be at the heart of the religious experience (Edmunds, 1959).

Some time later the law was written down into a code, but this code was mainly for the common people to follow. A Babylonian king codified Babylonian law and made it accessible to the people, but the code contained no laws for the king and very few for priests. Provisions in this code addressed the laws of witchcraft; the duties and privileges of royal servants; tenure, rents, and cultivated lands; deposits and prosecution for debt; family law; and so on, based on the principle "Law takes actual life as its starting point." The code also distinguished and provided for differential punishment based on the various social classes existing at that time. The same pattern was followed in India, where every Hindu belongs to the caste of his parents. The earliest codes of law incorporated the caste system. Later, they were superseded by the Laws of Manu, which interwove into the fabric of Hindu life but still allowed different treatment for people of different castes.

Feinerman (1994, pp. 100–101) pointed out that China, among its other historical features, can lay claim to one of the world's longest unbroken legal traditions. Documentation of early law, on bronze vessels and bamboo strips, stretches back almost three millennia. Throughout Chinese history, the essential moral norms of Confucian thought struggled to establish their superiority to the bureaucratic mechanisms of legalism. As a result, a long process of synthesis combined these two strands to create a unique Chinese conception of legality. By these examples we can see that law is always the product of a society's culture.

World Legal Systems

To classify the legal systems used by different political entities around the world, for the purposes of study and discussion, we have followed the classification framework of the University of Ottawa, Faculty of Law (*World Legal Systems*, 2002). Legal systems can be characterized as falling within one of the following six categories: civil law, common law, customary law, Islamic law, Talmudic law, or mixed law. Islamic law and Talmudic law are obviously systems based in religious law. Islamic law is included as a category because of its permanent, broadly based nature. Talmudic law is included because of the profoundly original nature of Israel's mixed legal system.

Civil law system. Civil law traditions trace their heritage back to Roman civil law, which was formalized into a set of statutes by the Napoleonic Code of 1804. This web of written law, organized into codes, can be conceptualized as a construction of the mind, designed to impose a rational and well-defined legal order on a particular society. Although judges do not "make law," because of the absence of the binding precedence of court decisions (i.e., *no stare decisis*), they are at the center of civil law systems. Not only do they issue the final decision in a case, they also decide all relevant interim questions. There are no juries to decide factual questions, because judges have been trained for and chosen to play this role (Bruno, 1994). In criminal cases judges have functioned in an "inquisitorial role," investigating cases as well as issuing verdicts. The civil system is characterized by a dogmatic and moralistic approach to legal principles, associated with extensive and integrated codifications (Zaphiriou, 1994).

Some 85 countries presently use a civil law system, including France, Germany, Greece, Italy, Mexico, and Spain. Many countries mix the civil law tradition with other systems. For example, China, Japan, and Korea use mixed systems of civil law and customary law; the Philippines, Scotland, and Thailand use mixed systems of civil law and common law; and Indonesia uses a mixed system of civil law, Muslim law, and customary law.

Common law system. Common law traditions are technically based on English common law concepts and legal organizational methods. These systems historically assigned a preeminent position to case law, as opposed to legislation, as the ordinary means of expressing general law. That is, judicial case law has precedential value, and judges actively create law when they decide cases. The judge acts as a referee, handling questions of law, whereas the jury is the final arbiter of questions of fact. Lawyers, however, are the engines of the judicial process. They file, interrogate, examine, cross-examine, object, dismiss, and constantly make motions to the court, inventing new procedural quirks and creating new rights. The lawyer makes the law as he or she goes along (Bruno, 1994, p. 6).

Twenty-two political entities use a common law system, including Australia, Canada, Ireland, New Zealand, the United Kingdom, and the United States. Although these countries historically have political ties with England, several other political entities that were less closely related to England in the past use this system. The common law system has taken on a variety of cultural forms throughout the world. In India, despite its British colonial past, a mixed system of common law, Muslim law, and customary law is used.

Customary law system. Customary law traditions are rooted in custom, which can take on many guises. Custom may be rooted in the wisdom borne of concrete daily experience or based more on great spiritual or philosophical traditions. Customary law still plays a significant role in matters of personal conduct in many countries or political entities with mixed legal systems. Obviously, it applies to a number of African countries and in very different circumstances in other parts of the world. The legal systems of China and India, for instance, incorporate customary law as part of their mixed systems. The customary law system is still used in a relatively pure form in some political entities, such as Cambodia and Laos.

Islamic law system. The Islamic law tradition is an autonomous legal system that is highly religious in nature and predominantly based on the Koran, the Muslim holy book. In a number of Muslim countries, the law tends to be focused on personal issues of ordinary people. Islamic law was previously observed in Afghanistan in its pure, unique form, although since the overthrow of the Taliban the country's legal system has been in the process of reformation. Islamic law is broadly used as part of a mixed system in many Muslim societies, including Egypt, Iraq, Pakistan, and Sudan in the Middle East, and in Indonesia and Malaysia in South Asia.

Cultural Backgrounds of Some Legal Systems

Cultural factors unique to every country around the world help determine and shape that nation's legal system, regardless of the type of legal system. A full explication of this process extends beyond the contours of this book. However, we will briefly illustrate culture's impact on the development of a few legal systems.

For those who see Western culture as essentially homogeneous, it may be surprising to note that different legal systems exist and are followed. For example, the common law system of the United States is historically rooted in the United Kingdom. This legal system places great value on the judgments of ordinary people. Attorneys on both sides present evidence and call witnesses, but the system entrusts to the ordinary people on the jury the task of sorting through the information and arguments presented in order to make a final judgment in a case. The judge functions only to determine how to properly carry out the legal process according to the law.

The basic spirit of the jury system, which values the commonsense view of ordinary people, contrasts with systems that rely primarily on the opinions and decisions of authorities or experts. The practice of entrusting such matters to ordinary people was influenced by a cultural attitude and belief that the judge (historically, often a noble or a person related to the royal system) was not trustworthy. This suspiciousness of authority, a characteristic of Americans since colonial times, finds its way into the constitutional right to trial by a jury, because a jury is thought to be better able to render a just and fair decision. Indeed, in the United States the jury even has the power of "nullification," which means that they can acquit even when there is clear evidence of a defendant's guilt. This allows the common person to disagree with the law or with its application when it is thought to be unfair.

A distinguishing difference is found in the civil law system, which is rooted in Roman law and the Napoleonic Code. The ultimate authority and decision maker in this system is the judge, who is considered the expert and the only person with enough knowledge of the law to make the final decision. Attorneys present their evidence and arguments to the judge, and no jury is involved. This system is based on a cultural attitude that trusts the authority of a legal expert to make decisions affecting people's lives. The lack of binding precedent (stare decisis) constrains the power of judges, however, because all power to make law is vested in the legislature. The removal of this power from judges—which is essentially the demise of the common law— occurred in France before the French Revolution. The judges at that time were from the nobility, and they routinely sabotaged moderate statutory reform proposals sought by the French crown to prevent revolution. It was thought prudent to take away from judges this power after the revolution, and this idea spread throughout Europe (Burnham, 2002, p. 42).

Inspired by Islamic principles, Islamic jurisprudence is unique in many aspects (Chaleby, 1996, 2001). For example, its family law, reflecting a profoundly patriarchal society, is strikingly different from that of the West. Only husbands can initiate divorce, and they may do so at will. In the event of divorce, the father will almost always be given legal custody of the children, although young children may be placed in the physical custody of their mothers until they grow up or their mother remarries. Furthermore, fathers are not punished for causing the death of a child if it occurs while they are disciplining their child. The law presumes that the father's discipline was for the child's own good, and in any case the child is the property of the father, who has the right to dispose of the child as he chooses.

Customary law traditions may observe unique family laws, as well, according to the cultural values of the family system. For example, in China and Singapore adult children may be legally punished if they do not support and take care of their aged parents. In Japan the law historically punished patricide, the killing of ones parent, more severely than it punished other killings. Although no longer true, it sheds light on the value placed on filial piety in Japan and throughout Asian culture. Thus, we can see the legal system as a cultural product that reflects many qualities emphasized in the culture where the law is established and practiced.

Incorporation of Cultural Consideration
in Legal Systems

A handful of legal systems explicitly recognize the importance of considering cultural factors in executing the law. For instance, Bloom and Bloom (1982) described how, when Micronesia came under United States trusteeship after World War II, the Anglo-American law-based Micronesian legal code (Trust Territories Code) was adopted to fit the local cultural situation in the early 1950s. This code (section 102) speaks to local customs and customary law as follows:

> The customs of the inhabitants of the Trust Territory, not in conflict with the laws of the Trust Territory, shall be preserved. The recognized customary law of the various parts of the Trust Territory shall have the full force and effect of law so far as the customary law is not in conflict with the laws mentioned in other sections of the code.

U.S. law also has begun to incorporate ethnic and cultural considerations in the legal system to accommodate the needs and rights of people of diverse cultural backgrounds. Levesque (2000) pointed out that in California, where many different ethnic groups reside, the law concerning child maltreatment explicitly provides that "cultural and religious childrearing practices and beliefs shall not in themselves create a need for child welfare services unless the practices present a specific danger to the physical or emotional safety of the child" (California Welfare & Institutional Code, 1996, § 16509). Similarly, Colorado law requires those who investigate reports of child abuse take into account accepted child-rearing practices of the parents' culture (Colorado Revised Statues, 1997, § 19-1-103[b]). In addition to using culture as a factor to assist in making determinations and formulating responses to potential child maltreatment, Levesque further indicated that the federal Indian Child Welfare Act, established in 1994, protects Native American populations against unnecessary removal of Indian children from their cultural heritage. New Mexico's statute requires the law "to provide for a culturally appropriate treatment plan, access to cultural practices and traditional treatment for an Indian child" (New Mexico Statues Annotated, 1996, § 32A-3B-19[G] [8]).

EFFECTS OF CULTURE IN COURT

Rules of practice and procedure of a court will obviously govern the course of legal proceedings. However, it is the human actors in the system who will conduct the proceedings and perform the various tasks during every stage in the legal process. If we consider how the people involved in court perceive, think, feel, and act, it is obvious that, with or without anyone's knowledge, the entire process will be affected by a variety of factors. These include professional, personal, and interpersonal factors. All elements of the system are products of human behavior and interaction and are affected by culture in various ways, obviously or subtly, consciously or unconsciously, but in significant, powerful ways. We elaborate on the culture of the legal system and then analyze the various ways culture can affect the court through the persons involved.

The Culture of the Legal System

Any established social organization operates in a certain style and according to particular rules and beliefs, whether spoken or unspoken. For instance, an army, besides being based on military principles and purposes, operates according to military culture, emphasizing hierarchy and absolute obedience toward authority. Medicine, in addition to operating based on medical knowledge and experiences, is carried out according to medical culture. This includes such things as observing the rules of the hospital, the separate functions of doctors and nurses, the patient following the doctor's orders, and so on. In the same way, the legal system is based on certain explicitly expressed ideas or unspoken rules in addition to the principles of law, forming a unique legal culture. This legal culture provides the spirit that determines the manner in which the law will be carried out.

Gutheil and Appelbaum (2000, p. 320) insightfully pointed out that the legal system operates on a distinctly different professional model from medicine or psychiatry. The law exists as a practical tool for maintaining order and resolving disputes in society. To deal with the infinite diversity and complexity of human beings (as conceptualized by psychiatrists), lawyers attempt to simplify the situation by postulating certain axioms and creating certain presumptions to redefine and create a more easily administered reality. Furthermore, given the law's need to rely on observable verities, lawyers are trained to be suspicious of any attempts to take people's words and actions at other than face value. In contrast, most clinicians are trained to understand behavior by assuming that people rarely say exactly what they mean. Finally, although lawyers generally prize autonomy and freedom to decide things for oneself, physicians may be more paternalistic and presume they know what is best for a patient (Saks, 2002). Thus, by training and orientation, the legal model and the psychiatric model operate according to different professional cultures.

Legal culture and legal practices will, as we elaborated previously, also be very much shaped by the culture of the society in which the law is processed. For instance, the American value of "having one's day in court" is incorporated into the American system of law, which strongly emphasizes due process, individual rights, and the opportunity for each side to speak up and make its case in court. The legal systems of other cultures will accordingly reflect different values, which will find their way into the legal culture of that society.

The Impact of Culture on Various Persons Involved in Court

Court proceedings involve a variety of individuals in different roles, including the judge, prosecutor and victim (criminal cases) or plaintiff and plaintiff's attorney (civil cases), defense attorney, jury, fact witnesses, experts of various kinds (including forensic psychiatrists and psychologists), and, of course, defendant. Besides the professional knowledge and experiences these individuals bring to their assigned roles, a variety of personal factors, including their personalities and predilections, individual experiences, ethnicity, race, and culture, will affect their perceptions, feelings, thinking, behavior, and decisions. Furthermore, the interpersonal relations and interactions that will take place among the various parties in court will affect the process and influence the outcome. We elaborate further on some of these cultural factors and issues specific to the various persons involved in court.

Judge. Beyond his or her professional knowledge of and experiences with the law, the judge's own personality and individual style will shape the ways in which he or she conducts the legal process. Cultural attitudes, values, and beliefs will shape thinking and decision making in a case. In criminal cases, for example, the degree and accuracy of the judge's understanding of the cultural backgrounds of the defendant and victim, as well as the cultural implications of the wrongful behavior alleged, will influence his or her views and judgments and how he or she exercises authority in court.

Attorney. The prosecutor and the plaintiff and defense attorneys will confront similar issues to that described previously for judges. In addition, because the attorneys are charged with managing each side of the case, the extent of their sensitivity and perceptiveness about cultural issues and their familiarity with the ethnic or cultural backgrounds of the accused and the victim is important. Not only must they have the needed cultural information, but they also must know that how they feel about it and how empathetic they are will have great significance. Furthermore, how they feel about and relate to the victim and the perpetrator, because of their existing ethnic or racial biases (either positive or negative) toward the group to which the victim or the perpetrator belongs (the kind of ethnic or racial countertransference that develops), is very significant. This will obviously affect the attorney's working relationships with all parties to a lawsuit.

Jury. A jury is a group of ordinary persons selected by the court to listen to and understand the evidence presented to them, to apprehend the behavior committed, and to make a layperson's judgment about the rightness or wrongfulness of the behavior committed. In capital cases, juries will participate in postconviction sentencing to decide whether imposition of the death penalty is appropriate.

Personal factors of jury members, including their individual backgrounds, personal experiences, and social, ethnic or racial, and cultural backgrounds, will shape their ways of thinking and their judgments. Indeed, attorneys commonly make use of consultants to help them select jury members with ethnic or racial backgrounds that will be favorable to their side. Although ethnic or racial background is relatively apparent and recognizable, cultural aspects such as how a person thinks, believes, and values things are more difficult to detect. The successful attorney will pay attention to the cultural backgrounds of the jury members and will know how to deal wisely with their cultures throughout the court process.

Witnesses. Witnesses include ordinary individuals who testify as to matters of fact, and experts who are allowed to tender professional conclusions. Fact witnesses must testify only to things about which they observe or have personal knowledge. Aside from deliberate falsehood, witness testimony may be faulty because of a number of factors, such as poor observation, imperfect recollection, bias toward one party or another, or the desire to make a good impression on the witness stand. Factors related to culture, ethnicity, and race may affect the ability or desire of a witness to give accurate testimony in any of these areas. For example, research has shown that identifying the face of someone from another race is more difficult and less accurate than identifying the face of someone from one's own race (Behrman & Davey, 2001; Meissner & Brigham, 2001). Witnesses who harbor prejudice toward persons of another race may be more willing to give false testimony. Furthermore, juries may be inclined to assign to witnesses of one race or culture more credibility than others.

Experts. Various professional people may be invited to become involved in the process of assessment and testimony. These experts include forensic psychiatrists and psychologists and other mental health personnel. The general considerations regarding attorneys apply to experts as well. Additional issues occur for forensic clinicians because they usually carry out their professional functions through close contact with the victim or the perpetrator. They not only should have some familiarity with the ethnic or cultural background of the subject but also should know the most culturally relevant and effective way to establish a relationship and communicate with the subject and to solicit culturally meaningful information in order to comprehend the whole picture. Understanding the cultural meaning of the circumstances in which the event occurred and the cultural implications of the behavior that took place is essential. Finally, experts should know how to explain their professional opinions, including the cultural issues involved, to the others involved in court.

Parties to the suit. The defendant and the plaintiff, in civil cases, and the defendant (and, to a lesser extent, the victim) in criminal cases are the primary persons involved in court. Their personal backgrounds (such as their ages, genders, educational levels, occupations, and so on), the admissible past personal and legal records, and the behavior they manifest in the process of evaluation and in court will affect how they will be viewed and judged. Their ethnic or racial backgrounds may additionally, and, in some cases, significantly, affect the decisions of the jury and the judge.

Important factors include not only their individual ethnic and racial backgrounds but also how they match with those of the opposing parties. This ethnic or racial match and interaction may occur in many circumstances in both criminal and civil law, but it may occur even more so in cases of murder, sexual harassment, or rape. For example, the different ethnic or racial matching involved when a Black man rapes a White woman or a White man rapes a Black woman, together with the ethnic or racial backgrounds of the jury members (either Black or White), will interact significantly and powerfully in shaping the decision of the jury. Many studies by mock trial have supported the tendency toward ethnic or racial bias (Hymes, Leinart, Rowe, & Rogers, 2001; Landweher et al., 2002; Wuensch, Campbell, Kesler, & Moore, 2002). (For details, see the section "Rape" in chapter 5 and the section "Sexual Harassment" in chapter 6.)

POSSIBLE IMPACT OF CULTURE ON THE LEGAL PROCESS AND DECISION

Cultural Evidence, Information, and Consideration

Certain terminology has come to be used in the legal system to describe cultural issues when they are introduced into the legal process. These terms, such as *cultural evidence, cultural information,* or *cultural consideration,* may be used with different connotations and implications from a legal perspective to describe various aspects of culture in the legal setting.

Cultural evidence. Cultural evidence is evidence about a cultural issue that is presented in the course of legal proceedings. There is an implication that significant and powerful "evidence" exists that will shape the judgment about the legal matter. From a theoretical point of view, there are problems inherent in the application of this term because culture by definition is amorphous, not objective, and cannot be easily described and presented as concrete evidence. Only ethnicity or nationality can be presented as concretely recognizable evidence for legal argument.

Cultural information. Cultural information refers to a set of "information" relating to cultural matters that can be presented and debated in court. It is assumed that the information is related to a rather unique or distinct cultural system, concerning a particular ethnic or minority group, and is going to have an obvious effect in court when it is presented.

Cultural consideration. Cultural consideration emphasizes that, in addition to other factors, cultural understanding and consideration are needed in the entire legal process, including the assessment and raising opinions to be judged and decided on. Cultural consideration not only focuses on the need for examination and use of cultural knowledge and information but also stresses the importance of adopting an orientation and approach to the legal procedure that is culturally relevant and fulfills the basic requirement of cultural competence. Thus, cultural consideration is broadly defined and applies to every case, no matter what the ethnic or cultural background of the parties involved.

The Impact of Culture on the Legal Process

Emphasizing Cultural Knowledge in Processing
Relevant Assessments

When the parties to a lawsuit have certain ethnic or cultural backgrounds there is a need for special cultural consideration in the legal process. This may include using cultural knowledge and transcultural skill in assessing and evaluating the case. Special consideration is particularly important when the parties in the suit have limited language abilities with the language spoken by the people of the mainstream. A well-trained and skillful interpreter should be available for the process of evaluation. Besides this, the examiner needs adequate cultural knowledge and experience in comprehending the cultural dimensions of thought and behavior of the person concerned. This is especially true when there is a wide gap between the cultures of the person concerned and the examiner.

Let us take the extreme example of making an assessment on a deaf person who is a part of the minority deaf culture within the mainstream society. Communicating with a deaf person whose only or primary language is sign language requires a skilled sign language interpreter. The interpreter must be able to sign in the same style as the deaf person (e.g., high visual, low language, signed English, American Sign Language, a foreign sign language such as Japanese sign, and so on). In addition, the interpreter must understand the cultural differences between the deaf community and the mainstream society and be knowledgeable about interpreting legal situations. The person making the assessment must also be aware of the impact of deaf culture on a deaf person's understanding and approach to mainstream culture and on his or her behavior.

Applying Cultural Insight in Forming an Opinion for the Court
In addition to performing a culturally sensitive and appropriate evaluation where suitable in a legal case, the forensic clinician may need to form a culturally competent opinion for the court's consideration. Every person has cultural beliefs, customs, and a value system, regardless of the ethnic or cultural group to which he or she belongs and whether he or she is a member of a minority or the majority. Evaluators' basic orientation already considers clinical and legal perspectives but may also need to display cultural understanding to assist the court.

Using Ethnic or Racial Heritage as a Defense
At times, the ethnic, racial, or otherwise unique background of the accused is used in the legal process as a defense against legal responsibility (Diamond, 1978). In some cases an attorney will emphasize lack of knowledge about a law, especially when it differs from the laws of the home country. The attorney may allege a person's inaccessibility to legal knowledge because of language problems or other reasons. Using culture as a defense in this way essentially argues that having a certain ethnic or racial heritage, or a special social background (such as being a tourist, a foreigner, or an immigrant, whose heritage or social status differs from the majority), should mitigate the "unlawful" behavior as defined by the society at large.

CASE 1: TOURIST ARRESTED FOR POSSESSION OF
AN ILLEGAL "TOXIC" SUBSTANCE

Tony, a young American man, took a trip to Asia and was arrested by police in customs. Tony had the habit of smoking marijuana and never encountered a legal problem at home.

Without thinking anything of it, he had packed some marijuana for use on his trip. However, when he was found in possession of this "toxic" substance he was put into detention and faced many years in prison for "smuggling" an illegal substance into the country. Tony's American attorney claimed that the defendant did not know of the existence of the law in the country he was visiting because he did not speak the local language. He further claimed that the defendant's free will and choice were hindered by social and cultural proscriptions. The local court, however, decided he should have known about the law because there was a clear warning statement, written in English, available to every passenger on the plane before entering the country. Furthermore, the court stated that if every visitor used not knowing the law as an excuse for bringing in prohibited material, the country would be harmed.

Using Cultural Beliefs, Values, or Information for Litigation

A defendant's cultural habits, beliefs, customs, or value systems are sometimes presented as legally significant information requiring special consideration from a cultural perspective. Often, an attorney will use this to suggest a penalty reduction, either during pretrial bargaining or during the sentencing stage. For example, the cultural background, attitude, and traditional child-rearing patterns and discipline of a parent accused of child abuse may be presented to explain the physical punishment applied by parents to their children.

CASE 2: CHILD DISCIPLINE OR ABUSE?

A Samoan man, Mr. Tutui, was arrested after the child protection service agency reported that he abused his young child, causing severe physical injury. Mr. Tutui's attorney claimed that disciplining children using corporal punishment was a culturally accepted practice on the Pacific island of Samoa. The attorney claimed his client was innocent because Mr. Tutui had neither a guilty mind when he hit his child nor should doing so be a guilty act from a legal perspective. Furthermore, he argued that if convicted for child maltreatment, the sentence should be reduced because of cultural considerations. The prosecutor, with the help of cultural experts, presented information that Mr. Tutui had recently learned that his wife had been unfaithful, and he had become angry and emotionally unstable. When he hit his child it was as an outlet for his anger not as an act of discipline because, according to neighbors, the child had not misbehaved. Most important, prosecutors pointed out that Mr. Tutui had lost self-control and hit his child's head, which is culturally forbidden because of the belief that a person's soul resides therein. Finally, the blow resulted in a skull fracture, which was far more severe than the kind of blow one might use in disciplining a child. The court ruled it to be a case of child maltreatment and sentence was passed accordingly. This case illustrates that a thorough investigation of background information in addition to adequate cultural knowledge may assist a court in making proper distinctions between a culture-based explanation and an emotional or behavior problem–related one, thus facilitating a proper legal decision for the case.

Following Local Customary Law Versus Primary Law

In some cases a defendant charged with violating a law of mainstream society might argue that his or her behavior followed the local custom or locally observed law. This situation usually happens when the community is isolated or culturally different from the majority or where people of a cultural minority follow a rather unique lifestyle that is very different from that of the larger society. This defense may challenge the validity of the primary law and seek to completely disregard its application.

CASE 3: MAN BURNS DOWN A MURDERER'S HOUSE (REVISED FROM BLOOM & BLOOM, 1982)

A man with a single name of Fiqir from the Micronesian island of Yap was arrested and convicted of arson. Fiqir burned down another man's house on the island. The man had killed Fiqir's father, and Fiqir claimed that "under traditional custom, it is the right and duty (and therefore not unlawful) to atone for or to obtain revenge for a prior homicide by killing the murderer or by burning down his house or taking his canoe." Fiqir claimed that his detention was illegal on the grounds that it was his "right and duty" to burn to the ground his father's murderer's house. Fiqir's father's murderer had been convicted of second-degree murder in the death of Fiqir's father. The argument was presented to the High Court of Micronesia (*Fiqir v. Trust Territory*), which ruled that the crime of arson under the written law of the Trust Territory necessarily superseded and replaced any applicable customs pursuant to this code.

From the cultural point of view, the conviction and imprisonment of the murderer of Fiqir's father that satisfied the primary law perhaps did not satisfy Fiqir's psychological needs. Following his culturally prescribed right and duty to personally take revenge on his father's murderer was perhaps the only way he could be satisfied emotionally that he did the right thing. He showed filial piety toward his murdered father, while gaining respect from his fellow villagers as a man because of the revenge he had taken. However, such behavior, although culturally understandable and justified, would not be accepted by the primary law and would be judged simply as a wrongful act. This illustrates the tension between the universal application of rules of law with issues of cultural relativism.

UNIVERSAL RULE VERSUS CULTURAL RELATIVISM

The fundamental spirit of the law is to provide a universal set of rules that will be applicable to all persons in a society. Legal systems seek to clearly define behavior that is lawful and unlawful, and provide punishment for wrongful behavior. Implicit is a basic assumption that what is right or wrong can be adequately defined and is conceptually quite clear. In contrast, knowledge accumulated from culture-focused behavioral science, through such disciplines as cultural anthropology, cross-cultural psychology, and cultural psychiatry, emphasizes that human life and behavior is full of variation. These disciplines hold that all matters should be considered from a cultural perspective and, when appropriate, adjusted accordingly (Tseng, 2001).

The difference in approach of these two ways of thinking— the universalism of law versus the relativism of ordinary human experience—guarantees they will at times come into conflict. We face both a theoretical and a practical challenge in sorting out how we are to follow the law, which stresses consistency with little room for exceptions, while balancing it with cultural relativism. Specifically, we must ask how we might best accommodate cultural issues in order to be fair to people of diverse ethnic and cultural backgrounds but still have an effective legal system. This issue is a key challenge for culturally oriented forensic psychiatry.

THE IMPACT OF CULTURE ON VARIOUS ASPECTS
OF FORENSIC PSYCHIATRY SERVICES

Forensic psychiatry operates at the interface of two disparate disciplines: law and psychiatry (Weinstock, Leong, & Silva, 2003). To serve people of diverse ethnic and cultural backgrounds, forensic psychiatry will benefit from the contribution of cultural psychiatry so that culturally competent forensic psychiatric services can be delivered in multiethnic societies around the world, including ours.

The scope of forensic psychiatric practice has expanded to embrace civil, criminal, correctional, and legislative matters, in association with accumulating knowledge and experience, clinical realities, and the demands of society (American Academy of Psychiatry and the Law, 1995). The major function of forensic psychiatry remains centered around the application of psychiatry to evaluations for legal purposes. To carry out culturally relevant forensic psychiatric work, several issues require special attention.

Providing Culturally Competent Clinical Assessment in Forensic Psychiatric Cases

Mental health workers now realize that "clinical competence" in psychiatric work requires some measure of "cultural competence," in order to provide assessment or care for people of diverse ethnic and cultural backgrounds. The importance of cultural competence applies to all aspects of psychiatric work, whether in inpatient or outpatient care, consultation liaison, or emergency service or whether related to child and adolescent, geriatric, or forensic psychiatry (Tseng & Streltzer, 2004).

In forensic psychiatry the major focus of cultural competence will be on providing a culturally relevant and appropriate psychiatric assessment of a person for legal purposes. This necessitates overcoming potential barriers in language, cognition, and concepts to comprehend culture-related beliefs, values, and attitudes held by the person and to provide a culturally relevant and meaningful assessment of the person's mental function. Extra effort may be needed when assessing foreigners, immigrants, people of ethnic or racial minorities, or people who are different from the majority in terms of age (such as children or aged persons) or gender (women), because contemporary psychiatric knowledge and experience is based primarily on male adults from society's major ethnic group. (We elaborate on these issues in detail in chapter 2.)

Carrying Out Culturally Appropriate Psychological Testing in Forensic Evaluations

In parallel with clinical psychiatric assessment, culturally relevant, appropriate, and valid psychological testing must be performed. This is true in ordinary psychiatric cases and even more so in forensic psychiatry cases, because the results of psychological tests may significantly influence the legal outcome of a case.

The transcultural application of psychological instruments, whether conventional psychological measurements or specialized forensic assessment instruments, deserves careful attention, so that test results may be appropriately interpreted and integrated with the clinical assessment. (We discuss this subject further in chapter 3.)

Comprehending Cultural Aspects of Psychiatric Disorders in a Forensic Context

To perform a clinically competent assessment, the psychiatrist must have adequate knowledge of various psychiatric disorders so that a professional assessment can be performed. From a cultural point of view, forensic psychiatrists should appreciate how psychiatric disorders may vary in their manifestation because of the influences of culture, and the different clinical and legal implications. Certain psychopathologies, such as psychopathy and psychoses—including delusional disorders, substance abuse, sexual disorders, and dissociation—are particularly important in forensic practice. (We examine the cultural aspects of certain psychiatric disorders in a forensic context in chapter 4.)

Understanding the Cultural Dimensions of Psychological and Behavioral Problems and Crimes in a Forensic Context

The law defines many human behaviors as crimes, and these may extend beyond the psychopathologies that can be categorized and labeled as psychiatric disorders. These problems often must be addressed in the forensic context. Spouse abuse, disputes associated with divorce, child custody, child abuse, violence against others, and sexual harassment are some examples. Cultural considerations should inform forensic assessment of these psychological and behavioral problems because the problems may be greatly subject to cultural factors and have significant social and legal implications. Comprehending these problems from a cultural perspective can be a great transcultural challenge. (We analyze this issue in detail in chapter 5.)

Cultural Considerations in Specific Types of Forensic Evaluations

Forensic clinicians may be involved in legal matters that are criminal, civil, or family-law related. In each case psychiatrists and other mental health professionals face tasks that must be performed for the court at different stages of the legal process. Forensic psychiatrists may be involved in issues such as the assessment of competency or insanity, and they must consult with attorneys, interact with judges, give testimony as an expert witness, and so on. In addition to the expectation of fulfilling the professional requirements of competent clinical knowledge and experience in these various aspects of forensic psychiatric work, there is the expectation that forensic psychiatrists will perform with cultural competency. Each task facing forensic clinicians presents its own culturally related challenges, in addition to general issues. (We examine and discuss this matter in chapter 6.)

Exercising Cultural Insight in the Legal Regulation of Psychiatry

Modern society regulates many aspects of medical and psychiatric care to ensure it is being appropriately carried out. These include the hospitalization of a mentally ill person, the right to treatment, proper therapist-patient relations, and special medical practices, such as physician-assisted suicide. In addition to approaching these issues from both the medical and legal perspectives, cultural consideration should become a part of the discussion to establish and execute culturally relevant and meaningful rules. This is an area in which culturally oriented forensic psychiatrists can make an additional and important contribution. (We examine this subject in chapter 7.)

Use of Cultural Information and Experiences in Correctional Psychiatry

Many legal offenders sentenced to prison come from minority cultural backgrounds. To effectively run a prison that accommodates these inmates while regulating their lives, maintaining order, and providing rehabilitation programs and counseling, is a challenging task. Attending to cultural issues will help effectuate such responsibilities as providing suitable care and counseling for these special populations. Forensic psychiatrists can become involved in the process of carrying out this care in a culturally competent manner. (We discuss these issues more fully in chapter 8.)

THE GOAL, SCOPE, AND NATURE OF THE BOOK

Our overall goal for this book is to present a complete and contemporary overview of cultural issues that should be considered in the practice of forensic clinical work. We aim to fulfill the newly developed expectation that culturally relevant and effective forensic mental health services will be provided for our multiethnic population. Three disciplines combine to form the core of this book, namely, cultural psychiatry, forensic psychiatry, and law. Culturally competent forensic psychiatry is a recently developed area in its early stages of growth.

To be useful to persons from a broad range of disciplines—forensic psychiatrists, forensic psychologists, attorneys, judges, general psychiatrists, clinical psychologists, and social workers—the contents cover a wide range of topics. Some topics are more relevant than others for different individuals. For example, comprehending cultural aspects of psychiatric disorders (chapter 4) is geared primarily toward persons from nonpsychiatric disciplines, such as attorneys and social workers. Cultural understanding of psychological problems in the forensic context (chapter 5) is aimed at general psychiatrists who, beyond their familiarity with psychiatric disorders, need more understanding of various behavioral and psychological problems in the legal setting from a cultural perspective. Legal regulation of psychiatry (chapter 7), a familiar topic for general psychiatrists, is addressed from the perspective of culture. This approach may make the chapter useful for both psychiatric and nonpsychiatric disciplines. Providing culturally suitable care for inmates is addressed (chapter 8) to all persons working in the prison system. In other words readers of different disciplines may have different degrees of interest in various chapters of this book, but the book as whole is organized in such a way as to cover various subjects widely and comprehensively to serve as an introductory guide.

Because it is a new field, there are not always distinct answers for some questions. When possible, explanations for problems and suggestions for dealing with them are provided. Furthermore, whenever issues involve culture, they tend to be broad in scope, relativistic, and sometimes judgmental in the value system that is attached. We are aware that the opinions and suggestions presented throughout this book reflect our professional opinions that are influenced by our own cultural heritages. Furthermore, although they represent our best assessment currently, we recognize that views may evolve over time and that other clinicians and scholars may hold different viewpoints. But we express our views with the hope that they might stimulate readers to explore their own.

REFERENCES

American Academy of Psychiatry and the Law. (1995). Ethics guides for the practice of forensic psychiatry (revised). American Anthropological Association (1999). AAA statement on race. *American Anthropologist, 100*(3), 712–713.

Appelbaum, P. S. (2002). Review of book: Forensic psychiatry in Islamic jurisprudence, by K. S. Chaleby (2001). *Journal of the American Academy of Psychiatry and the Law, 30*(3), 462–463.

Atkins v. Virginia, 536 U.S. 304 (2002).

Barnouw, V. (1963). *Culture and personality.* Homewood, IL: Dorsey Press.

Behrman, B. W., & Davey, S. L. (2001). Eyewitness identification in actual criminal cases: An archival analysis. *Law and Human Behavior, 25*(5), 475–491.

Bloom, J. D., & Bloom, J. L. (1982). An examination of the use of transcultural data in the courtroom. *Bulletin of the American Academy of Psychiatry and the Law, 10*(2), 89–95.

Bruno, P. (1994). The common law from a civil lawyer's perspective. In R. A. Danner & M. L. H. Bernal (Eds.), *Introduction to foreign legal systems* (pp. 1–13). New York: Oceana Publications.

Burnham, W. (2002). *Introduction to the law and legal system of the United States* (3rd ed.). St. Paul, MN: West Group.

California Welfare & Institutional Code, § 16509 (1996).

Chaleby, K. S. (1996). Issues in forensic psychiatry in Islamic jurisprudence. *Bulletin of the American Academy of Psychiatry and the Law, 24*(1), 117–124.

Chaleby, K. S. (2001). *Forensic psychiatry in Islamic jurisprudence.* Herndon, VA: International Institute of Islamic Thought.

Colorado Revised Statues, § 19-1-103[b] (1997).

Diamond, B. L. (1978). Social and cultural factors as a diminished capacity defense in criminal law. *Bulletin of the American Academy of Psychiatry and the Law, 6*(2), 195–209.

Edmunds, P. D. (1959). *Law and civilization.* Washington, DC: Public Affairs Press.

Feinerman, J. V. (1994). Introduction to Asian legal systems. In R. A. Danner & M. L. H. Bernal (Eds.), *Introduction to foreign legal systems* (pp. 94–121). New York: Oceana Publications.

Gonçalves, R. A. (1997). Criminological and legal psychology in Portugal: Past, present and future. In S. Redondo, V. Garrido, J. Péres, & R. Barberet (Eds.), *Advances in psychology and law: International contributions* (pp. 34–42). Berlin: de Gruyter.

Gutheil, T. G., & Appelbaum, P. S. (2000). *Clinical handbook of psychiatry and the law* (3rd ed.). Philadelphia: Lippincott Williams & Wilkins.

Hoebel, E. A. (1972). *Anthropology: The study of man.* New York: McGraw-Hill.

Hymes, R. W., Leinart, M., Rowe, S., & Rogers, W. (2001). Acquaintance rape: The effect of race of defendant and race of victim on white juror decisions. *Journal of Social Psychology, 133*(5), 627–634.

Kottak, C. P. (1999). *Mirror for humanity: A concise introduction to cultural anthropology* (2nd ed.). Boston: McGraw-Hill College.

Kroeber, A. L., & Kluckhohn, C. (1952). *Culture: A critical review of concepts and definition* (Papers of the Peabody Museum of Archaeology and Ethnology, 47 (1)). Cambridge, MA: Harvard University.

Kury, H., & Ferdinand, T. (1999). Public opinion and punitivity. *International Journal of Law and Psychiatry, 22*(3–4), 373–392.

Landwehr, P. H., Bothwell, R. K., Jeanmard, M., Luque, L. R., Brown, R. L., III, & Breaux, M. A. (2002). Racism in rape trials. *Journal of Social Psychology, 142*(5), 667–669.

Lawrence v. Texas, 123 S. Ct. 2472 (2003).

Levesque, R. J. R. (2000). Cultural evidence, child maltreatment, and the law. *Child Maltreatment, 5*(2), 146–160.

Meissner, C. A., & Brigham, J. C. (2001, March). Thirty years of investigating the own-race bias in memory for faces: A meta-analytic review. *Psychology, Public Policy, and Law, 7,* 3–35.

Neapolitan, J. L. (2001). An examination of cross-national variation in punitiveness. *International Journal of Offender Therapy and Comparative Criminology, 45*(6), 691–710.

New Mexico Statues Annotated, § 32A-3B-19[G][8] (1996).

Radin, M. J. (1978). The jurisprudence of death: Evolving standards for the cruel and unusual punishments clause. 126 U. Pa. L. Rev. 989.

Row over public floggings in Iran. (2001, August 15). BBC News. Retrieved from http://news.bbc.co.uk/2/hi/middle_east/1492852.stm; accessed 2 March 2004.

Saks, E. R. (2002). *Refusing care: Forced treatment and the rights of the mentally ill.* Chicago: University of Chicago Press.

Tseng, W. S. (2001). *Handbook of cultural psychiatry.* San Diego, CA: Academic Press.

Tseng, W. S., & Streltzer, J. (2004). *Cultural competence in clinical psychiatry.* Washington, DC: American Psychiatric Publishing.

Weinstock, R., Leong, G. B., & Silva, J. A. (2003). Defining forensic psychiatry: Roles and responsibilities. In R. Rosner (Ed.), *Principal and practice of forensic psychiatry* (2nd ed.). London: Arnold.

Wilkerson v. Utah, 99 U.S. 130 (1878).

World legal systems. (2002). University of Ottawa, Faculty of Law. Retrieved from http://www.uottawa.ca/world-legal-systems/eng-monde.html

Wuensch, K. L., Campbell, N. W., Kesler, F. C., & Moore, C. H. (2002). Racial bias in decisions made by mock jurors evaluating a case of sexual harassment. *Journal of Social Psychology, 142*(5), 587–600.

Zaphiriou, G. A. (1994). Introduction to civil law systems. In R. A. Danner & M. L. H. Bernal (Eds.), *Introduction to foreign legal systems* (pp. 47–55). New York: Oceana Publications.

2

General Cultural Issues in Forensic Psychiatric Assessment

BASIC CONSIDERATIONS IN TRANSCULTURAL FORENSIC ASSESSMENT

Culturally Competent Forensic Interviews

Forensic psychiatry, like general psychiatry, relies heavily on the assessment interview. We now recognize that in general psychiatry every examiner must have some degree of cultural competency to be truly clinically competent. Cultural competency improves diagnostic accuracy and enhances various aspects of treatment in the clinical setting. For clinical psychiatrists, especially those working in multiethnic or multicultural communities and providing care for patients of diverse backgrounds, cultural competency has become an important feature of practice. The requirement for competency in cultural matters should be extended to the practice of forensic psychiatry as well; forensic evaluees are drawn from a similarly diverse range of cultural and ethnic backgrounds (Matthews & Tseng, 2004). Forensic psychiatrists' lack of knowledge and familiarity with the specific culture of the examinee, coupled with emotional discomfort toward an examinee of diverse ethnic, racial, or cultural backgrounds, can result in impaired examiner-examinee relations and communication and in suboptional forensic evaluations (Silva, Leong, & Weinstock, 2003).

33

Cultural experts have identified fundamental qualities essential for cultural competency as a mental health clinician that are equally relevant to effective transcultural assessment (Foulks, 1980; Lu, Lim, & Mezzich, 1995; Moffic, Kendrick, & Reid, 1988; Tseng & Streltzer, 2001; Westermeyer, 1989; Yutrzenka, 1995). These qualities include cultural sensitivity, cultural knowledge, cultural empathy, and culturally relevant relations and interactions with examinees (Tseng, 2003, pp. 219–225).

Cultural Sensitivity

Examiners must have some measure of cultural sensitivity and openness to other cultures in order to appreciate the various lifestyles among human beings, their diverse views and attitudes, and the different ways of adaptation. Beyond this awareness, the examiner must be perceptive enough to sense cultural differences among people and know how to appreciate them without bias, prejudice, or stereotypes. The examiner must actively communicate and be receptive to learning as much as necessary from evaluees and their families about their opinions, understandings, beliefs, attitudes, values, ways of perceiving problems they encounter, and ways of dealing with problems. Cultural sensitivity embraces more than merely sensitive perception but includes an attitude of wanting to learn about others' lifestyles, rather than being trapped in one's own subjective perception and interpretation of others' behavior. In this way one can avoid cultural ignorance and minimize culture blindness ("cultural scotoma") and stereotyping.

Cultural Knowledge

In addition to having sensitivity, an examiner must develop a certain base of cultural information and knowledge about humankind as a whole, as well as of the particular examinee and family concerned. Obviously, not even a well-trained professional anthropologist will have a probing knowledge of every cultural system. Forensic clinicians are not expected to know about all the cultural systems that exist, but they should develop a basic understanding of anthropological knowledge about how human beings vary in their habits, customs, beliefs, value systems, and behavior relating to social regulation and the law. Furthermore, examiners must have a reasonable amount of specific cultural knowledge about the particular examinees with whom they are dealing. It seems self-evident that a forensic psychiatrist practicing, for example, in a predominantly Puerto Rican community should have a working understanding of the cultural practices of this population. If the examinee is a Jehovah's Witness, the examiner needs to understand the lifestyle of a Jehovah's Witness, particularly the beliefs and practices of the religion. Reading books and articles is one way to obtain basic cultural information. Consulting with cultural anthropologists on general issues or with experts on a particular cultural system is another approach, as is consulting with examiners of that particular cultural background (see the section "Spiritual Experience or Psychotic Breakdown?" in chapter 9). When informational sources are not easily available, one may use the examinee and his or her family or friends of the same ethnic-cultural background as resources, although careful judgment must be exercised to determine the accuracy and relevance of their information.

Cultural Empathy

Clinical experience suggests that factual information about an examinee's culture by itself may not lead to transcultural comprehension of the examinee. Another quality is often needed, namely, being able to feel and to understand at an emotional level from the examinee's own cultural perspective. Otherwise, a gap in understanding may remain, and the examiner will be unable to fully appreciate the emotional experience of the examinee, an ability that is useful in order to apprehend the intent, affect, and behavior at deep level. This ability is known as cultural empathy.

For instance, if a Samoan parent becomes extremely angry when someone hits his young child on the head, it is necessary to understand that the parent is upset not only because someone hit his child but because he hit the child's head, which, according to the parent's folk belief, is the location of the soul. The examiner should not only know about this belief but should also empathically appreciate the parent's fear that with even a minor blow, the child could lose his soul. That is, the emotional valence attached to the reaction will be much greater than the degree of the injury from the medical perspective. Historically, a Japanese woman who became pregnant without

being properly married would be greatly shamed. Friends, colleagues, and the society as a whole would shun her and the
child would be discriminated against all of his or her life as an
"illegitimate child." To avoid this result, an unmarried mother
might commit infanticide to remove the source of her shame,
the newborn baby (for example, see the section "Various Reasons for the Intentional Killing of Children" in chapter 5). This
contrasts with the situation in other cultures, such as Micronesia, in which it is not considered terrible for a woman to become
pregnant without being married. Not only is it important to
know about this cultural phenomenon, it is also important to
understand it at an emotional level, within the cultural context
of the case (namely, how a woman can become desperate if she
finds she is pregnant without being married).

Culturally Relevant Interactions

Competent clinicians realize the importance of knowing how
to adjust and maintain a proper professional relationship with
the patient in the clinical setting. The age, gender, and personality of the patient; the nature and severity of the psychopathology; and the purpose of interaction are elements to
consider in adjusting clinician-patient relations. By extension,
there is also a need to incorporate the patient's cultural attributes. Similar principles apply to examiner-examinee relations in
forensic psychiatric assessment as well.

Forensic evaluators should consider how the examinee's culture defines the proper relationship between a superordinate
and a subordinate figure, or risk misapprehending the behavior
of the examinee toward the examiner. When dealing with examinees with distinctly different ethnic or racial backgrounds, the
ability to detect, comprehend, and manage ethnic or race-related
transference and countertransference is also useful. This
becomes particularly important when negative and even hostile
relations exist between the ethnicity or racial backgrounds of the
examinee and the examiner or when there is an imbalance of
power due to one of them belonging to a minority group. These
issues may significantly influence the process of evaluation and
the results of the assessment. The willingness of the examiner to
give careful consideration to these issues, in order to properly
manage and make appropriate adjustments to the evaluation
process, is an important aspect of cultural competence.

Different Levels of Attention

Forensic assessments will be carried out in a manner that considers human psychology and sociocultural factors. This is particularly true when the assessment involves an examinee of a different ethnic and cultural background from the examiner. To assess an examinee's mind and behavior accurately and relevantly, the examiner must pay attention to the examinee's use of language, knowledge, emotion, behavior, and attitude.

Language: Communication and Understanding

Language is the basic tool we use to communicate with others and to understand another person's thoughts, motives, feelings, and behavior. If two people do not share a common language, communication between them will certainly be hindered. A third person may be required, functioning as an interpreter, to translate the spoken languages. This not only limits the amount and level of communication but also introduces the possibility of potential distortion and misunderstanding. A trained interpreter is useful in minimizing the miscommunications that may occur.

Even when two persons share a common language, the potential of miscommunication and misunderstanding exists, because the expression of thoughts, feelings, and motivation may not necessarily be open and direct within or between cultures but may be carried out indirectly or subtly. To understand the meaning behind words and the feelings concealed requires special effort and skill. Language remains the most significant obstacle in carrying out a cross-cultural psychiatric assessment in both clinical and forensic practice. (The following section, "Transcultural Assessments Using Interpreters," provides a more detailed elaboration of how to overcome this difficulty.)

Knowledge: Background Information

An examiner must view the examinee within the context of normal patterns of personality development and family dynamics and understand how psychopathology manifests itself in emotion, cognition, and behavior. Basic professional knowledge about these domains of functioning is needed in ordinary clinical or forensic practice. Furthermore, the examiner must have a degree of basic cultural knowledge about the examinee, such as the common attitudes, beliefs, and values held by his or her ethnic or cultural group; the customary behaviors; the common life stresses; and the usual help-seeking behaviors for coping with problems. On the basis of this cultural knowledge, an examiner can perform a more accurate and relevant forensic assessment.

Emotion: Feeling and Empathy

Although human beings share a basic, common, emotional response, every individual has a unique way of experiencing and expressing feelings. Similarly, cultural groups tend to share characteristic ways of experiencing and demonstrating emotion. Knowing the cultural variations in emotional experiences and sharing the feelings of another in a culturally relevant way is known as cultural empathy. Cultural empathy is a complicated matter that we touched on previously in this chapter and elaborate on further throughout this book. Attempting to understand and share the feelings experienced by persons from other ethnic or cultural groups is an important skill that is useful in carrying out culturally meaningful forensic assessments. Many U.S. statutes, for example, require the examiner to assess the examinee's ability to appreciate the wrongfulness of his or her conduct. Forensic psychiatrists and lawyers often think of "appreciation" as different from simple "knowing," although there is not agreement on the actual meaning of "appreciation"; still, studying an individual's ability to appreciate clearly moves the examiner closer to the necessity of understanding the individual in an empathic manner, attempting to include his or her emotional, cultural, and situational state in the interpretation of cognitive capacities.

Behavior: Customary Reaction and Appropriateness

As cultural anthropologists remind us, our behavioral patterns are molded from childhood through the process of "enculturation"—absorbing and introjecting the cultural norms from our surroundings, particularly from parents and other family members. Because our behavior patterns are shaped by our culture, culturally related behavior will vary from culture to culture. The patterns of socialization among people, the modes of celebrating special occasions, following certain etiquette and social rules, or the observance of certain taboos particularly illustrate this point. Culture defines "normal," "appropriate," and "correct" behavior patterns within a society. These patterns include desirable ways of dealing with problems encountered. Thus, a person's behavior should be appreciated and comprehended from the individual, family, group, and cultural perspectives.

Attitudes: Beliefs and Value Systems

Finally, examiners must pay attention to the attitudes, beliefs, and value systems held by an individual within the context of a group of people surrounding him or her. Cultural anthropologists remind us that these beliefs, attitudes, and value systems form the core of a culture. Beyond understanding individually related beliefs, attitudes, and value systems (manifested as a part of "personality"), we must comprehend the beliefs, attitudes, and value systems held by an individual as a member of his or her ethnic or cultural group. Attending to them will help us to understand the meaning and motive behind the behavior at a cultural level.

Interviewing and Communication

Interviewing is one of the basic approaches by which a forensic psychiatrist or other evaluator obtains needed information from the examinee for the purpose of making a diagnosis and addressing the relevant medicolegal issue at hand. Key areas of examiner-examinee communication include the way the examinee informs the examiner about events leading up to the interview and describes the intent of his or her behavior and patterns of reactions to situations. The examiner, reciprocally, listens and develops a relevant understanding about all the information received. The quality of this communication will affect the end product of the assessment. Skills required of the examiner include knowing how to address the examinee's suspiciousness and defensiveness. These are natural in most forensic situations, but they may seriously hinder the process of information gathering. Addressing these features of the examiner-examinee relationship may depend on the examiner's understanding of such cultural issues as patterns of relating to professionals across gender and social class.

Style of Interview: Direct Versus Open Inquiry

Like clinical interviews done for the purpose of evaluation and treatment, forensic interviews may be carried out using different approaches to questioning. The examiner sometimes takes a relatively active role, asking detailed questions to elicit specific needed information. This approach has the advantage of allowing the examiner to go through the areas that must be covered on the assessment most quickly and efficiently. A disadvantage of this style is that the examiner may miss areas with which the examinee is particularly concerned or, on the other hand, is attempting to conceal. Alternatively, the examiner may encourage the examinee to present freely any material that he or she may want to communicate. This allows the examiner to observe and examine the evaluee's thinking more broadly and permits the examiner to enter more easily into the examinee's subjective world. The shortcomings of this style are that it is time-consuming and may make the examinee feel uncomfortable in not knowing exactly what is expected of him or her.

These two basic approaches to interviewing can be applied alternately in suitable situations. Often a skillful interviewer will apply the direct style at the beginning of an interview, allowing time to shift to the open style later in the session. Another possible approach is to allow the examinee to cover all he or she wishes to say in an open-ended manner, then honing in with specific questioning. This may minimize the possibility of suggesting symptoms to the examinee through the interview process. We suggest, and the doctrine of informed consent implies, that the interviewer should try to determine to what extent the examinee is familiar with the nature of the interview process and should provide necessary explanation and assistance, particularly for those who are unfamiliar with professional interviews for cultural reasons.

Modes of Interview: Formal Versus Informal Approach

The forensic assessment interview must be conducted in a formal manner. The examiner should formally introduce himself or herself, explain the purpose of the forensic interview, discuss all relevant issues of confidentiality, obtain consent, inquire as to the examinee's understanding of these matters, and secure agreement to the assessment. The beginning examiner may wish to prepare a formalized statement that can be referenced in the process to ensure the disclosure and consent meets all applicable ethical and legal requirements, the latter varying by jurisdiction.

From a cultural point of view, this formal way of interacting with examinees can be somewhat counterproductive. People from many cultures are not used to beginning communication with others in a formal, standardized way. In some cultures members may greet each other by indicating where they come from and which (ethnic) group or tribe they belong to as a way of "knowing" each other first, before they start any important conversation. They may start an interview by attempting to chat about the weather, the surroundings, and the people.

Psychiatrists may be more comfortable with the informal interaction style in a clinical setting where friendliness and cordiality may be a normal part of the doctor-patient relationship. Because different parameters govern the forensic interview, the fact that it may not be taking place for the benefit of the examinee may induce an understandable and expected coolness. Forensic examiners might try to strike a balance by providing enough formality so as not to mislead the examinee into thinking routine doctor-patient rules apply, yet enough informality as not to stifle examinee responsiveness.

Interviewing Family or Friends: Individually or Collectively
Obtaining collateral information is an important part of the forensic assessment. The patient's family and friends will serve not only as a resource for information but also as a base from which to check the examinee's cultural reality. The interviewer can obtain from family members or friends information about the extent to which the examinee's thoughts and behaviors deviate from the sociocultural norm. This is particularly important in cases in which the normality or abnormality of the examinee's mental condition is a major concern.

Examiners must decide whether family members or friends should be interviewed separately or as a group. People may, for cultural reasons, hesitate to openly express their opinions individually, feeling more comfortable presenting their ideas in the presence of other family members or friends. The reverse may be true for individuals of other cultural backgrounds, who, by custom, may not feel at ease talking in front of other family members. They may fear, for example, that they will be criticized for revealing something shameful within the family and will feel comfortable expressing their views only outside of the presence of others. Trial and error may be required in developing an optimum approach to a particular case.

Relations Between the Examiner and the Examinee

Examiners must pay particular attention to the interviewer-examinee relationship when the interview is of an examinee of a different ethnic or cultural background. The relationship may vary according to a variety of cultural attributes.

Cultural Differences in Relations

Cultural factors contribute to interpersonal relations, particularly to authoritative-subordinate or male-female relations. Regarding cultural aspects of the physician-patient relationship, Nilchaikovit, Hill, and Holland (1993) explained that in some cultures, including American culture, the predominant form of the physician-patient relationship is egalitarian. It is based on a contractual agreement or, more correctly, a "fiduciary relationship" (because the doctor is obligated to act in the patient's best interests), between the two, influenced heavily by an ideological emphasis on individualism, autonomy, and consumerism. In contrast, in many other cultures, such as Asian cultures, the relationship is modeled after an ideal form of the culture's pattern of hierarchical relationships. The physician is seen as an authority figure endowed with knowledge and experience. An ideal doctor should have great virtue and be concerned, caring, and conscientiously responsible for the patient's welfare. In return the patient must show respect for and deference to the physician's authority and suggestions.

This culturally patterned authority-subordinate relationship needs to be considered in the examiner-examinee relationship in a forensic context as well. Transcultural challenges may be especially likely when an examiner and an examinee have distinctly different customs for relating to others, such as with an Asian examinee and an American examiner. An examinee unfamiliar with forensic assessments may incorrectly presume that an examination by a doctor is for the purpose of treatment and that the examiner will keep the examinee's best interests at mind. When the physician is an authority figure, a brief preexamination explanation of the purpose of the interview may not counteract the culturally conditioned tendency toward obedience. The examinee may be more likely to disclose sensitive or incriminating information to his or her detriment. On the other hand, the subordinately positioned examinee may not aggressively interact with the superior examiner or express feelings, frustrations, or opinions explicitly. In return the examinee may be seen as uncooperative or passive-aggressive by the examiner. Addressing this kind of culture-based misunderstanding may improve the quality of assessment.

Examiner-Examinee Matching

Mental health workers, perhaps stimulated by the human rights movement, have become increasingly concerned about the need for therapist-patient matching by ethnicity, race, and cultural background. Although the matching of therapist and patient by ethnicity, race, or cultural background sounds reasonable and desirable, it is not as simple as it might seem. Matching may be impractical and clinically it does not necessarily guarantee successful assessment and therapy. Therapeutic success depends on the therapist's personal ability to establish a positive relationship with and show empathy toward the patient. Although therapist-patient matching might be beneficial, matching alone will not guarantee positive therapeutic outcomes. In addition, when a therapist and patient have the same ethnic or racial background, ill effects may sometimes occur, such as when the patient does not want to reveal personal information to a therapist with the same background or when the therapist does not offer a proper figure for ethnic identification.

The same observations and limitations apply to forensic assessments. We believe that generally a homocultural match between examiner and examinee may be desirable, especially when the examiner can fluently speak the same language as examinee. In practice, however, finding examiners with backgrounds to match each examinee can be quite difficult. Because heterocultural matches are the standard of practice and will occur in most situations, examiners must know how to consult cultural experts when necessary, and the examiner must be equipped with the qualities necessary for cultural competence, such as cultural sensitivity, knowledge, and empathy, as we described in the foregoing section.

SPECIAL ATTENTION NEEDED FOR FORENSIC PSYCHIATRIC ASSESSMENTS

Transcultural Assessments Using Interpreters: Overcoming Language Barriers

Psychiatric assessment, whether forensic or clinical, relies heavily on information that comes from interviews with the subject as the major informant. When the examiner and the examinee do not share a common mother language, carrying out an assessment becomes problematic (Westermeyer, 1990). Examiners who must rely on the services of a translator may encounter limitations and the possibility of distortions and misunderstandings, depending on the skill and cultural knowledge of the translator.

Different languages use different sets of vocabulary to express meaning, a fact that interpreters must fully appreciate. One language may have only a few words to describe a particular concept, whereas another language may have many different words to elaborate the same thing. For example, Eskimo people living in cold weather have developed several different words to differentiate among different kinds of snow, whereas in English there is only one word for snow. Micronesian people living on tiny islands in the middle of a huge ocean, in order to precisely detect weather changes while sailing in small canoes, use different words to describe different kinds of clouds. We find the same tendency with behavior, psychology, or emotions. Japanese people have several different words centering around the key word *amae* (literally, "sweet") to elaborate the delicate, indulgent affection permitted between parent and child, because benevolent, dependent affection is valued and condoned in Japanese culture (Doi, 1973). However, it is difficult to find a concept equivalent to *amae* in Western thought, and it is even more difficult to translate the Japanese properly into English— "benevolent, dependent love" is probably the closest translation.

Language differences may have a serious impact on legal proceedings and important implications for forensic psychiatric practice. For example, a defendant may describe in his or her native language an action whose legal significance will vary depending on how the words are translated. A defendant on trial for murder might say, "I used a knife to 'fight' with him," "I injured him," "I stabbed him," "I killed him," or "I murdered him." An unskilled or inexperienced translator may interpret any of these simply as "I 'killed' him," which has significantly different implications from a legal perspective. Even for experienced and skillful translators, interpreting a word from one language into another accurately and with the equivalent cultural and semantic validity presents a challenge. Extra effort must be made to avoid potential mistakes that could result in differences in legal outcome.

Psychiatrists working in forensic settings should have knowledge about the potential problems and challenges related to language, in addition to a cultural orientation. To minimize error, the translator needs proper selection and adequate orientation, guidance, and training. The translator must be competent in language and interpretation and also should have a basic knowledge of clinical psychiatry (understanding the nature and various types of psychopathology), culture and behavior (cultural variation of behavior in general, and case-related culture in specific), and the legal system (the rules that must be followed in court, and how the interpretations may affect the legal decision). The following cases illustrate the problems of language and challenges for translators.

CASE 1: INTERPRETATION ERRORS IN COURT

A Chinese man living in the United States was charged with homicide in the death of his boss. Interpreters were used for the defendant as well as for the witnesses, because they did not speak English. In court the defendant complained in Chinese about how he had been mistreated by his boss in his work situation. He described his boss as repeatedly cursing and shouting at him: (I will) "fuck your mother's vagina!" The translator for the defendant, reluctant to translate word for word what the defendant said, simply translated that the boss had used "dirty words" when swearing at the defendant. She was a highly educated, well-mannered woman who balked at putting the actual (dirty and disgraceful) curse words in her mouth in front of others in the courtroom. On her own, she decided to "simplify" the translation by just saying that the boss always "swore" at the defendant. The defendant's description of the situation, which was important in defense of his case, lost its emotional impact because the actual meaning was not conveyed. The interpreter failed to communicate the weight and impact of the defendant's words and explanation to the court, and his situation became significantly less favorable.

When a prosecution witness was called and asked by the prosecutor to reveal what he had heard from the defendant after the incident, the witness said in Chinese, which was translated by the prosecutor's interpreter, that the defendant had told him that he had "killed" the boss more than 10 times with a knife. On hearing this translation, the defense interpreter disagreed with the interpretation, pointing out that the witness actually said that the defendant tried to "stab" the boss 10 times. In Chinese *ci* (stabbing) others, *ci-shang* (stabbing and injuring) others, *sha* (killing) others, or *mou-sha* (murdering) others with a knife are different words semantically. In court the witness used the word (trying to) "stab" the boss rather than (trying to) "kill" the boss more than 10 times. In other words the defendant said that, after seeing the boss take a knife to kill him, he used his own knife to stab the boss to defend himself. To "stab" someone (as a defensive, protective measure) obviously has different implications from trying to "kill" someone (an active, aggressive action, with the intention of taking someone's life).

The same witness also disclosed that the defendant had said the boss was a person of *gu-tou-ying*, which literally means "a hard bone." Interpreters on both sides argued about whether the defendant used that Chinese word to say that he found the boss had "a hard bone" when he stabbed him or whether he meant that the boss was "a tough guy" (the symbolic meaning of this word), who was difficult to fight in self-defense.

Transcultural Understanding: Culturally Relevant Interpretation of Behavior

People follow certain cultural rules and guidelines when manifesting behavior. In some cultures certain behavior is prohibited and certain other actions are permissible or even desirable and encouraged. In Micronesia, a culture practicing a matrilineal system (in which power passes from mother to daughter, rather than from father to son as in a patrilineal system), the bond between brother and sister is considered the most important among family relations. As a result, there is a strong taboo against close physical relations between brother and sister. Traditionally, the taboo was observed to such an extent that a brother and sister were not allowed in the same room together when there was no other person present. This taboo was practiced to protect their close relationship (from a psychological and functional perspective) in the matrilineal family system. Meanwhile, in the same island society, the concept of virginity is not stressed like it is in other cultures. In the past, sexual relations were permitted between young boys and girls, and even childbearing was allowed prior to formal marriage.

What constitutes a "normal" or "unusual" relationship between a man and a woman needs careful interpretation within their cultural system. Because cultural factors greatly influence patterns of communication, interaction, and relationships between men and women, they deserve careful assessment and understanding in legal situations. For example, when a person says, "I like you," shakes hands or hugs a person of the opposite sex as a form of "social greeting," or telephones someone of the opposite sex at night (whatever the purpose of the call), these actions, personally, socially, and culturally, must be further investigated to determine their meaning. When a woman complains that she was stalked, sexually harassed, or assaulted, her complaint must be understood and analyzed from the perspective of both the alleged victim and the person accused of wrongdoing. Particularly if the accusing and the accused persons are of different ethnic, racial, or cultural backgrounds, both perspectives must be given consideration in order to understand and comprehend the intercultural interaction that took place.

CASE 2: CULTURAL MISUNDERSTANDING OR EROTOMANIA?

A hospital asked a psychiatrist to perform a psychiatric assessment of an Asian (female) nurse, who believed that a Caucasian (male) doctor working in the same hospital was in love with her. She repeatedly contacted the doctor and made moves that led the doctor to complain to the hospital administrator. The assessment revealed that the nurse had emigrated from a conservative, traditional Asian country a year before. Her English was barely sufficient for her work as a nurse, and she clearly lacked an adequate social life in the hosting society. In the interview she presented the "facts" of how the doctor had indicated his affection for her, leading her to believe that he was in love with her. She stated that the doctor, who happened to live in the hospital dormitory next to hers, always gave her a big smile and asked, "How are you today?" when they bumped into each other. She revealed that, in her home country, a man never asks such a "personal" question about a woman unless he is interested in her. Besides, she explained that, one day, he knocked on her door to borrow sugar for his coffee. She explained that in her country a man did not find such an excuse to "intrude" on a lady's private life unless he had special intentions. Other "evidence" that indicated his affection for her included asking for her apartment phone number and calling her one time (about a trivial matter). Once she believed that he was in love with her, she became upset when she found out he was dating another woman. She felt betrayed by him and, in her anger, had called to annoy him.

The psychiatrist's task was to assess whether this was merely a case of intercultural misunderstanding between a man and a woman, related to different cultural expressions of affection, or a matter of erotic delusions on the part of the nurse. Clinical information from the past, her personality, her behavior patterns in general, and her relations with others, particularly with men in working and social situations, would all be helpful in assessing the case comprehensively. Most of all, consultation with other women from the same home country would be of great assistance in making a final assessment.

In this case, after the psychiatrist explained to her the cultural differences between American and Asian people in male-female interactions and discussed with her the possibility that she might have misunderstood the (American) male doctor's behavior toward her, she refused to entertain such a possibility or any other alternative reasons and continued to hold fast to her belief that he was in love with her. Her unshakable belief led the psychiatrist to conclude that she was suffering from an erotomanic delusion, and cultural misunderstanding was thought to have merely functioned as a basis for the development of the delusional state.

CASE 3: WOMAN DELAYS REVEALING SHE WAS RAPED

A middle-aged, married woman accused her boss of raping her almost a year before. She did not complain immediately after the alleged incident occurred, not even informing her husband about what had happened. Her attorney was concerned initially with why she had delayed her accusation and he consulted a psychiatrist for an assessment.

The woman's history revealed that she had come to this country two decades before. She had married a local man, who was more than 15 years older than she was. She said that she did not have a child, but that her husband was kind to her and that they had a good marital relationship. Her aged husband was already retired and financially depended mostly on her income from work. As an immigrant, her English was only fluent enough for her to work in a shop doing unskilled work. The boss was a married man, originally from Asia himself. He hired two or three female employees, mostly immigrants from Asia, to work in his shop.

The woman reported that, about a year before, her boss asked her to work late in the evening, as usual. When she was alone with him, he asked her to come into his office, and, on the sofa, he played with her body and eventually removed her clothes and had sexual relations with her. She was surprised by what was happening but stated that she was too scared to resist, run, or shout out for help, because he was physically very strong and there was no way to resist or escape. Besides, she added that he was her boss and was very authoritative. (She explained that she was raised in a culture in which it was very difficult for a woman to say no to an authoritative man.)

She did not dare mention this incident to her husband because she was afraid that he might divorce her. (In her home country, a husband had the right to desert his wife if she were "contaminated" by a man other than her husband.) Besides, she needed her job to support her family, and there was no easy way for her to find another one. She kept quiet about the incident and continued to work there, making an effort to avoid any opportunity for her boss to take advantage of her again.

The previous month, she had come upon a young female coworker, also an Asian immigrant, who had started to work in the store several weeks before. The woman was crying and looked unhappy, so she asked what was wrong. The coworker revealed that the boss had raped her, in almost the same manner that he had raped the older woman. When she heard about her boss taking advantage of another woman, she became very angry and without hesitation decided to take legal action to "punish" this terrible boss and stop him from damaging other innocent young women.

The psychiatrist's investigation revealed the woman's motivation and psychology regarding her reaction to the incident and why she had delayed so long to take legal action. However, it would take further work by the psychiatrist, in collaboration with the attorney, to convince the judge and the jury that the woman's explanation had merit on its own, with cultural considerations.

A CULTURALLY APPROPRIATE APPROACH TO
EXAMINING MENTAL STATUS

General Considerations and Proper Preparation

In the process of any psychiatric evaluation, especially those assessing competency in its various manifestations, the examiner carries out a mental status examination in which he or she systematically evaluates the examinee's state of mind by going through various aspects of mental function. These usually include orientation, cognition, thought process, perception, affection, intellectual function, psychomotor action, insight (awareness of one's own mental problems), and so on. The examination is often carried out in a format that allows a clinical judgment to be made about the responses given by the examinee. However, this stylized way of examining mental functioning warrants cultural concern. Examinees who are not familiar with psychiatric mental status examinations may be confused and puzzled and react in an unusual way, which may mislead the results of the assessment and diagnosis. Careful explanation and guidance to the examinee can help avoid this.

For instance, how questions are asked to elicit correct responses are very important. Asking the question "Do you hear any voices?" may not be understood correctly by the examinee as inquiring into the presence of auditory hallucinations. Instead, he may answer that his hearing ability is intact. "How do you feel?" and "Are you depressed?" are other examples that sound simple in daily English but can be very confusing from the language and conceptual perspectives of those who do not commonly refer to "feeling" or states of "depression." "Do you feel tired?" "Have you lost energy for daily work?" "Have you lost your appetite to eat?" and "Have you lost interest in everyday life?" may be more suitable questions to ask.

Cultural Modification of the Examination

As a part of the mental status examination, an examiner may ask questions such as "Who is the president of the United States?" as a way to examine the examinee's fund of social information. This is a proper question to ask if the examinee is a citizen of the United States, currently living in the country, with adequate contact with the social environment through the news media. However, such a question is irrelevant when it is addressed to a foreigner or someone with limited access to social media.

The interpretation of proverbs provides another example. To assess the examinee's abstraction ability, an examiner may routinely ask for interpretations of various proverbs, such as "A rolling stone gathers no moss" or "The grass is greener on the other side of the fence." These standard proverbs have their roots in English language and culture and may be undecipherable to many non-Westerners who are entirely unfamiliar with them. In other words proverbs are cultural products and are often difficult to understand across cultures. Proper selection of proverbs to suit the individual examinee is very important if proverb interpretation is used in the mental status exam.

Some Mental Symptoms Needing Special Attention

Certain psychiatric symptoms must be clarified and assessed with extra effort and caution to avoid any possible confusion from semantic and conceptual perspectives, particularly when we are performing transcultural assessment. The following are some areas that need special attention.

Hallucinations. A hallucination is a disturbance in perception, causing the individual to hear, see, or experience sensory stimulation without stimuli from outside. The occurrence of this symptom is interpreted generally as a sign that the person is suffering from a psychotic condition. Clinical skill is required when inquiring about the presence or absence of hallucinations, particularly auditory or visual ones. Experiences that have occurred in the absence of external stimulation must be clarified. The individual must explain carefully the "unusual" experience of hearing and seeing things that are not shared by other people. Because this kind of pathological symptom is due to a disorder of perception experienced subjectively by the individual and is difficult for outsiders to validate, the examiner has to rely solely on the patient's description. This becomes a complicated matter when the examiner does not speak the same language as the person being examined. Even when an interpreter is used, the meaning of the examiner's questions and the examinee's answers may still be misunderstood. The difficulty may be compounded because people from some cultures may take the view that hearing voices is "natural" or "a blessing" rather than a "pathological" experience.

Delusions. A delusion is defined as a "false" belief that has no basis in objective reality and is not culturally based but is firmly believed by the individual. Delusions are subjective experiences that result from the misinterpretation of information from the outside reality. They are a mental symptom that is difficult to detect if an individual refuses to reveal them, and even when disclosed, they may be difficult to differentiate from nonpathological beliefs or overvalued ideas. Adequate information and knowledge about the reality base is necessary to make a proper determination. If the examiner is not familiar with the reality system of the examinee's culture, or has difficulty understanding it, the examiner will have great difficulty identifying delusional beliefs. This is a common situation that may occur when the examinee belongs to a cultural group with which the examiner is not very familiar or if there is a significant obstruction in communication due to language problems.

Delusions that are associated with political issues, religious matters, or affection between a man and a woman often fall into a gray area of possible reality and are especially difficult to distinguish from nonpathological beliefs. Special efforts are warranted in evaluating such beliefs. Interviewing family members, friends, or people from the same cultural background as the examinee and consulting with clinicians who are familiar with the norms of the culture is helpful.

Disturbed thinking process. Normal people think and process information in a rational and intellectual way, whereas mentally disordered persons, particularly schizophrenic individuals, do not. The examiner's judgment as to whether the examinee is suffering from a psychotic condition, particularly schizophrenia, is based on how the examinee thinks, either rationally, logically, linearly, comprehensibly, or otherwise. However, it is not easy to evaluate and judge rational, logical, or comprehensible thought processes when we encounter a person who is used to thinking quite differently, not only semantically but also conceptually. Whether it is an idiosyncratically manifested individual psychopathology or a culturally shared thought process, it deserves careful consideration before any judgment is made. Again, obtaining opinions from family members, friends, and other people from the same cultural background or consulting with cultural experts is necessary to avoid error.

Elevated or apathetic mood. There is generally no problem identifying an elated mood or manic condition because it is obvious. However, caution is still needed, because some groups of people, by nature or ethnic character, tend to be cheerful, happy, and talkative and should not be labeled in haste as manic without checking against the norm of mood presentation. On the contrary, if some people fail to express their moods openly, showing little emotion, particularly without obvious fluctuation, they may be labeled apathetic, particularly from the point of view of an examiner who tends to show emotion more openly. Judgment of mood or emotion is a relative matter and should be checked against the norm of other people and the examiner. It is important to distinguish those people who, by culture, are taught not to express emotion openly in public (particularly in front of strangers) from those who suffer from withdrawal of emotion (namely, are pathologically apathetic). This kind of mistake tends to occur when the Western examiner (who is used to demonstrating emotion rather freely) is assessing a non-Western patient who looks apathetic, adding one more "findings" to support a clinical diagnosis of a psychotic disorder, particularly schizophrenia. Similarly, an irritable mood that may be attributable to an individual's difficulties in interacting with a culturally foreign examiner and legal system may be misinterpreted as evidence of mood pathology.

Insight (awareness of one's illness). Finally, a part of the mental examination evaluates the extent to which the examinee is aware, is able to admit to, and is able to seek treatment for his or her mental illness. This ability is called having insight or awareness of one's own mental disorder. However, we must consider what it might mean for the examinee to admit that he or she has a mental disorder. In some cultures, being mentally disordered means being sent to a mental institution for custodial care, without much hope of being discharged. Even if the person is discharged, he or she may be subject to a strong stigma in society for the rest of his or her life. Therefore, the examinee has a good reason to deny that there is a mental problem. However, the examinee may still be assessed in Western culture as having no insight into his or her mental condition. In contrast, in other cultures, being a psychiatric patient means being admitted to a well-maintained psychiatric hospital, with a comfortable bed and warm food every day, and being treated well and cared for by the staff. In this case, it would be relatively easy for a person to admit that he or she had mental problems. Therefore, in judging if an examinee is aware of and will admit to a mental disorder, the examiner needs to take into consideration the examinee's understanding of mental disorders and, in particular, how he or she feels about having such a disorder from a cultural perspective. Furthermore, individuals raised in traditional societies may not view psychological phenomena as biomedically based. Levels and kinds of distress that in Western technological culture are seen as symptomatic of mental illness may have very different explanations in other societies.

In summary, beyond knowing how to conduct a forensic interview and assess and incorporate the information obtained, an examiner should carefully consider whether there are cultural factors influencing the process and results of a mental examination. This is particularly true when the examiner is evaluating an individual from a cultural background that is greatly different from the examiner's own. In that case, the examiner is faced with examining the individual and making decisions without an appropriate baseline, without the sound ground of a norm against which to compare one's findings.

CERTAIN LEGALLY RELATED ISSUES REQUIRING CULTURAL CONSIDERATION

Concepts of Right and Wrong

One important task of forensic psychiatrists providing consultation to the legal system is deciding if a defendant knew right from wrong at the time of the crime and was aware of the wrongfulness of his or her behavior. Not only are the concepts of right and wrong defined by the legal system they also are shaped by culture. They may vary from society to society and in this sense are not absolute. Right and wrong depend on a variety of factors: the motivation behind the behavior, the meaning assigned to it, the implications and consequences, and how others in the society perceived it (Matthews & Tseng, 2004). For example, in the French story *Les Misérables*, stealing bread was considered wrongful behavior deserving of severe punishment, but today such an act would likely be regarded as a minor transgression not meriting lengthy imprisonment or harsh treatment. Right and wrong are often judged by varying social standards that lead different societies and cultures to different conclusions about how wrongful a behavior is.

This point is well illustrated by a cross-cultural study. To investigate how cultural factors influence the perception of stress, Masuda and Holmes (1967) carried out a study of Japanese and Americans. They used the Social Readjustment Rating Questionnaire to rank items that were perceived as stressful and required considerable readjustment in the participants' lives. The researchers arranged the data obtained in order of the severity of the items. The results indicated a high concordance between the Japanese and the American samples in the manner in which they establish a relative order of magnitude of life events, such as "death of spouse" or "divorce." However, cultural variants also were evident that distinguished members of one industrialized society from another. Many life-event items were scored significantly differently by Japanese and Americans. The item "detention in jail" was ranked 2nd by Japanese but 6th by Americans. "Minor violation of the law" was ranked 28th by Japanese and 43rd by Americans. Clearly, to offend the law was considered a more serious matter in Japanese than in American culture.

Following Masuda and Holme's investigation, Rahe (1969) added a survey of additional cultural groups, namely, African American, Mexican American, Hawaiian, Danish, and Swedish, in his comparative study. Again, even though the investigator claimed that general patterns were similar for all the subject groups studied, there were considerable differences among the groups. Among the items relating to legal matters, "jail term" appeared to represent less of a life change for the Mexican American (19th ranking order) and Hawaiian (10th ranking order) groups than for the Japanese, Danish, and Swedish, who ranked it 2nd, and Caucasian Americans, who ranked it 6th. Life events that could cause life changes had considerably different ranking orders in the various cultural groups investigated, which Rahe associated with different cultural influences. Different cultural groups also perceived legal problems differently in terms of severity.

Generally speaking, the extent to which behavior is regarded as wrong can vary among different cultures regarding many legally related matters, such as telling a lie, cheating on taxes, bankruptcy, bribery, embezzlement, rape, or even homicide of an "enemy," depending on how these issues are perceived by the cultures.

Concept of Responsibility

The question of who should take responsibility and shoulder blame for a wrongful act deserves careful consideration from a cultural perspective. In an individual-oriented society, an individual will assume sole legal responsibility for his or her actions. That is, a person's parents, spouse, or children will not have to share responsibility for criminal behavior unless they participated in it. However, in a family-oriented society, the responsibility does not necessarily end with the individual. For example, in some cultures parents, a spouse, or children must satisfy a person's legal or financial debts if necessary. History illustrates the extreme example in which all immediate family members of the criminal were executed if the person committed a serious offense, such as offending a monarch. Responsibility did not end with the individual who committed the offense.

Judging Normality Versus Abnormality

Judging whether a defendant's behavior is normal or pathological, or usual or unusual, is important in transcultural assessments in general, but it is particularly crucial in forensic evaluations. To assess the influence of culture on psychopathology, one must take into account the operating definition of normality versus pathology, because the distinction between normal and abnormal, as certain psychopathologies are concerned, may vary greatly among different cultures. Clinically, as pointed out by Offer and Sabshin (1974), there are four ways to distinguish normality from pathology. We discuss them in the following paragraphs.

By Professional Definition
According to this approach, normality or pathology can be differentiated clearly by the nature of the phenomenon and judgment

made about it by professionals. Certain conditions (manifested as signs or symptoms) are considered to be absolutely pathological in nature. A diagnosis can be made on conditions that are applicable universally, beyond cultural boundaries. Gross organic brain disorders, such as severe dementia, a delirious state, or a severe psychotic condition, with pathological thought disorders or disorganized behavior, tend to be easily and confidently diagnosed by experts, even cross-culturally.

By Deviation from the Mean

This approach relies on mathematical measurement and uses a range of deviations from the mean to distinguish between normal and abnormal. For example, having hypertension and being underweight are medical conditions that are defined as normal according to certain scales and measurements; a pathological condition is diagnosed when the measurement goes beyond the average range. In psychiatry the measurement of IQ serves to distinguish normal or subnormal intelligence. Although the concept of the mean is universal, the range of the mean often needs to be adjusted for different populations. This is true when personality is assessed by questionnaires cross-culturally. The cutting point for defining behavior disorders as measured by questionnaires is another area that requires careful cross-cultural adjustment. For example, determining what amount of drinking is excessive requires biological, social, and cultural adjustments. (For details see chapter 3.)

By Assessment of Function

This approach considers the effect of a person's mental condition on his or her actual functioning in daily life. The basis for this judgment is whether the condition provides (healthy) function or (unhealthy) dysfunction in the individual. Memory disturbance is determined by the extent to which a person can retain information and reproduce it through recollection. For instance, if a person living in an urban setting cannot recall the street number of his or her house or the name of the street where he or she lives and thus does not know how to return home, the individual is clearly suffering from memory dysfunction. In contrast, if a person living in a remote rural area, where a street number is not significant, does not recall it, the individual may not be considered dysfunctional unless he or she forgets where the village is located or how it looks and cannot return to it. Thus, it is the purpose and function of memory that needs to be considered, rather than the information to be recollected (Thompson, Donegan, & Lavond, 1986).

Openly aggressive behavior that frequently disturbs family, neighbors, or society generally will be perceived by the family or community as dysfunctional and, therefore, pathological. On the other hand, quiet, seclusive, and asocial behavior, if it does not cause problems for other people, may not be considered dysfunctional and thus may not be labeled pathological. Studies have shown that examiners' evaluations of hyperactive children vary greatly in different cultures (Mann et al., 1992). In other words, from a functional point of view behavior tends to be judged primarily by its impact on the individual, others, and the environment.

By Social Definition

This approach uses the judgment of a society or culture about what behavior is normal and what is pathological. The decision is subject to the limitations of knowledge and the attitudes found among the members of a society. The conclusion is subjective and made collectively.

For instance, walking seminude in a public area may be considered normal behavior in one situation (such as on Waikiki Beach in Honolulu), unusual in another (such as on Fifth Avenue in New York), and obscene in a third (such as at the Meiji Shrine in Tokyo), depending on how each society defines and tolerates such behavior. When a man continues to live with his parents after age 25, he may be considered dependent in the United States but ordinary in Filipino society. Speaking out against authority figures (such as parents, teachers, or the police) may be regarded as brave behavior in a democratic society but antisocial in an autocratic one. The judgments made by a society may vary greatly, depending on customs, beliefs, and values. In general social behavior tends to be assessed and defined by sociocultural judgments.

Evaluators might consider which approach is being used, recognize the limitations of each approach, and make whatever sociocultural adjustments are necessary before making a final assessment.

Judging normality versus abnormality is relatively easy for certain psychopathologies, such as severe dementia and a disorganized psychotic condition, and difficult for others, such as a delusion (Levy, 1996). One of the best ways to assess if an individual's idea is pathological and delusional in nature is to rely on objective information from family, friends, or others persons of the same ethnic or cultural background in the community. However, it is often very valuable to consult with expert, professional, cultural psychiatrists who are familiar with the language and culture of the defendant and have psychiatric knowledge of and experience with the individual's society of origin.

Definition of Insanity

The jury in a criminal case decides whether the defendant was sane at the time of the crime, but the determination of insanity is influenced by many factors in addition to the forensic professional's expert opinion. Juries bring to bear their commonsense perceptions about what constitutes insanity. In many cases this may have a direct impact on their perception and judgment regarding sanity. Opposing forensic experts often provide conflicting opinions about a defendant's sanity, and at times this may be due to differing interpretations about the meaning of insanity. Insanity is a medico-legal concept rather than a diagnostic category in the official psychiatric classification system. A number of other psychiatric conditions that may be claimed by a defendant, such as dissociated states, borderline personality disorders, and multiple personality disorders (dissociative identity disorders) have also generated controversy among experts.

Lying, Manipulating, and Malingering

People in litigation may deny, distort, rationalize, manipulate, malinger, and lie if they perceive doing so to be advantageous. Depending on one's cultural background, such behavior may be considered to be very bad, and the person will lose creditability, regardless of the excuses he or she gives. In other cultures the same behavior may be understood and tolerated as more or less acceptable. In an authoritarian society in which punishment is severe, a person may learn from childhood to use denial or distortion as a survival defense for use in dealing with difficult situations. In a society that places a high value on honesty as a virtue (exemplified by the story of a young George Washington admitting that he cut down a cherry tree), being dishonest is considered unreliable and disgraceful. Acts of dishonesty should be understood and evaluated against the cultural norm, although properly assessing and judging whether a person is lying or malingering can be challenging (Bunnting, Wessels, Lasich, & Pillay, 1996).

ASSESSMENT OF MALINGERING: CULTURAL CONSIDERATIONS

General Issues

A routine part of forensic assessment is the detection of malingering. Assessment of malingering may involve clinical evaluation, structured interviewing, and psychometric testing. Detecting malingering can be difficult even for experienced forensic psychiatrists and psychologists, requiring specialized knowledge and skill (Resnick, 2002, 2003).

Understanding cultural permission and the habit of "lying." Everyone lies sometimes, either for convenience or for personal and social adaptation or gain. However, the extent to which people lie, how often they lie, the extent to which they are permitted to lie, and the reasons for which they lie differ from one society to another. In some societies honesty and truth are stressed so greatly that any lie is regarded as morally unacceptable, whereas, in other societies lying for certain reasons is permitted behavior and is even considered normal (or useful) for coping in certain situations.

To evaluate lying, one needs to know the issues about which people lie and their motivation for doing so. Individual and sociocultural judgments will determine whether lies are serious, or minor matters, such as when a man says he is too busy to visit and turns down an invitation from a friend (when in reality he is not interested in visiting the friend), or a woman does not tell her true age to a new boyfriend, or when someone cheats a little on his or her tax return.

Distinguishing between partial "lying" and total "malingering." Clinically, forensic examiners must differentiate between a person who lies for a particular reason and someone who deliberately lies to intentionally achieve the goal of malingering. This is an entirely different clinical condition with different legal implications. Both normal people and those with serious mental disorders may exaggerate or minimize mental symptoms or psychological problems for various reasons. These people need to be differentiated from those who consciously and intentionally provide misinformation to obtain certain gains (to avoid legal punishment, to get better care, or to gain certain financial benefits).

General Cautions and Special Attention

Interpretation of "lying." Professional experiences teach clinicians how to make rough and ready judgments as to whether a person is lying. They note whether the examinee is maintaining eye contact with the examiner, blinking his or her eyes, or changing his or her voice when answering about a critical matters, as well as many other nonverbal signs. Nonverbal communication is subject to cultural shaping. For example, not maintaining eye contact with an authority figure or a stranger may be appropriate cultural etiquette within some groups. One sign examiners may rely on in assessing lying is hesitation and taking time to think before answering; this may be interpreted as a sign that the examinee is searching for the "right" answer and that he is "guarded and defensive." Before making such an interpretation, the examiner should rule out the possibility of a language or cultural factor. When a person with a language difficulty or limitation is asked about a critical subject (that may shape the legal decision to be made concerning him), the person is advised to take time to understand the question, think carefully, and search for the correct words with which to answer. In such a case, the person is not manipulating the answer.

Subject falsified. Under certain circumstances people will change their names, ages, or other identifying personal information. For example, an underage person who is economically stressed may add years to his or her age to qualify for a wanted job. A person may make a name change to avoid being identified as a member of an ethnic group that is out of favor. Although some people may interpret this behavior as dishonest according to their moral standards, others may be less critical. A cultural understanding of the circumstances under which the person falsified the information and his or her practical reasons for doing so must precede any interpretation that the person is simply lying.

Reinterpretation of "Ordinary" Indicators for Malingering

Forensic psychiatrics have accumulated a body of clinical knowledge on the detection of malingering (Rogers, 1997). The signs of malingering in the majority population, however, deserve careful cultural consideration and adjustment. The following are some behaviors thought to indicate malingering (Melton, Petrila, Poythress, & Slobogin, 1997, pp. 53–58), elaborated here from a cultural perspective.

An overplayed and dramatic presentation. Some individuals may present problems or symptoms in a theatrical style, display an eagerness to discuss them, report extremely severe symptoms, or indiscriminately endorse symptoms. Such behaviors often indicate that the examinee is eager for the examiner to believe that he or she is suffering from a mental disorder, and a severe one at that. Although this may be a useful marker in many cases, it may also be influenced by other factors. Besides personality influences (such as histrionic personality features), complaining in a particular way—loudly, for example—may be acceptable in certain cultures.

Deliberateness and carefulness. In contrast, an examinee might respond to inquiries with extreme caution. Slower rates of speech, hesitation, or a tendency to clarify with deliberation are some features of this style. Such behavior usually indicates that the examinee is being careful not to make a mistake and does not want to be misunderstood by the examiner as not having a mental disorder. As elaborated previously, if the examinee is not fluent in the language being spoken, he or she may require time to think about how to reply correctly; this may be misinterpreted as being deliberately defensive. In addition people from some cultural groups simply tend to think and speak more slowly than others.

Complaints inconsistent with true psychiatric illness. This is another useful indicator of malingering in ordinary circumstances. This indicator is based on the medical assumption that different psychiatric disorders tend to manifest a distinct set of clinical features. For instance, an epileptic convulsion, which is a neurological disorder, has certain unique features that are quite different from a hysterical conversion. Knowing this will help the clinician discern a hysterical convulsion (which occurs as the result of a psychological reaction) from an epileptic convulsion (which is induced by a neurological disturbance). However, caution needs to be taken from the cross-cultural standpoint. Even though most major psychiatric disorders (e.g., psychoses) share a more or less similar clinical picture among patients of different cultures, there still exist atypical cases that are different from the disorders usually recognized by (Western) standardized psychiatric classifications, for example, culture-specific clinical syndromes. These may not fit well with the clinical descriptions that Western-trained psychiatrists know and encounter routinely and thus may easily be misinterpreted as a sign of malingering.

Inconsistency of self-report. Inconsistency of self-report is when an examinee tends to report contradictory symptoms and there is a disparity between reported and observed symptomatology. Although this inconsistency is useful as an indicator for detecting malingering, an examinee who is not well equipped with the proper language skills to communicate and elaborate symptoms may have inconsistencies that might be detected and incorrectly attributed to malingering by the examiner.

Instruments for Assessment of Malingering

Objective testing may be very useful in detecting the presence of malingering. In addition to the use of general psychological testing, such as intelligence testing, the Minnesota Multiphasic Personality Inventory (MMPI) (Hathaway & McKinley, 1940), or neuropsychological testing, there are instruments designed specifically for the assessment of malingering, such as the Structured Inventory of Reported Symptomatology (Lewis, Simcox, & Berry, 2002).

Ganellen, Wasyliw, and Haywood (1996) studied people trying to malinger psychosis. They reported that the participants in the malingering group did not differ from the honest responders on Rorschach variables that distinguish psychotic from nonpsychotic patients, but they did differ in the number of dramatic responses produced. They suggested that the combination of an objective instrument, such as the MMPI, and a projective instrument, such as the Rorschach test, provides a powerful psychometric technique for detecting deliberate malingering for psychosis. Heinze and Purisch (2001) echoed this point of view; that is, that any one test alone is not sensitive enough to be employed as a single malingering test.

Few studies have focused on the cross-ethnic aspects of malingering assessment. Bunnting and colleagues (1996) focused on African American forensic participants and developed a rating scale for assessing malingering. They reported that some items have a high positive predictive value (suggesting universal applicability). That is, "There is a marked discrepancy in the performance of the same specific intellectual task on two different occasions and/or the intellectual performance is not in keeping with the education," and "The accused has altered consciousness with subsequent amnesia for the event and yet was able to defend himself or herself." In contrast there are some items that have a low positive predictive value, such as, "There is a past history of criminal behavior as shown by one of more periods of imprisonment and/or having faced criminal charges on at least two occasions in the past," and "The accused presents for the first time to the medico-legal team at a relatively young age (i.e., below 30 years)." This low positive predictive value is because some African Americans have relatively frequent legal charges, sometimes starting in an early stage of life, so that these two items are not as (ethnically) valid as they are for other ethnic groups.

The MMPI–Second Revision (MMPI-2), one of the commonly used instruments for measuring personality and psychopathology, also is used as an instrument to detect any tendency of malingering. The MMPI-2, by design, has several specific scales constructed to check the validity of responses made by the examinee (Graham, 1990, pp. 22–51). The Cannot Say (?) Scale is based on the number of omitted items, including those answered both true and false. It is interpreted as the examinee being unwilling or uncertain about how to reveal himself, a possible sign of being "guarded." The L scale is constructed to detect a deliberate and rather unsophisticated attempt to present in a favorable light. The items deal with minor flaws and weaknesses, to which most people are willing to admit. However, those who are deliberately trying to present themselves in a very favorable way are not willing to admit even a minor shortcoming. The F scale is constructed to detect deviant or atypical ways of responding to test items. It shows that the examinee answered in the scored direction by less than 10% of ordinary (American) adult participants. The K scale is constructed to examine in a subtle way the tendency of test distortion. It intends to detect any attempts by examinees to deny psychopathology and to present themselves in a favorable light or, conversely, to exaggerate psychopathology and to try to appear in a very unfavorable light.

Although these scales are useful in general to help clinicians check for the validity of responses made by the examinees, there is still a need for cultural consideration and adjustment before making any final interpretation of the data. Besides the common issues that are inherent in various instruments for psychological testing for transcultural application (for details, see chapter 3), there is room for cultural consideration of the same issues that were elaborated on previously in the clinical examination. Regarding the Cannot Say (?) Scale, some examinees, because of language or conceptual problems, may have difficulty understanding the items written in English and will not know how to respond to them. Hesitation in making responses should not be interpreted hastily as a sign of faking. When interpreting the L scale, it needs to be known that some examinees, because of their cultural heritage, have a common tendency to present themselves as "good" that is not directly related to "faking." If examinees produce high scores on the F scale for giving many atypical responses, one must determine whether that is related to idiosyncratic culture-related responses before a judgment concerning validity is made. Examiners should remember that the MMPI-2 norms are based on the data obtained from the American population, without validation on populations of other ethnic or cultural groups. The judgment of "typical" is based on ordinary American adults, and examiners should not make the conclusion of "atypical" responses without taking culture into account. Finally, examiners discovered that the K scale is not as reliable as originally thought by the developers. Scores are influenced by educational level and socioeconomic status of the examinees, with better educated and higher socioeconomic-level participants scoring higher (Graham, 1990, p. 27). Thus, even though objective testing provides additional information for clinicians in making judgments, additional caution and reinterpretation is always necessary if the examinee is not from the ordinary (American) population.

Third-Party Information

Collateral information provided by third parties may be very useful in determining if an examinee is malingering. For example, staff working on the wards of a forensic hospital who can observe the examinee's daily behavior and interactions with others are very useful to the clinician as an additional source of information. Information offered by the examinee's family members or friends or by law enforcement should be considered when making a judgment. Other sources of information are particularly important when communication with the examinee is hindered by the absence of a common language or when there are concerns that the report made by the examinee is inconsistent with the behavior observed by others.

In summary the detection of malingering requires clinical knowledge, skill, and judgment, sometimes augmented by findings from objective psychological testing that support the clinical impression. Detecting malingering may be affected by various cultural factors that have been enumerated, such as language problems or the examinee's (culture-rooted) overreaction to the formal interview or interrogation setting. Persons from other cultures may not be used to being interviewed by an authority figure and may become overanxious in responding. They may not fully understand the meaning of being interviewed or the potential consequence of not providing "true" responses. The situation may be compounded by the examiner's own reaction, the personal and ethnic countertransference, toward "lying" by the examinee. Careful explanation and instruction may reduce the tension, minimize the overreaction by the examinee, and decrease the possibility of misrepresentation of clinical features.

PARTICULAR CONCERN IS NEEDED FOR CERTAIN POPULATIONS

Certain populations deserve special care and consideration in the legal system. These populations include foreigners, ethnic or racial minorities, children and adolescents, women, and the hearing and speech impaired. We elaborate on how to care for these populations in the correctional system in chapter 8 (see the section "Care for Specific Populations"). Here we briefly touch on matters relating to assessment.

Assessing Foreigners or Immigrants

The term *foreigner* refers to a person who has temporarily moved into another society with the intention of returning to the home country. Students from foreign countries or international business persons and their family are good examples. When they commit legally wrongful behavior, and are subject to forensic evaluation, special attention is warranted. They may not be familiar with the legal system in the host society and problems with language often are involved. Their attorney must make an extra effort to explain the local legal system, the implications of the charges, their legal options, and the legal rights they may exercise.

Some foreigners are afraid of authority, particularly law enforcement officers, because they have been treated badly by such authorities in their home countries and have difficulty trusting governmental agents. Time may be required for them to feel comfortable with and trust the persons they must work with within the legal system.

If a foreigner does not speak the language of the host society, proper translation through a competent interpreter should be provided. Even foreigners who speak the language of the host society rather fluently may experience problems in terms of how to interpret the words and concepts properly and grasp their meanings and implications correctly.

Many legal concepts, such as confidentiality, legal rights, and the role of the jury, may be unfamiliar to foreigners, and adequate explanations are always in order. As we mentioned previously, too formal of an approach in conducting interviews for assessments may frighten a foreigner and increase his or her defensiveness. Exceptions need to be considered and less formal approaches may be considered, at times, to gain the needed information.

The term *immigrant* refers to persons who emigrate from their home country to the hosting society with the intention to stay permanently in the hosting society. As new members of the hosting society, they theoretically need to learn the language, lifestyle, and rules of the hosting society. In reality, however, many new immigrants—particularly first-generation ones—may not speak the common language used in the hosting society and may not be familiar with local laws. Their situation will resemble that of foreigners in this aspect, and it needs careful consideration from the legal perspective

(Fromkin & Friedland, 1995). Immigrants who moved to the hosting country many years before, as well as their descendents (second generation and after), may still think and behave like new immigrants, depending on their motivation for accommodating to the hosting society's culture, their level of education, and their level of communication and degree of interaction with others in the majority community. Immigrants who enter the hosting society illegally face certain additional complications from the legal process. Because of the fear of being deported back to their home countries, they may tend to respond in such a way that is pleasing to the examiner in the hope of being allowed to stay in the hosting society. When making an evaluation the evaluator must carefully consider the immigrants' motivation.

Evaluating Ethnic or Racial Minorities

When the examinee has an ethnic or racial background of an unprivileged minority, and the examiner is from the majority, special concern is needed to deal with any bias, misunderstanding, or mistreatment that may occur in the process of assessment. The examiner must be mindful of and minimize stereotypes, discrimination, or even unfair treatment. One approach is to bring up and discuss at the beginning the difference in ethnic, race, or cultural backgrounds. The examiner may make suggestions on how to overcome the possible gaps between them. For a more proper assessment to be performed, the examinee should feel comfortable, if necessary, in taking the role of guiding the examiner in learning about the examinee's cultural system.

If the relations between the examinee and the examiner are reversed in terms of majority and minority, namely, the examiner belongs to a minority group and the examinee is of a majority background, the same cautions apply. Any ethnic or racial transference or countertransference needs to be observed and managed if it affects the objective process of evaluation.

Examining Children or Adolescents

Children and adolescents differ from adults in their stages of cognitive, social, and physical development. Children and adolescents have different levels of understanding of legal issues and different abilities in communicating, particularly in expressing their intrapsychic material. They need more guidance and encouragement than adults do in relating to the examiner and providing information from their perspectives. As in the practice of child and adolescent psychiatry, an indirect approach (such as playing a game, telling a story, or revealing wishes) should be considered and applied in clinical forensic assessment and psychological testing (Clark & Clark, 2002; Shetky & Benedek, 2002). In addition, collateral information from parents, siblings, peers, schoolteachers, or counselors should be included in the assessment. Finally, examiners should have special training and experience if they wish to evaluate young children.

Evaluating Women

Men and women have different psychologies, including different perceptions, beliefs, attitudes, values, and techniques of problem solving. The gender of the evaluator may affect the process or outcome of the evaluation, depending on the issues involved and the cultures of examinee and examiner. For example, when a male clinician evaluates a female examinee regarding sex-related issues, she may be more reticent to reveal information than she would be if the clinician were female. The same might also be true if the examinee were male and the examiner female. The male examinee may be unwilling to discuss sexual issues with the female examiner (as would be likely in Islamic cultures), or the male examinee may purposely talk about sexual matters crudely to intimidate the female examiner.

Although it may be useful for the examiner and examinee to be of the same gender, this does not provide a total solution, any more than ethnic or racial matching does. In clinical situations some male patients may feel more comfortable communicating with female therapists, and female patients may prefer to talk to male therapists. This phenomenon has been observed in the examiner-examinee relationship in a forensic context as well. No matter what matching takes place, generally speaking, cultural sensitivity, in addition to basic clinical competence and experience, is an important variable that will improve the total result of the assessment process.

Hearing- and Speech-Impaired Persons

Hearing- and speech-impaired persons not only experience limitations in communication by spoken language, they also, in contrast to unimpaired people, often go through different pathways of personal development, experience different life circumstances, and may be underprivileged and subject to discrimination by the majority of people in the society. When they encounter legal problems, they face the added difficulty of being unable to defend themselves through spoken language. Even if they use sign language to communicate, they may be limited in expressing and perceiving many detailed issues. This puts them at a serious disadvantage when it comes to legal matters. There are very few mental health workers or psychiatrists who understand sign language. Furthermore, there is a shortage of sign language interpreters who are qualified to interpret in court. Many states require special legal certification to interpret in court or court-related settings. There is a great need to train special interpreters to work with people who suffer from an inability to communicate through spoken language, especially in forensic situations.

REFERENCES

Bunnting, B. G., Wessels, W. H., Lasich, A. J., & Pillay, B. (1996). The distinction of malingering and mental illness in black forensic cases. *Medicine and Law, 15,* 241–247.

Clark, B. K., & Clark, C. R. (2002). Psychological testing in child and adolescent forensic evaluation. In D. H. Shetky & E. P. Benedek (Eds.), *Principles and practice of child and adolescent forensic psychiatry* (pp. 45–57). Washington, DC: American Psychiatric Publishing.

Doi, T. (1973). *The anatomy of dependence.* Tokyo: Kodansha International.

Foulks, E. (1980). The concept of culture in psychiatric residency education. *American Journal of Psychiatry, 137,* 811–816.

Fromkin, I. B., & Friedland, J. (1995). Forensic evaluations in immigration cases: Evolving issues. *Behavioral Sciences and the Law, 13,* 477–489.

Ganellen, R. J., Wasyliw, O. E., & Haywood, T. W. (1996). Can psychosis be malingered on the Rorschach? An empirical study. *Journal of Personality Assessment, 66*(1), 65–80.

Graham, J. R. (1990). *MMPI–2: Assessing personality and psychopathology.* New York: Oxford University Press.

Hathaway, S. R., & McKinley, J. C. (1940). A multiphasic personality schedule (Minnesota): I. Construction of the schedule. *Journal of Psychology, 10,* 249–254.

Heinze, M. C., & Purisch, A. D. (2001). Beneath the mask: Use of psychological tests to detect and subtype malingering in criminal defendants. *Journal of Forensic Psychology Practice, 1*(4), 23–52.

Levy, A. (1996). Forensic implications of the difficulties of defining delusions. *Medicine and Law, 15*(2), 257–260.

Lewis, J. L., Simcox, A. M., & Berry, D. T. R. (2002). Screening for feigned psychiatric symptoms in a forensic sample by using the MMPI–2 and the Structured Inventory of Reported Symptomatology. *Psychological Assessment, 14*(2), 170–176.

Lu, F., Lim, R., & Mezzich, J. (1995). Issues in the assessment and diagnosis of culturally diverse individuals. In P. Ruitz (Ed.), *Annual review of psychiatry* (pp. 477–510). Washington, DC: American Psychiatric Press.

Mann, E. M., Ikeda, Y., Mueller, C. W., Takahashi, A. M., Tao, K. T., Mumns, E., Li, B. L., Chin, D. (1992). Cross-cultural differences in rating hyperactive-disruptive behaviors in children. *American Journal of Psychiatry, 149*(11), 1539–1542.

Masuda, M., & Holmes, T. H. (1967). The Social Readjustment Rating Scale: A cross–cultural study of Japanese and Americans. *Journal of Psychosomatic Research, 11,* 227–237.

Matthews, D., & Tseng, W. S. (2004). Culture and forensic psychiatry. In W. S. Tseng & J. Streltzer (Eds.), *Culture competence in clinical psychiatry* (pp. 121–141). Washington, DC: American Psychiatric Publishing.

Melton, G. B., Petrila, J., Poythress, N. G., & Slobogin, C. (1997). *Psychological evaluations for the court: A handbook for mental health professionals and lawyers* (2nd ed.). New York: Guilford.

Moffic, M. S., Kendrick, E. A., & Reid, K. (1988). Cultural psychiatry education during psychiatric residency. *Journal of Psychiatric Education, 12,* 90–101.

Nilchaikovit, T., Hill, J. M., & Holland, J. C. (1993). The effects of culture on illness behavior and medical care: Asian and American differences. *General Hospital Psychiatry, 15,* 41–50.

Offer, D., & Sabshin, M. (1974). *Normality: Theoretical and clinical concepts of mental health* (2nd ed.). New York: Basic Books.

Rahe, R. H. (1969). Multi-cultural correlations of life change scaling: America, Japan, Denmark, and Sweden. *Journal of Psychosomatic Research, 13,* 191–195.

Resnick, P. J. (2002). The clinical assessment of malingered mental illness. In *Forensic psychiatric review course* (pp. 251–292). Bloomfield, CT: American Academy of Psychiatry and the Law.

Resnick, P. J. (2003). Malingering. In R. Rosner (Ed.), *Principles and practice of forensic psychiatry* (2nd ed., pp. 543–554). London: Arnold.

Rogers, R. (Ed.). (1997). *Clinical assessment of malingering and deception* (2nd ed.). New York: Guilford.

Shetky, D. H., & Benedek, E. P. (2002). *Principles and practice of child and adolescent forensic psychiatry.* Washington, DC: American Psychiatric Publishing.

Silva, J. A., Leong, G. B., & Weinstock, R. (2003). Culture and ethnicity. In R. Rosner (Ed.), *Principles and practice of forensic psychiatry* (2nd ed., pp. 631–637). London: Arnold.

Thompson, R. F., Donegan, N. H., & Lavond, D. G. (1986). The psychobiology of learning and memory. In R. C. Atkinson, R. J. Herrnstein, G.

Lindzey, & R. D. Luce (Eds.), *Steven's handbook of experimental psychology* (2nd ed.). New York: Wiley.

Tseng, W. S. (2003). *Clinician's guide to cultural psychiatry.* San Diego, CA: Academic Press.

Tseng, W. S., & Streltzer, J. (Eds.). (2001). *Culture and psychotherapy: A guide for clinical practice.* Washington, DC: American Psychiatric Press.

Westermeyer, J. (1989). *The psychiatric care of migrants: A clinical guide.* Washington, DC: American Psychiatric Press.

Westermeyer, J. (1990). Working with an interpreter in psychiatric assessment and treatment. *Journal of Nervous and Mental Disease, 178,* 745–749.

Yutrzenka, B. A. (1995). Making a case for training in ethnic and cultural diversity in increasing treatment efficacy. *Journal of Consulting and Clinical Psychology, 63*(2), 197–206.

3

Psychological Testing for Forensic Evaluation

TRANSCULTURAL APPLICATION OF PSYCHOLOGICAL INSTRUMENTS: GENERAL ISSUES

Although a thorough psychiatric evaluation forms the core of forensic psychiatric assessment, psychological testing often is useful to evaluate an examinee's personality, neuropsychological status, psychopathology, competency (for a specific function), level of functioning, pattern of coping, or other issues. Psychological testing provides supplemental objective data that, in addition to other sources of information, can lead to a comprehensive diagnostic and forensic assessment of the examinee.

In applying the tools of psychological measurement we must keep in mind that Western behavioral scientists or clinicians have designed most standardized tests for use in predominantly Caucasian populations with European American backgrounds. Questions may therefore be raised about the reliability and usefulness of the instruments when applied to respondents of other ethnic-cultural backgrounds living in European American societies or when, after translation and perhaps some modifications, they are applied to subjects or examinees with non-Western cultural backgrounds. The transcultural applicability of instruments employed in forensic evaluations deserves careful attention (Brislin, 2000; Lonner, 1990;

Lonner & Berry, 1986; Ratner, 1997; Segall, Dasen, Berry, & Poortinga, 1990). Depending on the testing situation, issues of the admissibility of findings under the Daubert or Frye standards (legal standards for the admissibility of scientific evidence) may arise.

Basic Considerations: Methodological Issues

Area and Scope of Measurement

Many basic issues need to be addressed when testing in different cultural settings. We must ask whether the method and instrument are applied appropriately and adequately to cover the scope of the topic being investigated: intelligence, personality, psychopathology, and other subjects. Despite our common humanity, our intellects do not perform in the same ways, our behavior patterns are not necessarily demonstrated within the same dimensions, and our pathological mental conditions are not manifested within the same scope of abnormality, because of cultural variations. Following the concept of the "netting effect," namely, that different kinds of fishing nets will catch different sizes and kinds of fish (Tseng, 2003, pp. 240–241), there is always a need to design or modify instruments to cover different areas or scopes of mental functions manifested by respondents of diverse cultural backgrounds in order to conduct culturally appropriate psychological evaluations.

Problems of Administration

In the administration of psychological tests in cross-cultural situations, examiners should question the examinee about his or her familiarity with testing. As pointed out by Lonner (1990, pp. 58–59), no other country can likely match the United States in test usage. Most current tests were developed in the United States and are based on the assumptions that individuals can order or rank stimuli linearly, can readily make judgments about social and psychological stimuli, and are capable of self-assessment and self-reflection (Trimble, Lonner, & Boucher, 1983). Clearly, such assumptions may not apply to people in many other cultures, even those whose populations are well educated or psychologically sophisticated, not to mention those in which people have never heard of, or experienced, testing.

Closely related to this are examinees' attitudes and reactions to testing, how they feel about revealing their private selves to strangers (test administrators), their attitudes toward authority (the examiners), and the meaning they ascribe to being tested. People may respond to testing in various ways. They may agree with just about everything (acquiescence), respond in socially approved directions (social desirability), or respond with answers in the middle (positional) of the spectrum. These response styles, in addition to personality, often are shaped by cultural factors and greatly affect the results of measurement.

Interpretation of Results
Even if the data are obtained in a manner that minimizes confounding influences of culture, bias may creep in during the interpretation stage. That is, examiners must take care to be sure that the data are interpreted in a culturally meaningful and relevant way. In court opposing experts and opposing counsel may assert that, unless an examiner is very familiar with the culture of the person being tested, the examiner may interpret the data incorrectly in a cross-cultural evaluation. Generally speaking, the collaboration of evaluators who are both inside and outside the culture produces a more meaningful and relevant interpretation of the data obtained both subjectively and objectively.

Equivalence and Validity

Equivalency of Meaning
If researchers are to meaningfully compare cultures, they need to meet several kinds of equivalency. Berry (1980) discussed functional, conceptual, and metric equivalence; Brislin (2000) described translation, conceptual, and metric equivalence; whereas Flaherty and colleagues (1988) were concerned with content, semantic, technical, criterion, and conceptual equivalence.

Conceptual equivalence. Conceptual equivalence requires that our tests and concepts have identical meaning in the cultures being examined. Researchers must find out the local meaning of concepts within the cognitive systems of the people and groups being compared. Only if a common meaning is discovered can comparison legitimately take place (Berry, 1980, p. 9). Therefore, it is a precondition of comparison.

Functional equivalence. Functional equivalence is concerned with whether two or more behaviors (in two or more cultural systems) are related to functionally similar problems. For example, generosity toward others in one culture might be measured by how much money one donates to a church; in another culture it might be measured by how much food one gives to other clan members.

Semantic or translation equivalence. When an instrument designed in one language is to be translated into another for transcultural application, semantic translation becomes an important issue from the standpoint of conceptual equivalence. Researchers have suggested the forward and back translation of words (Brislin, 1970, 1976, 2000), which means that an item is translated initially into a target language by one bilingual person then translated back into the original language by another bilingual person. For instance, the English words, "I had problems with the police this morning," if translated into another language and translated back as "I committed a crime this morning," would obviously illustrate a conceptual gap between the two cultures in the understanding of "had problems with the police." Discrepancies indicate conceptual nonequivalence. Through back translation and semantic differential analysis, conceptual equivalence can be ensured (Osgood, 1965).

Technical equivalence. The key issue in technical equivalence is whether the method of data collection affects the results differently in different cultures (Flaherty et al., 1988). Technical equivalence must be assessed because certain cultures may be uncomfortable and unfamiliar with the technical aspects of testing and data collection.

Metric equivalence. Metric equivalence centers on the analysis of the same concepts across cultures and assumes that the same scale (after proper translation procedures) can be used to measure the concept everywhere (Brislin, 2000, p. 103). This is important when mean scores between cultures are to be compared. To demonstrate metric equivalence in any two cultures, researchers must establish that the statistical behavior of the items in each culture is the same (Kline, 1983). Therefore, a score in one culture can be directly compared with a score in another.

Validity of the Measurement

Validity concerns whether a test, questionnaire, or set of observations measures what it is supposed to measure. The validity of the measurement is the most critical issue in the cross-cultural application of testing. What is the value of the results obtained from testing? Do the results really represent the issues being measured? How do we know that the bases of comparison are equivalent across cultures? These are questions that must be raised and answered (Rogler, 1999).

Validity for Threshold or Cutoff Point

In addition to determining measurement validity, researchers must determine at what point the results should be considered deviant or psychopathological. In other words there is a need to determine the threshold or cutoff point for inclusion of a case as positively manifesting the examined variable. Decisions about the criteria for the threshold will be subject to sociocultural considerations (Hicks, 2002) and it is foreseeable that the results will differentially affect different cultural groups.

In summary, in designing, administering, scoring, and interpreting psychological tests, several factors need to be considered from a cultural perspective. A comprehensive consideration of these factors as they affect the various available psychological tests is beyond the range of this book. Next we discuss some of the commonly used general instruments in forensic mental health practice and those used for various specialized aspects of forensic assessment, such as competency, psychopathy, or risk of violence.

CONVENTIONAL PSYCHOLOGICAL TESTS

Personality Evaluation: Minnesota Multiphasic Personality Inventory–Revised Edition

Development and revision of the instrument. The Minnesota Multiphasic Personality Inventory–Revised Edition (MMPI-2) is one of the most widely used questionnaires for the objective assessment of personality and psychopathology. It was originally developed in 1937 by psychologist Starke R. Hathaway and neurologist and psychiatrist John C. McKinley (Hathaway & McKinley, 1940). The norms were based on data collected from nonpatient samples (mostly patients' relatives and other visitors to a university hospital) in Minnesota. The questionnaire was composed of more than 500 items, which presented eight scales with clinical names: Hypochondriasis, Depression, Hysteria, Psychopathic Deviate, Paranoia, Psychasthenia, Schizophrenia, and Hypomania. Subsequently, two scales were added: Masculinity-Femininity and Social Introversion. Because the clinical scales are not pure measurements of the syndromes suggested by their names, researchers assigned numerals to the original scales, replacing the clinical labels. Four scales were developed to examine validity. The scales do not reflect simply the total number of items either omitted or responded to as both true and false by the individual taking the test. The L scale (originally called the Lie scale) was designed to detect participants who present themselves in an overly favorable light. The F scale (also called the Infrequency scale) was designed to detect individuals who tend to give responses in an atypical direction. The K scale was constructed to identify participants who tend to give responses that are lower than expected for the clinical status they manifest.

Since the development of the MMPI in the 1940s, remarkable changes have taken place in American society. Besides a marked improvement in living standards, increased levels of education, the impact of the feminist movement, and the liberalizing of religious and moral views in our technological society, there have been changes in family structure. A need developed to revitalize the MMPI. On the basis of this, Colligan and Offord (1985) carried out a project to develop contemporary norms. From the same geographic area, Minnesota, through random sampling of household residents, they systematically included a normative sample in the survey. This survey disclosed that MMPI response patterns among the sample had changed. Analysis of data yielded scores and profiles higher than those obtained from the original standardization group in the 1940s. The differences were more apparent for men than for women. The investigators speculated that the response-pattern changes were probably more due to changes in social attitudes and perceptions than to a change in mental health status. These changes illustrate that, even within the same society and (Caucasian American) ethnic group, the norm of an instrument needs to be adjusted to reflect social changes that have occurred. Culture changes over time as well as with location or social group.

In 1989 the MMPI-2 was published. This revision of the MMPI was based on several concerns (Graham, 1990, pp. 8–13). One concern was the item content of the original MMPI. Some of the language and references in the items had become archaic or obsolete. For instance, the children's game "drop the handkerchief" described in one item had not been popular among children for many years, the term "sleeping powder" was no longer used and needed to be replaced by "sleeping pill," some sexist language was no longer in accord with contemporary American standards, and some language changes were needed to eliminate subcultural bias. For example, "I go to church almost every week" was revised to read "I attend religious services almost every week." Again, this illustrated the need for considerable changes in the instrument even for administration within the same society to reflect cultural changes over time.

Obtaining normative data was another reason for revision. To obtain a large normative group that was broadly representative of the U.S. population and that ensured proper geographic representation for the MMPI-2, examiners selected seven testing sites nationally. In addition to the Caucasian sample, other ethnic groups were included to make the instrument more broadly applicable. However, the distribution of ethnic backgrounds was still skewed, as reflected by the percentage of ethnic group samples: Caucasian, 81%; African American, 12%; Hispanic American, 3%; American Indian, 3%; and Asian American, 1%. Thus, the norms developed for the MMPI-2 still predominantly reflect a Caucasian population and do not adequately represent other ethnic groups that comprise a relatively large percentage of the population, such as the Hispanic American group.

Cross-ethnic application. There have been several reports on the application of the original MMPI to minority ethnic groups in the United States. Early in the 1970s Gynther (1972) reported that African American respondents generally obtained higher scores than Caucasian American respondents on scales F (Infrequency scale), 8 (Schizophrenia), and 9 (Hypomania). In his interpretation, these differences represented differences in values, perceptions, and expectations of respondents, rather than levels of adjustment.

Pollack and Shore (1980) reported that Native American respondents from various Pacific Northwest tribes all had similar

MMPI profiles and, compared with the norm of Caucasian respondents, had significant elevations in scales Sc (Schizophrenia), Pd (Psychopathic Deviance), and Pa (Paranoia). The authors believed that the similarity of all subgroup profiles demonstrated a significant cultural influence on the results of the MMPI in the Native American population investigated.

Using an external criterion analysis of the MMPI, Megargee, Cook, and Mendelsohn (1967) derived a 31-item Overcontrolled-Hostility (O-H) Scale, which discriminates extremely assaultive from moderately and nonassaultive probation applications. Hutton, Miner, Blades, and Langfeldt (1992) used the O-H Scale on male forensic psychiatric inpatients of mixed racial backgrounds. Regression analysis using the total study sample disclosed that African American patients scored higher than Caucasian American patients. On the basis of these findings, they commented that using the O-H Scale with African American patients could lead to an erroneous interpretation of a propensity for aggressive or violent acts.

Since the revised MMPI-2 became available, scholars and clinicians have carried out several studies examining the cross-ethnic application of the test to nonclinical samples in the United States. Research by Timbrook and Graham (1994) revealed that the empirical correlates for MMPI-2 scales apply equally for African Americans and Caucasian Americans. Similarly, McNulty, Graham, Ben-Porath, and Stein (1997) studied a group of male outpatients undergoing court-ordered evaluations. They showed similar results and demonstrated empirically the relative unimportance of ethnic group differences on the MMPI-2, among some populations under certain circumstances (Pope, Butcher, & Seelen, 2000). Ben-Porath, Shondrick, and Stafford (1994) compared African Americans and Caucasian Americans who had been ordered by the court to take the MMPI-2 as part of their pretrial evaluation. They found relatively few scale-level differences between the groups, indicating that the MMPI-2 normative sample is appropriate to use for African Americans, for the majority of individuals. Only scale 9 on the clinical and validity profile and CYN (Cynicism) and ASP (Antisocial Practices) on the content scale profile were significantly different; these differences were slight, although statistically significant (Pope et al., 2000).

International application. When Song (1985) applied the MMPI to Chinese individuals in China, she reported that, among both male and female normal respondents, the scores for D (Depression) and Sc (Schizophrenia) were elevated in contrast to the norms of American respondents. According to Song, this reflected Chinese character traits that were completely different from those of Americans. As manifested in the test results, the Chinese are emotionally more reserved, introverted, fond of tranquility, overly considerate, socially overcautious, and habitually self-restrained. These results indicate the need to use modified norms in measuring Chinese personality traits. In other words if Chinese norms were applied in the measurement of American respondents, the scores for the D and Sc scales would be degraded; that is, from the Chinese perspective, Americans are more extroverted, express emotion freely, are less considerate in interpersonal relations, and are socially less cautious. This reflects the relativity of trait descriptions, depending on the perspective from which the data are measured and interpreted. It also points to the need for adjustment of norms in the transcultural application of the MMPI. On the basis of these findings, Cheung and Song designed a Chinese version of the personality assessment inventory, similar to the MMPI in its basic structure, with special items for the Chinese, and they labeled the instrument the Chinese Personality Assessment Inventory (Cheung, Chang, & Song, 1996).

Evaluation of Depression: Inventory for Assessing Depression

There are many instruments designed for the systematic assessment of psychopathology for diagnostic purposes. Some have major clinical and forensic application, whereas others are primarily research tools. We discuss only the assessment of depression, because it is often of forensic importance and it lends itself to an apt illustration of cultural impact on its clinical measurement.

The Composite International Diagnostic Interview is a standardized instrument developed by the World Health Organization (1997) for administration by laypersons in psychiatric epidemiological studies. This instrument was originally derived from the National Institute of Mental Health Diagnostic Interview Schedule, developed for U.S. populations for the Epidemiological Catchment Area study, and the World Health Organization adopted it for international use. Although identifying the symptom items of depression was not difficult, there was a problem in identifying cases for clinical purposes. In other words this instrument was designed not only to explore symptoms but also to determine whether the case was positive for a clinical disorder. The clinical significance of symptoms is determined by such criteria as whether the person has told a doctor or other professional (such as a nurse or a social worker) about the symptoms, whether the person has been told to take medication for them, and whether the symptoms have interfered very much with the person's life or activities.

According to Hicks (2002), when the Composite International Diagnostic Interview was used to detect major depression among Chinese American women, underdetecting the disorder became a potential problem because the inclusion criteria addressed help-seeking behavior. Socioeconomic conditions and cultural factors, such as coming from a non-U.S. political environment (such as mainland China) or living in deprived social conditions, significantly modified help-seeking behavior. For example, in the past political atmosphere of China, patients were not comfortable complaining about depression to a doctor, fearing that such complaints might be misinterpreted as a sign that they were resentful toward the government. In addition individuals physically or economically isolated from sources of medical care are per force unable to tell a doctor or other professional about their symptoms or take recommended medications for them. Furthermore, if living conditions are gravely undesirable and depression is an ongoing part of everyone's daily existence, the conditions will not be considered to interfere with life. In other words because of inclusion criteria or the threshold determined, researchers may underdiagnose depression among patients living in certain sociocultural environments. Such research indicates that the instrument is culturally unsound, inadequate in its design, and not applicable cross-culturally or internationally, despite its design as an instrument for international epidemiological surveys.

In clinical application the Beck Depression Inventory and Zung's Depression Inventory are among the most commonly used tools for the assessment of depression in the United States. Both inventories contain a set of questions related to the symptomatic complex regarded as depression. However, it is common knowledge among cultural psychiatrists that the clinical condition of depression may be manifested differently according to a patient's cultural background, with variations in how the condition is perceived, experienced, and expressed. Examiners must exercise care when using and interpreting results from these instruments. In some cases alternative versions of these instruments, tested and normed on the target population, have been developed to address these tests' shortcomings.

A group of American cultural psychiatrists (Kinzie et al., 1982) working with Vietnamese refugees in Oregon for many years found that it was difficult to use existing depression scales, such as the Beck Depression Inventory, to assess the Vietnamese patients under their care. Therefore, they developed a depressive scale in the Vietnamese language that contained culturally consistent items describing the thoughts, feelings, and behaviors of depressed individuals and items describing the common clinical characteristics of depressed Vietnamese patients. They claimed that this culturally relevant depressive scale was much more useful for clinical application with this particular group of people.

For similar reasons Chinese psychiatrists developed the Chinese Depression Inventory (Zheng & Lin, 1991) for depressed patients in China. The psychiatrists constructed the inventory according to the culture and verbal styles used to express emotional and somatic experiences relating to depression. For instance, the words *suicide, sexual drive,* and *sense of failure,* which were considered sensitive and negative in their culture, were replaced by more euphemistic expressions, such as "being alive is not interesting," "not interested in the opposite sex," and "feeling like a weak person in life." The word *depression,* which is not common in the Chinese language, was substituted with "being uncomfortable in one's heart." Zheng and Lin claimed that their inventory was a more culturally sensitive and useful self-report scale for measuring the severity of depression in Chinese than was the Beck Depression Inventory, which was designed for Americans in the United States.

Community Survey of Antisocial Personality Disorder

Although not designed for the psychological assessment of an individual in the forensic setting, many research instruments have been developed for the epidemiological surveys of various psychiatric disorders in the community setting. The questionnaire-based Diagnostic Interview Schedule, developed by the National Institute of Mental Health for use in the Epidemiological Catchment Area study in the United States, is one of them. The Diagnostic Interview Schedule questionnaire was translated into Chinese and applied in an epidemiological study in Taiwan (Hwu, Yeh, & Chang, 1989). Among psychiatric disorders in the community survey relevant to forensic psychiatry is the disorder of antisocial personality disorder (ASPD). The prevalence of ASPD in Taiwan was found to be only 0.14%, which was remarkably less than the 3% that was found in the United States (Comton et al., 1991). Potential explanations advanced for this result include the possibility that the prevalence of ASPD is actually very low in Taiwan or that the instrument itself has problems in its equivalence and validity in detecting ASPD through a one-time questionnaire survey in the Taiwanese population.

Close examination of the questionnaire content concerning items designed to detect the ASPD reveals potential problems for cross-cultural application to a population of different social and cultural background. For example, Taiwan has a different educational system and social setting from the United States. Items intended to reveal aspects of ASPD in childhood, as manifested by "repeating the class" (item 208), "to be excluded from the class" (item 211), "truancy" (item 212), and "run away from the home" (item 215), do not take into consideration the cultural context. The family and educational system do not allow such behavioral problems to occur easily. As for the indirect index for antisocial personality in adulthood, items such as "having extramarital affairs more than three times" (item 244), "having sex with more than 10 persons within a year" (item 245), or "to be paid to have sex with others" (item 246) reflect sexual behaviors that are unlikely to happen in a society where, generally speaking, sexual relations with others are more tightly restricted by culture. The response to these items will accordingly be reduced, which influences the total score needed for diagnosing ASPD (as done in the United States).

Furthermore, on many of the items the people surveyed will be less likely to answer the examiner honestly in the home setting where the verbal survey was conducted. For example, items such as "to earn money illegally, such as to sell stolen objects, illegal drug" (item 248), to "physically abuse spouse or sexual partner" (item 251), and to be "fired from work more than two times" (item 256). They concern issues that people, in a society in which "no family disgrace should be revealed to the outside" is stressed and "saving face" is very important, would find difficult to admit to a stranger (the surveyer). Clearly, the administration of the instrument gives rise to a culture-related problem.

Questions about ordinary psychiatric disorders, which survey the mental symptoms that patients are suffering, will arguably be less subject to problems in cross-cultural study because those people having such suffering will be less hesitant to reveal them to an examiner. On the other hand, socially undesirable behavioral problems are a different matter, requiring careful cultural consideration when conducting a community survey.

SPECIALIZED FORENSIC ASSESSMENT INSTRUMENTS

Psychopathy Assessment: Hare Psychopathy Checklist

Construct of the checklist. The Hare Psychopathy Checklist–Revised (PCL-R) was developed by Robert Hare in 1991 to assess psychopathy categorically and dimensionally, particularly within the adult male forensic population (Hare, 2000). The concept of "psychopathy" has a long history in European and American mental health. The term refers to a particular group of persons (psychopaths) who, by their characters, tend to manifest behavioral patterns that are against society and that undertake actions that are harmful to others. Psychopathy describes a special kind of personality disorder manifesting a core of problems in interpersonal, affective, and behavioral attributes. On the interpersonal level, individuals with this disorder typically present as grandiose, arrogant, callous, dominant, superficial, deceptive, and manipulative. On the affective level, they are short-tempered, unable to form strong emotional bonds with others, and lack empathy, guilt, remorse, or deep-seated emotions. On the behavioral level, they tend to live a socially deviant lifestyle, with irresponsible and impulsive behavior and a tendency to ignore or violate social conventions and morals (Hare, 1991).

The PCL-R was designed as a clinical construct rating scale that uses a semistructured interview, case-history information, and specific scoring criteria to rate each of 20 items on a 3-point scale of 0, 1, or 2, according to the extent to which each item applies to a given individual. Thus, the total score can range from the minimal of 0 to the maximum of 40, reflecting an estimate of the degree to which the individual matches the conceptualized prototypical psychopath. A cutoff score greater than or equal to 30 can be used to classify individuals with psychopathy (Hare, 2000). In addition to figuring the total score, the PCL-R figures scores according to two factors. Factor 1 reflects the interpersonal and affective components of the construct. Factor 2 reflects behavioral components and is more closely allied with a socially deviant lifestyle. In addition there are items that do not belong to Factor 1 or 2 but are calculated in the total score. The items in each factor are as follows.

Factor 1
    1. glibness or superficial charm
    2. grandiose sense of self-worth
    4. pathological lying
    5. conning or manipulative
    6. lack of remorse or guilt
    7. shallow affect
    8. callous or lack of empathy
    16. failure to accept responsibility for own actions

Factor 2
    3. need for stimulation or proneness to boredom
    9. parasitic lifestyle
    10. poor behavioral controls
    12. early behavioral problems
    13. lack of realistic long-term goals
    14. impulsivity
    15. irresponsibility
    18. juvenile delinquency
    19. revocation of conditional release

Additional Factors
11. promiscuous sexual behavior
17. many short-term marital relationships
20. criminal versatility

Cross-ethnic comparison in the United States. The evidence for the validity of the PCL-R was originally primarily derived from male Caucasian subjects. Several studies have examined how well the checklist applies to other ethnic groups, particularly those with minority backgrounds in the United States. Evaluating the construct validity of psychopathy in African American and Caucasian American male inmates, Cooke, Kosson, and Michie (2001) indicated that no cross-group difference in factor structure could be found. However, in a previous study concerning the differences between African American inmates and Caucasian American inmates, Kosson, Smith, and Newman (1990) found a mean score of 25.74 for the Caucasian Americans and a slightly higher mean score of 28.04 for the African Americans. Furthermore, there was a difference in the distribution of psychopathy scores between the two groups. With a score of 31.5 or higher categorized as psychopathic, a score between 20 and 31.5 as intermediate psychopathic, and a score of 20 or lower as nonpsychopathic, the distribution of these three groups among Caucasian American male inmates was 23.7%, 54.7%, and 21.6%, respectively; for African American male inmates it was 36.3%, 8.9%, and 54.8%, respectively. Taking into account the results of other studies, Kosson and colleagues concluded that psychopathy, as measured by the PCL-R, does exist in African American male inmates, with the overall pattern showing more parallels than disparities. However, there were important differences in the expression of psychopathy between these two groups of inmates. Kosson and colleagues speculated that many possible factors were responsible for these differences, including bias in the PCL-R and the fact that all the raters in the studies were Caucasian Americans, inducing examiner-examinee racial interaction effects. Furthermore, they considered the possibility that the personality dynamics and the reasons for the antisocial behavior of psychopaths in these two ethnic groups may be somewhat different.

International application. Since its introduction, the PCL-R has been used not only in the United States and Canada but also gradually in Europe, providing data for international comparison.

According to Hare (1991), in North America the mean score for prison samples was 23.6 (SD = 7.9) and the mean score for forensic psychiatric samples was 20.6 (SD = 7.8). In contrast, in some European countries (e.g., England, Scotland, and Sweden) the mean scores appeared to be several points lower than in North America (Cooke, 1998).

A detailed examination of the application of PCL-R in England and Sweden, as well as in Germany, Belgium, Spain, and Portugal, when compared with North America, led Hare, Clark, Grann, and Thornton (2000) to conclude that the ability of the PCL-R to predict recidivism, violence, and treatment outcomes could be generalized considerably across cultures. A similar situation was found to occur in Sweden by Grann, Langstrom, Tengstrom, and Kullgren (1999). However, it should be noted that the countries in which the PCL-R has been studied in this manner all had predominantly Caucasian populations. At the time we wrote this book, there had not yet been a study involving participants from non-Western societies for wider cross-cultural comparison.

Comments from a cultural perspective. When examining cultural factors, researchers note that comparing cultural groups with relatively remarkable differences makes the cultural dimension more readily apparent. Most of the so-called cross-cultural comparative studies reviewed thus far have involved societies in Europe and North America. There is almost no information available from ethnic, racial, or cultural groups living in societies whose cultural systems are far different from Caucasian groups. The method of examination and the content of the checklist, however, point to several issues that deserve attention from a cultural perspective.

First, besides relying on information from past records, the examination is based on clinical inquiries through semistructured interviews of individuals. It may thus be subject to cultural variations to the extent to which the individual is willing to reveal "bad" personality traits and affirm "undesirable" past behavior to the interviewers. (See the section "Psychopathy and Antisocial Personality Disorder" in chapter 4, concerning the low rate of the disorder found in Taiwan in contrast to that found in the United States.)

Second, the instrument's design requires that the examiner score the test while making judgments and subjective interpretations of the data. The results will depend not only on the examiner's professional views and personal factors but also on his or her ethnic and cultural background as they influence the scoring and interpretation.

Finally, a review of the content of the checklist indicates that many items are influenced by social and cultural factors. For instance, telling lies or being manipulative is regarded and expressed differently among different cultural groups. A parasitic lifestyle (item 9), promiscuous sexual behavior (item 11), and lack of realistic or long-term goals (item 13) are related directly to social background and regulations, as well as cultural definition and expectations of lifestyle, and responses to them may vary greatly among different societies. Short-term marital relationships, which are common in many Western cultures, may be uncommon and socially prohibited in societies in which marriage is considered a lifetime commitment. In other words many items on the checklist may be open to challenge in rating and scoring by questions of cultural equivalence. This instrument deserves further cross-cultural examination, particularly involving cultural samples that vary more widely than the predominantly Caucasian cultures investigated to date.

Competence to Stand Trial

In Western jurisprudence it is a generally accepted legal principle that an individual who is not mentally competent should not be allowed to stand trial. The U.S. Supreme Court, in *Dusky v. United States* (1960), defined the minimum standard for competency as whether the defendant "has sufficient present ability to consult with his lawyer with a reasonable degree of rational understanding—and whether he has a rational as well as factual understanding of the proceedings against him." A fundamental task of forensic psychiatry and psychology is to assist the court in its determination of trial competency issues. Toward that end, a number of assessment instruments have been developed, two of which we discuss next.

MacArthur Competency Assessment Tool–Criminal Adjudication (Mac CAT-CA). Bonnie and colleagues (1997), in association with the MacArthur Foundation, developed this set 22-item instrument for the assessment of criminal competencies. The test consists of a standardized instrument in which a hypothetical case is presented to the defendant and a number of questions asked about legal procedures and strategies. The instrument contains three scales, understanding, reasoning, and appreciation, which reflect the three aspects of the Dusky standard, and it is scored accordingly. Although considered to be an instrument with good internal reliability, it might create problems for some defendants, particularly those from ethnic minority groups, who may find working with a hypothetical case difficult. In addition to the defendant's age, level of education, intelligence, and mental condition, the defendant's knowledge of and familiarity with legal settings and procedures will closely relate to sociocultural factors, including socioeconomic level and status and length of time since immigration to the host society. This will be compounded by problems of culture-related responding style, such as giving excessive affirmative responses without knowing the facts or giving negative responses because of excessive caution and hesitation. If the defendant has language problems, his or her response may be distorted further through translation. Thus, communication problems may dramatically affect the results of the assessment.

When applying the Mac CAT-CA to juvenile populations, Burnett (2000) reported significant differences in the scores of African American juveniles and Caucasian American juveniles on the Understanding and Reasoning scales but not on the Appreciation scale. Regression analysis showed that estimated intelligence accounted for a significant amount of the variance in Understanding scores and educational level accounted for the Reasoning scores.

McGarry's Competency Assessment Instrument (CAI). Psychologists Paul Lipsitt and David Lelos, in conjunction with A. Louis McGarry, a psychiatrist who directed a large-scale research project to improve pretrial competency evaluations, developed this semistructured interview assessment in the 1970s. Items, which are scored on a 5-point scale, include appraisal of the quality of available legal defenses' relating to attorneys, planning of legal strategy, understanding of court procedure, appreciation of charges and range of penalties, and related matters. Scoring is not standardized and there are no norms for interpreting scores. The same potential communication problems that exist for the Mac CAT-CA apply to assessment by the CAI; in addition, however, the examiner does the scoring subjectively, and the results of the scoring may be affected by the examiner's cultural knowledge of the defendant examined.

Impulse-Control Assessment: Violence Risk Appraisal Guide and Barratt Impulsiveness Scale

Assessing the risk of future violence is a practical need in the legal system, particularly when a detained person is to be released or a decision about parole is pending. Mental health professionals face a considerable challenge in performing this task, because of limitations in adequate knowledge or information on which to base the assessment. Some variables that are useful to consider include antisocial personality style, impulsiveness, anger, and a history of violence, as well as aspects of the current offense (Wang, 1999).

The PCL-R has been found useful in predicting violence and recidivistic behavior, subject to the limitations described previously. The Violence Risk Appraisal Guide (VRAG) takes an actuarial approach to risk assessments and incorporates the PCL-R (Harris, Rice, & Quinsey, 1993). Harris and colleagues studied the files of 618 offenders with mental disorders released from a secure facility and followed them for an average of 7 years (later for 10 years). They then determined how the variable they had measured related to recidivism and found the best predictor of subsequent recidivism to be the participant's score on the PCL-R. Additional contributing factors included separation from a parent before age 16, never having been married, maladjustment to elementary school, and failure on prior conditional release. The correlations were derived for any subsequent violent offense, including relatively minor ones such as "simple assault." The period of risk extended over 7 years. Accordingly, the legal use of the VRAG may be significantly limited (Litwack & Schlesinger, 1999). Furthermore, as the authors of the VRAG fully recognized, use of the instrument for assessment may be limited only to members of populations similar to those in the study populations. It may be said that its use is limited not only in clinical and legal applications but very likely in cross-cultural applications as well.

The Barratt Impulsiveness Scale (BIS) was developed for use in the assessment of control over impulsive behavior (Barratt, 2000). In addition to testing its use among North American populations, researchers have tested it in Europe and Asia. Fosati, Di Ceglie, Acquarini, and Barratt (2001) used the BIS, after translation, on college undergraduates in Italy. The results indicated that first-order factors and oblique second-order factors were consistent with the number identified in the English version, whereas subfactor item loadings differed.

After translating the BIS, Someya and colleagues (2001) applied the 11th version of the scale (BIS-11) to Japanese samples. They judged the Japanese version of the BIS-11 to have a factor structure similar to that of the original English version. They considered it to be a reliable and valid measure for Japanese people.

Sexual Harassment Assessment: Sexual Experiences Questionnaire

Over the past three decades, sexual harassment in the workplace has developed as a legal cause of action resulting in increasing numbers of claims filed. The court has called on forensic mental health professionals to assist in determining the nature and extent of harm suffered, causation of the harm, and damages.

The Sexual Experiences Questionnaire (SEQ) is one instrument developed to facilitate assessment of sexual harassment. Fitzgerald and colleagues designed this instrument in 1988 for application to the majority group of European Americans. The SEQ was revised further (Fitzgerald, Gelfund, & Drasgow, 1995), based on the three-dimensional model of sexual harassment; namely, gender harassment, unwanted sexual attention, and sexual coercion.

Concerned that the questionnaire was not suitable for Latinas working in the United States, particularly Mexican American women with moderately low acculturation, Cortina (2001) made revisions and developed the SEQ–Latina (SEQ-L). Cortina added six new items relevant to Latina experiences to the dimensions in the original SEQ. Two items were added regarding verbal behavior: (A man) "addressed you informally when a formal manner of address was more appropriate (for example, used *tu* rather than *usted*)" and "called you inappropriate 'pet names' in Spanish (such as: *manacita* or *mi hija*)." Four items were included regarding sexual behavior: (A man) "made you uncomfortable by standing too close," "gave you a sexual 'look' that made you feel uncomfortable or dirty," "slowly looked at your entire body (up and down)," and "made kissing noises or whistled at you." These revisions were based on Mexican cultural practices in which people are expected to address each other more politely and formally, to keep an appropriate physical distance, to not maintain eye contact for too long, and to not stare at others, particularly when the interaction is between a man and a woman. Any man who ignores this social etiquette and these cultural norms in his behavior toward a woman is considered rude and sexually harassing.

In addition five new items were included to check any sexual racism shown by non-Latino people; namely, "said things to insult Latina women specifically (such as Latins are 'hot-blooded' and 'loose')," "told jokes or stories that described Latina women negatively," "displayed pictures or cartoons that showed Latina women negatively," "called you insulting names that referred to your gender and ethnicity (such as 'Mexican bitch')," and "said they expected you to behave in certain ways because you are a Latina woman (for example, expecting you to wear sexy clothes)."

This example clearly illustrates that what is considered sexually offending or harassing behavior toward women is significantly affected by cultural factors and deserves careful cultural adjustment, and even expansion, for assessment and measurement.

Assessments for Child Custody

To assist the court in determining the "best interests of the child," the legal standard currently used to decide most child custody disputes, clinicians have developed various sets of instruments. These include specialized instruments such as the Bricklin Perceptual Scales and Perception of Relationship Test, the Child Abuse Potential Inventory, the Parent-Child Relationship Inventory, and the Parenting Stress Index, which clinicians use to assess the mental health of parents and children, the nature and quality of the relationship between parent and child, and other relevant matters (Heinze & Grisso, 1996). A primarily test-based approach is used to measure how successful each parent is at the job of parenting (Bricklin, 1995). These psychological tests may provide useful information augmenting the forensic interviews.

When using psychological measurements in custody cases one should be mindful of their shortcomings from the cultural perspective. Azar and Cote (2002) pointed out that psychologists have given insufficient attention to sociocultural factors, both in basic theory building and in the practice of determining a specific parent's competencies to adequately meet the needs of a specific child. The database has been found to be quite narrow, focusing primarily on the majority group and raising questions regarding the representativeness of findings and the relevance of constructs identified for measurement.

Azar and Cote (2002) noted that cultures differ in their use of affect, as well as in the value each attaches to parental control and monitoring. For example, African American parents often are seen as overly strict and restrictive. However, this behavior may result from a parental belief that their children must outperform other ethnic children in a society that is predisposed to seeing them as incompetent (Greene, 1990). Research suggests that Korean adolescents with highly controlling parents perceive their parents as warm and loving, whereas Caucasian adolescents with the same type of parents perceive them as hostile and rejecting (Rohner & Pettengill, 1985). Some cultural groups that are viewed (by Westerners) as engaging in harsher punishment and less overt positive affection (e.g., Chinese Americans) still have more positive child outcomes, as measured by academic achievement (Uba, 1994).

Azar and Cote (2002) concluded that sociocultural factors, including ethnic and racial background and socioeconomic status, are critical to a discussion of parenting practices and how they match a child's needs. They suggested that more cross-cultural research is needed regarding parenting behaviors and more caution is needed in assessing and making suggestions regarding child custody, particularly for families of diverse cultural groups.

IMPLICATIONS FOR FORENSIC APPLICATION

As the use of psychological measures in performing assessments has become more common, the need for caution in how the results of tests will be used has become more important. In court the results of psychological measurement may be used or interpreted incorrectly by the attorneys, the judge, and the jury. Attorneys for either side may attempt to misuse the psychological instrument and test results, either deliberately or because of a lack of professional knowledge. For example, instead of making a general assessment from the integrated results obtained from the instrument as a whole, an attorney may try to focus on a single item. On cross-examination the attorney may ask how the examinee responded to an item and suggest an interpretation based on that response (Clark & Clark, 2002, p. 55).

When taken out of context and reported in this manner, the response to any single item can be meaningless or even misleading. Indeed, psychologists facing demands from attorneys or others for raw test data that might give rise to such error should recall their ethical code allows them, within the bounds of the law, to "refrain from releasing test data to protect a client/patient or others from substantial harm or misuse or misrepresentation of the data" (American Psychological Association, 2003, 9.04). The greater the cultural ignorance of the instrument, the greater is the potential for this difficulty to arise.

The impact of the examinee's culture on the psychological assessment can be either entirely ignored or, alternatively, overemphasized in forensic reports and testimony; in both cases, it can be misleading. Of course this problem is not limited to psychological testing and can occur in the interpretation of the results obtained from interviews as well.

Comments From Cultural Perspectives

Different degree of cross-cultural comparison made. To assess cultural influence, examiners need to make cross-cultural comparisons, and this, as has been seen, requires caution. If the study samples compared do not belong to widely different cultural systems, then what is being compared are samples from different ethnic subgroups within a larger cultural group or different societies with similar groups that do not illustrate remarkable cultural differences. For instance, comparing populations from the United States and European countries means comparing samples with little "cultural distance"; that is, there are relatively fewer remarkable differences in their cultural attitudes, views, and value systems. The results from such a "cross-society" comparison will be different from more divergent cross-cultural comparisons. The claim that there is no cultural impact in a cross-society comparison can be misleading.

Different range of cultural influences. The degree of cultural influence on the application and results of a psychological assessment, as with the different degrees of cultural impact on various types of psychopathology (see the section "Culture and Psychiatric Disorders: General Review" in chapter 4), varies along a spectrum. At one end, we find little cultural impact on the measurement of basic neuropsychological functions, which have a largely neurobiological base. On the other end, we find extensive cultural influence on the assessment of socially related psychological issues. For instance, the measurement of stress encountered in daily life or life attitudes and living habits is significantly subject to cultural bias. The assessment of child custody issues will be subject to certain basic questions, such as, "What are healthy parents?" "What are desirable parent-child relations and interactions?" and "What is best for the children as well as for the parents?" The answers to these questions are inextricably bound to culture.

The measurement of the symptoms of psychopathology lies midspectrum, depending on whether the psychopathology is major or minor and what kind of symptoms are being examined. The assessment of possible delusional thinking requires social and cultural judgment, beyond technical knowledge, to determine the extent to which the purportedly delusional idea deviates from the reality in the society.

Multiple sources of cultural impact. As we have seen, the impact of culture on psychological assessment stems from multiple factors. It may simply be related to the way in which the measurement is administered, how it is translated, or, if there are basic problems in its design and construction, the scope of the mental functions assessed. The problem may be a matter of the norm and can be resolved by modifying the cutting point. Problems also may originate from the validity of the assessment that is applied.

A distinction must be drawn between the so-called culture-free and culture-fair measurements. The culture-free label would be applied to an instrument that actually measures some inherent quality of human capacity equally well in all cultures. Obviously, there can be no such thing as a perfect culture-free test. Culture-fair instruments aim to contain the same number of test items that are familiar to participants from different cultural backgrounds, to ensure fairness in making assessments. Clearly, that modification is needed when an instrument is applied to different cultural groups.

Suggestions for Transcultural Application

The correct approach to culture in psychological measurements is to assume that there will always be problems and limitations in their transcultural application, rather than to search for a culture-free or universally applicable method of measurement. Most useful is to examine and disclose the ways in which measurements are influenced by cultural factors and determine how to resolve the problems involved in transcultural application. The following are some ways with which to deal with the transcultural application of psychological measurements.

Adjustment of the norm or cutting point. When the instrument is designed to distinguish between normality and abnormality by a score, such as Hare's PCL-R, the cutting point may require adjustment when applied to participants from other cultural backgrounds. Clinical validation is needed for such an adjustment.

Making special efforts in translation. If a participant speaks a language other than that of the original instrument, extra effort and caution are needed in translating it. Problems of language equivalency as well as conceptual equivalency need to be resolved.

Modification of the test instrument. Items included in the instrument that are not relevant and valid for transcultural application need to be removed, modified, or substituted by new items that are more relevant to the culture. (This is illustrated by the revision of the MMPI to adjust for social changes that had occurred in the United States over the past half century.) If certain areas are not included in the instrument, causing problems due to a "netting effect," additional items or even areas need to be added. New factors will be developed for application based on these revisions or additions, even though the basic conceptual structure of the instrument is maintained.

Reconstruction of the tool. When the existing inventory is found to be unsuitable for transcultural application in the investigation of a particular cultural group, one solution is to construct a new, culturally appropriate and valid inventory. (This is illustrated by the development of the Vietnamese-Language Depression Rating Scale for Vietnamese Americans or the development of the Chinese Personality Inventory for assessment of the Chinese personality.)

Psychological measurements have the unique and valuable function of providing objectivity in making quantitative comparisons—comparing the psychological status of the same person at different times, comparing different subgroups (identified either by social demographic factors or clinical conditions) in the same society, or comparing groups of people from different societies. Although it is difficult to expect universally applicable instruments for pancultural use, and there is often a need for modification or reconstruction of the tool, it is desirable to maintain a certain commonality of the instrument so that a degree of comparison can be made or, at least, inferred. That is the core nature of culturally competent forensic practice.

REFERENCES

American Psychological Association. (2003). *Ethical principles of psychologists and code of conduct.* Retrieved from http://www.apa.org/ethics/code2002.html#9_04; accessed 3 March 2004.

Azar, S. T., & Cote, L. R. (2002). Sociocultural issues in the evaluation of the needs of children in custody decision-making: What do our current frameworks for evaluating parenting practices have to offer? *International Journal of Law and Psychiatry, 25*(3), 193–217.

Barratt, E. (2000). Barratt Impulsiveness Scale, version 11 (BIAS-11). In *Handbook of psychiatric measure* (pp. 691–693). Washington, DC: American Psychiatric Association.

Ben-Porath, Y. S., Shondrick, D. D., & Stafford, K. P. (1994). MMPI-2 and race in a forensic diagnostic sample. *Criminal Justice and Behavior, 22,* 19–32.

Berry, J. W. (1980). Introduction to methodology. In H. C. Triandis & J. W. Berry (Eds.), *Handbook of cross-cultural psychology, Vol. 2: Methodology.* Boston: Allyn & Bacon.

Bonnie, R. J., Hoge, S. K., Monahan, J., Poythress, N., Eisenberg, M., & Feucht-Haviar, T. (1997). The MacArthur adjudicative competence study: A comparison of criteria for assessing the competence of criminal defendants. *Journal of American Academy of Psychiatry and the Law, 25*(3), 249–259.

Bricklin, B. (1995). *The custody evaluation handbook: Research-based solutions and applications.* New York: Brunner/Mazel.

Brislin, R. (1970). Back translation for cross-cultural research. *Journal of Cross-Cultural Psychology, 1,* 185–216.

Brislin, R. (1976). *Translation: Applications and research.* New York: Wiley-Halsted.

Brislin, R. W. (2000). Some methodological concerns in intercultural and cross-cultural research. In R. W. Brislin (Ed.), *Understanding culture's influence on behavior* (2nd ed.). Fort Worth, TX: Harcourt.

Burnett, D. M. R. (2000). Evaluation of competency to stand trial in a juvenile population. *Dissertation Abstracts International, B: The Sciences and Engineering, 61*(2-B), 1074.

Cheung, M. C., Chang, J. X., & Song, W. Z. (1996). Chinese character as reflected in psychological measurement: (1) Application of the inventory. In W. S. Tseng (Ed.), *Chinese mind and therapy.* Taipei, Taiwan: Laureate Publisher. (In Chinese).

Clark, B. K., & Clark, C. R. (2002). Psychological testing in child and adolescent forensic evaluation. In D. H. Schetky & E. P. Benedek (Eds.), *Principles and practice of child and adolescent forensic psychiatry* (pp. 45–57). Washington, DC: American Psychiatric Publishing.

Colligan, R. C., & Offord, K. P. (1985). Revitalizing the MMPI: The development of contemporary norms. *Psychiatric Annals, 15*(9), 558–568.

Comton, W. M., Helzer, J. E., Hwu, H. G., Yeh, E. K., McEvoy, L., Topp, I. E., &
Spiztnagel, E. L. (1991). New methods in cross-cultural psychiatry: Psychiatric
illness in Taiwan and the U.S. *American Journal of Psychiatry, 148,* 1697–1704.

Cooke, D. J. (1998). Psychopathy across cultures. In D. J. Cooke, A. E. Forth,
& R. D. Hare (Eds.), *Psychopathy: Theory, research, and implication for society*
(pp. 13–45). Dordrecht, the Netherlands: Kluwer.

Cooke, D. J., Kosson, D. S., & Michie, C. (2001). Psychopathy and ethnicity:
Structural, item, and test generalizability of the Psychopathy
Checklist–Revised (PCL-R) in Caucasian and African American partici-
pants. *Psychological Assessment, 13*(4), 531–542.

Cortina, L. M. (2001). Assessing sexual harassment among Latinas: Development of an instrument. *Cultural Diversity and Ethnicity Minority Psychology,
7*(2), 164–181.

Dusky v. United States, 362 U.S. 402 (1960).

Fitzgerald, L. F., Gelfand, M. J., & Drasgow, F. (1995). Measuring sexual
harassment: Theoretical and psychometric advances. *Basic and Applied
Social Psychology, 17,* 425–445.

Flaherty, J. A., Gaviria, M., Pathak, D., Mitchell, T., Wintorob, R., Richman, J.,
& Birz, S. (1988). Developing instruments for cross-cultural psychiatric
research. *Journal of Nervous and Mental Disease, 176*(5), 257–263.

Fosati, A., Di Ceglie, A., Acquarini, E., & Barratt, E. S. (2001). Psychometric
properties of and Italian version of the Barratt Impulsiveness Scale-11
(BIS 11) in nonclinical subjects. *Journal of Clinical Psychology, 57*(6), 815–828.

Graham, J. R. (1990). *MMPI-2: Assessing personality and psychopathology.* New
York: Oxford University Press.

Grann, M., Langstrom, N., Tengstrom, A., & Kullgren, G. (1999). Psychopathy
(PCL-R) predicts violent recidivism among criminal offenders with personality disorders in Sweden. *Law and Human Behavior, 23*(2), 205–217.

Greene, B. (1990). Sturdy bridges: Role of African-American mothers in the
socialization of African-American children. In J. P. Knowles & E. Cole (Eds.),
Women-defined motherhood (pp. 205–225). New York: Harington Park Press.

Gynther, M. D. (1972). White norms and Black MMPIs: A prescription for discrimination? *Psychological Bulletin, 78*(5), 386–402.

Hare, R. D. (1991). *The Hare Psychopathy Checklist–Revised.* Toronto, ON: Multi-
Health Systems.

Hare, R. D. (2000). Hare Psychopathy Checklist–Revised (PCL-R). In *Handbook
of psychiatric measure* (pp. 729–732). Washington, DC: American Psychiatric
Association.

Hare, R. D., Clark, D., Grann, M., & Thornton, D. (2000). Psychopathy and
the predictive validity of the PCL-R: An international perspective. *Behavioral Science and the Law, 18*(5), 623–645.

Harris, G. T., Rice, M. E., & Quinsey, V. L. (1993). Violent recidivism of mentally disordered offenders: The development of statistical prediction instrument. *Criminal Justice and Behavior, 20,* 315–335.

Hathaway, S. R., & McKinley, J. C. (1940). A multiphasic personality schedule (Minnesota): I. Construction of the schedule. *Journal of Psychology, 10,* 249–254.

Heinze, M. C., & Grisso, T. (1996). Review of instruments assessing parenting competencies used in child custody evaluations. *Behavioral Science and the Law, 14*(3), 293–313.

Hicks, M. H. R. (2002). Validity of the CIDI probe flow chart for depression in Chinese American women. *Transcultural Psychiatry, 39*(4), 434–451.

Hutton, H. E., Miner, M. H., Blades, J. R., & Langfeldt, V. C. (1992). Ethnic differences on the MMPI Overcontrolled-Hostility Scale. *Journal of Personality Assessment, 58*(2), 260–268.

Hwu, H. G., Yeh, E. K., & Chang, L. Y. (1989). Prevalence of psychiatric disorders in Taiwan defined by the Chinese Diagnostic Interview Schedule. *Acta Psychiatrica Scandinavica, 79,* 136–147.

Kinzie, J. D., Manson, S. M., Vinh, D. T., Tolan, N. T., Anh, B., & Pho, T. N. (1982). Development and validation of a Vietnamese-Language Depression Rating Scale. *American Journal of Psychiatry, 139*(10), 1276–1281.

Kline, P. (1983). The cross-cultural use of personality tests. In S. H. Irvin & J. W. Berry (Eds.), *Human assessment and cultural factors.* New York: Plenum.

Kosson, D. S., Smith, S. S., & Newman, J. P. (1990). Evaluating the construct validity of psychopathy in Black and White male inmates: Three preliminary studies. *Journal of Abnormal Psychology, 99*(3), 250–259.

Litwack, T. R., & Schlesinger, L. B. (1999). Dangerousness risk assessments: Research, legal, and clinical considerations. In A. K. Hess & I. B. Weiner (Eds.), *The handbook of forensic psychology* (2nd ed.). New York: John Wiley.

Lonner, W. J. (1990). An overview of cross-cultural testing and assessment. In R. W. Brislin (Ed.), *Applied cross-cultural psychology* (pp. 56–76). Newbury Park, CA: Sage.

Lonner, W. J., & Berry, J. W. (Eds.). (1986). *Field methods in cross-cultural research.* Newbury Park, CA: Sage.

McNulty, J., Graham, J. R., Ben-Porath, Y. S., & Stein, L. A. R. (1997). Comparative validity of MMPI-2 scores of African-American and Caucasian mental health clients. *Psychological Assessment, 9,* 464–470.

Megargee, E. I., Cook, P. E., & Mendelsohn, G. A. (1967). Development and validation of an MMPI scale of assaultiveness in overcontrolled individuals. *Journal of Abnormal Psychology, 72,* 519–528.

Osgood, C. (1965). Cross-cultural comparability in attitude measurement via multilingual semantic differentials. In I. Steiner & M. Fishbein (Eds.), *Current studies in social psychology.* Chicago: Holt, Rinehart & Winston.

Pollack, D., & Shore, J. H. (1980). Validity of the MMPI with Native Americans. *American Journal of Psychiatry, 137*(8), 946–950.

Pope, H. S., Butcher, J. N., & Seelen, J. (2000). *The MMPI, MMPI-2, MMPI-A in court: A practical guide for expert witness and attorneys* (2nd ed.). Washington, DC: American Psychological Association.

Ratner, C. (1997). *Cultural psychology and qualitative methodology: Theoretical and empirical consideration.* New York: Plenum.

Rogler, L. H. (1999). Implementing cultural sensitivity in mental health research: Convergence and new directions. Part I: Content validity in the development of instruments from concepts. II. Translation of instrument. *Psychline, 3*(1), 5–11.

Rohner, R., & Pettengill, S. (1985). Perceived parental acceptance-rejection and parental control among Korean adolescents. *Child Development, 56,* 524–528.

Segall, M. H., Dasen, P. R., Berry, J. W., & Poortinga, Y. H. (1990). *Human behavior in global perspective: An introduction to cross-cultural psychology.* New York: Pergamon Press.

Someya, T., Sakado, K., Seki, T., Kojima, M., Reist, C., Tang, S. W., & Takahashi, S. (2001). The Japanese version of the Barratt Impulsiveness Scale, 11th version (BIS-11): Its reliability and validity. *Psychiatry and Clinical Neurosciences, 55*(2), 111–114.

Song, W. Z. (1985). A preliminary study of the character traits of the Chinese. In W. S. Tseng & D. Y. H. Wu (Eds.), *Chinese culture and mental health* (pp. 47–55). Orlando, FL: Academic Press.

Timbrook, R., & Graham, J. R. (1994). Ethnic differences on the MMPI? *Psychological Assessment, 6,* 212–217.

Trimble, J. E., Lonner, W. J., & Boucher, J. (1983). Stalking the wily emic: Alternatives to cross-cultural measurement. In S. Irving & J. W. Berry (Eds.), *Human assessment and cultural factors.* New York: Plenum.

Tseng, W. S. (2003). *Clinician's guide to cultural psychiatry.* San Diego, CA: Academic Press.

Uba, L. (1994). *Asian Americans: Personality pattern, identity, and mental health.* New York: Guilford.

Wang, E. W. (1999). The use of structural modeling techniques to predict violence potential in mentally ill male prisoners. *Dissertation Abstracts International, B: The Sciences and Engineering, 59*(7-B), 3719.

World Health Organization. (1997). *Composite international diagnostic interview (core version 2.1).* Retrieved May 4, 2004, from http://www.who.int/msa/cidi/cidilt.pdf

Zheng, Y. P., & Lin, K. M. (1991). Comparison of the Chinese Depression Inventory and the Chinese version of the Beck Depression Inventory. *Acta Psychiatrica Scandinavica, 84,* 531–536.

4

Cultural Aspects of Psychiatric Disorders in the Forensic Context

To perform a competent evaluation and render an informed decision, a forensic psychiatrist must know how psychiatric disorders, under the influences of culture, may vary in manifestation and clinical course. For this reason, we elaborate in this chapter on the cultural aspects of psychiatric disorders, particularly for certain psychopathologies, which often give rise to forensic problems, such as psychopathy, psychoses, delusional disorders, substance abuse, sexual disorders, and dissociation. We aimed this chapter primarily at persons who are relatively unfamiliar with cultural psychiatry, including professionals from other disciplines.

CULTURE AND PSYCHIATRIC DISORDERS: GENERAL REVIEW

Contemporary psychiatrists generally consider mental illness to be the product of multiple factors, including biological neurochemical psychological and social-cultural, in different combinations and in an integrated, dynamic way. The term *psychiatric disorders* refers to a mental, emotional, or behavioral condition that is pathological and different from the normal. Disorders are

103

viewed as morbid entities manifesting certain pathological mental conditions. Mental symptoms or signs recognized by professionals (such as disorientation, hallucination, delusion, depression, and anxiety) lead to distress or disability in an individual. Psychiatric disorders may impair the person's cognition and judgment, and may manifest in behavior that is harmful to self or others.

From the beginning of modern psychiatry, clinicians and scholars have debated whether psychopathology is "continuous" or "discontinuous" (Berrios, 1994). The continuity model posits a continual spectrum from normal (nonpathological) to pathological psychic phenomena. Manifestations of mild degrees of anxiety, fear, or depression fit this model. Intellectual impairment, substance-use behavior, or personality problems can exist within the continuity spectrum as well. In contrast to this, the discontinuity model holds that there are pathological psychic symptoms that have no counterparts in normal behavior. Bizarre psychotic symptoms or specific organic mental conditions belong to this model and are explained according to the concept of mental disease, rather than viewed merely as exaggerations of normal into abnormal behavior.

In general psychiatrists prefer to use the term *psychiatric disorders*, implying that the disordered condition is related to the morbid entity of disease, whereas behavioral scientists, such as psychologists, tend to use the term *abnormality*, meaning dysfunctional behavior that measurably deviates from the normal range. In this chapter we focus on psychiatric disorders, and we address criminal behaviors and related behavioral problems in the following chapter. Because the distinction between psychiatric disorders and abnormal behavior is somewhat arbitrary, the boundary between them can be blurred.

Cultural Contributions to Psychopathology

Although psychopathology may be attributed to multiple factors, including biological and psychological ones, we will focus primarily on cultural contributions to psychopathology. Conceptually, culture may contribute to psychopathology in several ways, as we describe in the following sections (Tseng, 2001, pp. 177–193).

Pathogenic effects. Pathogenic effects refer to situations in which culture is a direct causative factor in forming or generating psychopathology. There are several ways that cultural ideas and beliefs can contribute to stress, which, in turn, produces psychopathology. Many culture-related specific syndromes, such as *koro* (genital-retraction anxiety disorder), *daht* syndrome (semen-loss anxiety disorder), and *voodoo* death (magic-fear-induced death) are closely related to and induced by cultural beliefs (Tseng, 2001, pp. 211–263). Most of the psychiatric disorders that are caused by cultural beliefs are manifested as minor psychiatric disorders, nonpsychotic in nature, and legally usually not considered severe enough to meet criteria for an insanity defense.

Pathoselective effects. At a cultural level people in a society, as a result of cultural influences, tend to select certain reaction patterns for coping with problems, resulting in the manifestation of certain psychopathologies. Without their knowing it, culture has a powerful influence on the choices people make in reacting to stressful situations and it shapes the nature of the psychopathology that occurs as a result of those choices. Running *amok* (indiscriminate mass homicide attacks) or family suicide (parental suicide and child homicide) are clinical examples of ways of coping with desperate situations. The clinical manifestation of this culturally selected behavior can be severe and associated with homicide, leading to forensic involvement for its legal resolution.

Pathoplastic effects. Pathoplastic effects are the ways in which culture contributes to modeling or plastering the manifestations of psychopathology, which can occur on two different levels: shaping the content of symptoms or modeling the clinical picture as a whole. Culture can shape symptom manifestation at the level of the content presented. The content of delusions, auditory hallucinations, obsessions, or phobias is subject to the environmental context in which the pathology is manifested. For instance, an individual's grandiose delusions may be characterized by the belief that he or she is a Russian emperor, Jesus Christ, Buddha, or the president of the United States, depending on which figure is more popular or important in the individual's society. When psychiatric symptoms are significantly shaped by cultural factors, manifesting a substantially different clinical picture, they may cause a diagnostic dilemma both clinically and legally.

Pathofacilitative effects. Pathofacilitative effects imply that, although cultural factors do not change the manifestation of the psychopathology too significantly, that is, the clinical picture can still be recognized and categorized diagnostically without difficulty in the existing classification system, they do contribute to the frequent occurrence of certain mental disorders in a society. In other words the disorder potentially exists and is recognized globally; however, because of cultural factors, it becomes prevalent in certain cultures at particular times. Clinically many psychiatric disorders that are intimately tied to psychological and sociocultural variables in their development are found to have a wider range of variation of prevalence. Suicidal behavior, alcoholism, and substance abuse are examples of disorders whose frequency varies among different societies and whose occurrence is significantly influenced by the sociocultural context.

Pathodiscriminating effects. Sociocultural factors may not influence the occurrence or manifestation of the psychopathology, but they may determine whether society and professionals regard the mental condition or behavior as "abnormal" or "pathological." There are several different ways to discriminate normal from abnormal. Some examples include decision by professional judgment and definition, by means, by function, or by sociocultural factors. Several mental conditions or behaviors, such as personality disorders, sexual deviation, and substance abuse (including smoking or drinking), can be seen as socially acceptable, normal behaviors, or pathological conditions, depending on the cultural perspective. Because the boundary between normal and pathological is socioculturally determined, serious legal debate may result.

Pathoreactive effects. These effects indicate that although cultural factors do not directly affect the manifestation or frequency of the mental disorder, they influence people's beliefs and understanding of the disorder and mold their reaction toward it. Culture influences how people label a disorder and how they react to it emotionally, and this guides them in expressing their suffering. As a consequence the clinical picture of the mental disorder is colored by the cultural reaction, at a secondary level, to such an extent that the total process of the illness may vary. The so-called *ataques de nervios* (attack of nerves) and *susto* (loss of soul), observed mainly among Latin Americans, or *hwabyung* (fire sickness) among Korean Americans are examples of how local people interpret and react to certain emotional conditions.

Cultural Impact on Different Kinds of Psychopathology

We have clarified the different ways culture contributes to psychopathology. Next, we must recognize that culture affects different groups of psychiatric disorders in different ways, depending on the nature of the psychopathology. Generally speaking, psychopathology that is predominantly determined by biological factors (major psychiatric disorders, such as psychoses) is less influenced by cultural factors and any such influence is secondary or peripheral. In contrast psychopathology that is predominantly determined by psychological factors (minor psychiatric disorders, such as anxiety) is more attributable to cultural factors. This basic distinction is necessary in discussing different levels of cultural impact on various types of psychopathology.

There exists a range of psychopathologies, from the universally uniform ones to the culture-elaborated specific psychopathologies. The degree of cultural input on psychopathology varies between the extremes of distantly culture related to closely culture related. These integrated conceptual views will assist us in elaborating on the subject of culture and psychopathology.

Implications for Forensic Psychiatry

Culture, as we have seen, has different kinds and degrees of impact on different psychiatric disorders.

In general, predominantly biologically caused psychiatric conditions, such as organic mental disorders, schizophrenia, or bipolar affective disorders, are less likely to be caused or substantially influenced by cultural factors. Cultural factors contribute largely in the process of assessment and diagnosis. However, for predominantly psychologically induced, minor psychiatric disorders, such as anxiety disorders or culture-related specific syndromes, in the extreme, culture plays a considerable role from an etiological perspective. There is much more room to argue whether such conditions as normal or abnormal. This is particularly true for personality disorders.

Instead of examining the full range of psychiatric disorders from a cultural perspective, which has been done in detail elsewhere (Tseng, 2001, pp. 291–431), we address in the following sections only those psychiatric disorders that have significant legal implications.

PSYCHOPATHY AND ANTISOCIAL PERSONALITY DISORDER

Definition of Psychopathy and Antisocial Personality Disorder

Some scholars and clinicians use the terms *psychopathy, sociopathy,* and *antisocial personality disorders* as if they are the same; others distinguish them clearly. Antisocial personality disorder generally refers to a particular personality disorder defined in the *Diagnostic and Statistical Manual of Mental Disorders–Fourth Edition–Text Revision (DSM-IV-TR)* (American Psychiatric Association, 2000), characterized by a pervasive pattern of disregard for and the violation of the rights of others (beginning at the age of 15 years) and often indicated by failure to conform to social norms, deceitfulness, impulsiveness, aggressiveness, reckless disregard for the safety of the self and others, consistent irresponsibility, and lack of remorse. Psychopathy, on the other hand, refers to a person who meets special criteria as described by Hare and others, because the term is not used diagnostically in the *DSM-IV-TR* (Hare, Hart, & Harpur, 1991). Characteristic features include glibness or superficial charm, egocentricity or grandiose sense of self-worth, proneness to boredom or low frustration tolerance, pathological lying and deception, cunning or lack of sincerity or manipulative, lack of emotional depth, and lack of empathy, as well as a life history of early behavior problems, poor behavioral control, a parasitic lifestyle, lack of realistic or long-term plans, and promiscuous sexual relations or many short-term marital relationships, as reflected in the Hare Psychopathy Checklist–Revised (PCL-R) (Hare, 1991). Antisocial personality disorder, sociopathy, and psychopathy are pathological personality disorders.

According to the *DSM-IV-TR* (American Psychiatric Association, 2000, p. 633) the identification of personality disorders in general is based on the diagnostic criteria of "an enduring pattern of inner experience and behavior that deviates markedly from the expectations of the individual's *culture*" [emphasis added] and "the enduring pattern leads to clinically significant distress or impairment in *social*, occupational, or other important areas of functioning." Diagnosis depends on how the society views and tolerates the behavior concerned. In other words it is subjective, relative, and culturally defined. Naturally, there is ample room for cross-cultural bias and differences in making diagnoses and identifying the disorders of personality. As stressed by Foulks (1996), different cultures have tended to emphasize different personality traits as ideal. Defining or labeling deviancies from normal personality is clearly a culture-relative exercise, and its boundaries are reflective of the specific values, ideas, worldview, resources, and social structure of the society.

This relative view of personality disorders applies to personality disorders, termed antisocial, psychopathic, or sociopathic as well. These disorders are defined by the failure to conform to social norms, problems maintaining culturally desirable interpersonal social relations (such as reckless disregard for the safety of others, deceitfulness, or aggressiveness), and a lack of socially expected guilt feelings for wrongful behavior. Sociocultural judgment is needed to define the disorders. Even measuring psychopathy is subject to the limitations of cross-cultural application. Certain items used for scoring, particularly those related to life history, such as parasitic lifestyle, promiscuous sexual behavior, irresponsibility (for one's behavior), and failure to accept responsibility for one's own actions are subject to social judgment and cultural definition, which can potentially be different from one society to another and need careful adjustment and redefinition (for details, see the section "Psychopathy Assessment: Hare Psychopathy Checklist" in chapter 3).

Prevalence Rates in Various Societies

The frequency of various personality disorders is difficult to examine through epidemiological studies, because, methodologically, the surveys are one-time studies and do not examine a person's life thoroughly or objectively enough to make it possible to diagnose a personality disorder. Of all the recognized personality disorders, antisocial personality disorder, because of its nature, is the easiest to identify and study, with epidemiological data relatively available for cross-societal comparison.

Moran (1999) reviewed the available literature and epidemiological data from studies of antisocial personality disorder conducted around the world. He pointed out that despite the different survey methods and diagnostic categories used, the lifetime prevalence rates of antisocial personality disorder are remarkably consistent, with the majority of studies reporting prevalence rates of between 2% and 3% of the sample population. He mostly used data from North America (the United States and Canada) and downplayed the lower rates given by other surveys, including those from Asia.

There is cross-socially a limited amount of reasonably comparable epidemiological data about personality disorders. Unless similar methodology and criteria are used, there is no point in making cross-cultural comparisons. To date there have been few cross-cultural comparisons of personality disorders using data obtained with the same epidemiological survey methods. The questionnaire used in the National Institute of Mental Health's Epidemiological Catchment Area study in the United States was translated into Chinese and applied in an epidemiological study in Taiwan (Hwu, Yeh, & Chang, 1989), as we described previously in chapter 3 (see the section "Community Survey of Antisocial Personality Disorder"). The authors found the prevalence of antisocial personality disorder to be 0.14% in Taiwan, which was remarkably less than the 3% that was found in the United States (Comton et al., 1991). However, the results may be criticized on methodological grounds (see the section "The Issues of Equivalence and Validity" in chapter 3).

Cross-Ethnic Comparisons in the United States

The Epidemiological Catchment Area study carried out in the United States examined data for antisocial personality disorder among the three ethnic groups surveyed, namely, Caucasian American, African American, and Hispanic American. The lifetime prevalence rates were found to be 2%, 2.3%, and 3.4%, respectively. Robins, Tipp, and Pryzbeck (1991) therefore claimed that in the United States there were no racial differences in the prevalence of antisocial personality disorder. At the same time, the racial distribution of the prison population in the United States reflected racial disparity. Kosson, Smith, and Newman (1990) reported that African Americans, who comprise less than 13% of the general population, represented 45% of the prisoners in the United States. These results suggest an overpathologizing bias toward African Americans and lower-class individuals relative to Caucasian American and female individuals in the diagnosis of antisocial personality disorder (Lopez, 1989). Alarcón and Foulks (1995) pointed out that as many as half of America's inner-city youth may be misdiagnosed with antisocial personality disorder. They argue that the criteria are inappropriate for settings in which value systems and behavioral rules encourage learning to be violent as a protective strategy for survival.

Racial and Ethnic Differences in Psychopathic Personalities

Lynn (2002) intensively reviewed the data on whether there are racial or ethnic differences in psychopathic personalities. He examined all available literature on psychopathy and related antisocial behavior among various racial or ethnic groups: Black (African American or African), Eastern Asian, Hispanic, (Native) North American, and White (Caucasian American or European). The data reviewed came in multiple forms, such as scores from the Minnesota Multiphasic Personality Inventory Psychopathic Deviate scale; early childhood histories of reported conduct disorders, school suspensions and exclusions, and attention-deficit/ hyperactivity disorder; sociobehavioral problems in honoring financial obligations, irresponsible parenting, aggressive behavior, and crime; various kinds of reckless behavior, such as nonuse of contraception, unplanned pregnancies and births, and automobile accidents; and heterosexual behaviors, such as long-term monogamous relationships, extramarital sex, and multiple sexual partners. Lynn concluded that psychopathic personality as a continuously distributed trait is distributed differently among different racial and ethnic groups. He pointed out that higher values are present in Blacks (African American or African) and Native Americans, intermediate values in Hispanics, lower values in Whites (Caucasian American or European), and the lowest values in Eastern Asians (mainly Chinese and Japanese).

Cooke and Michie (1999) reported that even among members of the Caucasian group—the North American and Scotland participants—there were some differences in the presentation of psychopathy. They analyzed the Hare PCL-R ratings obtained from a sample of North American male prisoners and forensic patients with those of Scottish male prisoners. They reported that although the items had equal relevance to the description of psychopathic personality disorder in both settings, the Scottish prisoners needed higher levels of underlying latent traits before certain characteristics became apparent (see the section "Psychopathy Assessment: Hare Psychopathy Checklist" in chapter 3).

Cultural Issues Relating to Antisocial Behavior

The data obtained from different societies provide us with the general picture that psychopathy, sociopathy, and antisocial personality disorders are universally observed in various societies. However, the data also suggest that antisocial behavior, broadly defined, varies among different societies and even among different ethnicities in the same society, in terms of observed frequency and, possibly, the way it is manifested.

From a cultural perspective, important issues include how a society views and defines antisocial behavior, how the society reacts to it and deals with it, and the degree to which the society punishes the behavior through the legal system.

SCHIZOPHRENIA

The Nature of the Disorder

Among all major psychiatric disorders, schizophrenia has been of greatest concern to general psychiatrists since the history of psychiatry began, because it is one of the most severe, chronic, and prevalent mental disorders in humankind. Closely related to this, from a forensic psychiatric point of view, is that schizophrenia is also one of the mental disorders most commonly giving rise to an insanity defense.

Even laypersons today may easily grasp the term *schizophrenic* as describing a person who has severely lost touch with reality, who manifests a disintegration of personality, who exhibits various strange behaviors or peculiar mental phenomena. The professional definition and conceptualization of schizophrenia have changed considerably over time. During the late 18th century, the German psychiatrist Emil Kraepelin, the father of modern psychiatry, called schizophrenia "dementia praecox," indicating that some people become "demented," starting from the age of puberty (in contrast to senile dementia, which starts in old age). The term was discarded when clinicians learned that dementia was not necessarily the ultimate outcome of the disorder. At the turn of the 19th century, Swiss psychiatrist Eugen Bleuer invented the term *schizophrenia* to emphasize the split and disintegration of various dimensions of mental functions (such as cognition, affect, and perception). Furthermore, association disturbance, affect disturbance, autism, and ambivalence (the four A symptoms) were considered the primary symptoms of schizophrenia; whereas, hallucinations, delusions, and a catatonic state were secondary. According to the current official diagnostic classification system used in the United States, the *DSM-IV-TR*, the characteristic positive symptoms of schizophrenia, manifested during the psychotic state, are delusions, hallucinations, disorganized speech, and grossly disorganized behavior. The negative symptoms of schizophrenia, including affective flattening, alogia (not talking), or avolition (loss of motivation in life), are observed even during the nonpsychotic state.

No matter how schizophrenia is precisely defined, one might assume that explaining this mental disorder to those in court, including a jury, would be easy. However, in actuality, the situation is complicated by the fact that the diagnosis of schizophrenia sometimes may not be made easily, even by a professional, because the disorder may manifest in different forms. To what extent the condition is subject to ethnic and cultural factors deserves special attention.

Cross-Cultural Comparison

Clinical manifestation. From 1966 to 1969 the World Health Organization (WHO) launched the International Pilot Study of Schizophrenia to systematically study the possible cross-cultural variations of the symptomatology of schizophrenia. Nine study centers around the world—Aarhus (Denmark), Agra (India), Cali (Colombia), Ibadan (Nigeria), London (United Kingdom), Moscow (USSR), Prague (Czechoslovakia), Taipei (Taiwan, China), and Washington, DC (United States)—collected data using standardized methodology to compare the clinical picture of schizophrenia in various societies with divergent ethnic and culture backgrounds (WHO, 1973). The study found average percentage scores to be very similar across all centers. All schizophrenic individuals had high scores on certain measures: lack of insight, predelusional signs, flatness of affect, auditory hallucinations (except the Washington center), and experiences of control. The results indicated that schizophrenic patients from diverse cultural settings shared similar basic symptomatology.

Among all the patients studied (811 cases in total), the single largest subtype was paranoid schizophrenia, comprising a total of 323 cases (39.8%). This was also the largest single diagnostic subgroup in most of the individual centers, except Agra, Cali, and Moscow. This subtype accounted for 75% of all schizophrenic patients in London, 53% in Aarhus and Washington, and 40% or more in Ibadan and Taipei. The second-largest single subgroup was the schizo-affective type, comprising a total of 107 cases (13.2%). There were only 54 cases (6.7%) of the catatonic subtype—22 cases from Agra, 13 from Cali, and 10 from Ibadan. The distribution of the catatonic subtype was thus rather uneven among the nine study centers and was found mainly in the three centers in the developing societies. These findings support the clinical impression held by clinicians that catatonic schizophrenia is diminishing and paranoid schizophrenia is rising in developed societies.

Frequency of the disorder. Stimulated by the success of the International Pilot Study of Schizophrenia in studying internationally the clinical picture of schizophrenia, the WHO launched another multisociety investigation several years later: the WHO Collaborative Study on the Determinants of Outcome of Severe Mental Disorders. In the late 1970s 12 study centers around the world were selected as study sites. The results revealed that if a broad definition of schizophrenia was used, incident rates of schizophrenia were different among the different centers investigated (Jablensky et al., 1991). However, the annual incidence rates merely ranged from 1.5 to 4.2 per 10,000 population ages 15 to 54 years. If a more strict research definition of schizophrenia was used, the incidence rates did not differ among the centers, with a range of 0.7 to 1.4 per 10,000 population ages 15 to 54 years.

This finding of incidence rates is compatible with findings from other epidemiological studies carried out in the past in several different countries, even though each investigation used its own methods. According to Jablensky and his colleagues (1991, p. 53), for example, there was an incidence rate of 2.4 in Norway, 1.7 in the United Kingdom, 5.4 in Germany, and 1.1 in China—all defined in terms of incidence rate per 10,000 for the geographically defined population.

Legal Implications

Even though the frequency of the disorder varies within a small range among different societies and ethnic groups, suggesting that schizophrenia is predominantly determined by biological factors, recognizing and diagnosing this disorder can still be a challenge from a practical point of view. This is particularly true when the patient speaks a different language from the examiner. Diagnostic assessment becomes more difficult, particularly when the examiner has to determine to what extent the examinee's mental condition deviates from the norm (for details, see chapter 2). This difficulty may result in a wide discrepancy of assessment results among different examiners in the forensic setting.

Beyond this general difficulty in making clinical assessments, the situation may be more complicated cross-culturally, because the subtype of disorders may vary among different societies and ethnic groups. For instance, the catatonic type is more prevalent in developing societies, whereas the paranoid type is more prevalent in developed societies. Also, the prognosis of schizophrenia varies cross-culturally, being more favorable in rural-agriculture-oriented developing societies and less favorable in urban-industry-oriented developed societies.

Thus, deciding upon the correct diagnosis can be a challange from a clinical perspective and also for legal purposes. Acute psychoses and organic psychoses, particularly substance-induced psychoses, are diagnoses within the differential deserving of careful consideration in forensic examinations.

DELUSIONAL DISORDERS

The Nature of the Disorders

A delusional disorder is a psychotic condition. A delusion is defined as a consistent, firm, false belief that is not shared by others. The content of a delusion can be erotomanic (the individual believes another person is in love with him or her), grandiose (the person has an inflated sense of worth, power, knowledge, or identity or believes to have a special relationship to a famous person), jealous (the individual believes his or her sexual partner is unfaithful), persecutory (the person believes he or she is being malevolently treated or persecuted in some way by others), or somatic (the person believes he or she has some physical defect or medical condition), or it may have other content. Although the delusion is unlikely to be true, there is at least a remote possibility it could be true (e.g., "Madonna is in love with me"), unlike the delusions of a person with schizophrenia, which may be bizarre (e.g., "Martians are beaming messages into my head"). In delusional disorder, the explained delusion is often systematical and "logically" explained by the individual, even if it is false. Because of such disordered, delusional thoughts, the person may have attitudinal, affective, and behavioral changes. For example, a person with persecutory delusions may manifest a suspicious or hostile attitude, not trust others, become guarded, and believe he or she is being watched and followed, or even poisoned, by others. In reaction to such persecutory beliefs, individuals may attack others (in "self-defense"), harm others (to eliminate the "enemy" or the "persecutor"), or attempt to end their own life to avoid the situation. The legal system has seen abundant examples of people harming others under the influence of persecutory delusions.

Acute Delusional Episode

According to the American Psychiatric Association classification system, the *DSM-IV-TR*, the delusion must be present for a period of at least 1 month for a delusional disorder to be diagnosed. This criterion reflects the clinical experience that delusional disorders tend to run a long-term course. This is partly because delusional patients tend not to seek treatment and often refuse treatment because of a lack of insight (being unaware that he or she is suffering from a mental disorder). Besides, even when a patient receives treatment, response to treatment (by medication) is presently not optimal. In other words a delusional disorder is considered by American psychiatrists to be a relatively long-term, difficult-to-treat disorder that may continue for many years.

On the basis of clinical observation, psychiatrists in other parts of the world, however, recognize a type of delusional disorder that can be transient and refer to the condition as an acute delusional episode. The disorder can occur as an episode, psychotic in nature, manifested mainly by delusional thoughts of various kinds. The episode may last for several days, weeks, or months at most. After the episode is over, the patient returns to his or her ordinary mental condition. From a forensic point of view, it is important to recognize the existence of this brief delusional paroxysm, because by the time a forensic examination is carried out, the patient may no longer be psychotic.

Cultural and Legal Implications

In contrast to schizophrenia, delusional disorders may be controversial from a legal perspective. Apart from the impact and ramifications of the delusion(s), a person's general functioning typically is not markedly impaired and behavior is not obviously odd or bizarre. This is particularly true if the person is suffering from an erotomanic or religious delusion. The person can function occupationally in society reasonably successfully, as long as conditions do not touch on his or her delusion. For this reason, some scholars call delusional disorders partial psychoses, indicating that there is potential difficulty in detecting the existence of the disorder unless the individual manifests overt, strange thoughts or behavior. Convincing laypersons the person is suffering from psychotic delusions and has severely lost the ability to make judgments regarding reality often is difficult. Jurors, who do not have a real understanding of the psychotic nature of this disorder, may be hard to persuade.

Clinically, identifying delusions can be quite difficult (Levy, 1996). Furthermore, because a delusion is defined as a false belief by an individual, and is not shared by others, assessing it can be quite challenging from a cultural point of view. What appears to be a delusion to a person from one culture may be a common belief for a person of another culture. Members of a large group of people may share, in particular, religious beliefs that seem odd to others. Clearly, sociocultural definition often is involved in judging to what extent the belief departs or deviates from reality. Information regarding how others within the examinee's cultural group view the subject will be necessary to sort this out.

MOOD DISORDERS

Types of Mood Disorders

Mood disorders are mental disorders that are characterized by mood disturbances. They tend to occur episodically. They can be manifested as a manic episode (with an elevated mood) or a depressive episode (with a low mood), and, based on its clinical manifestation, it can be given various specific clinical diagnostic labels, such as major depressive disorder, dysthymic disorder, bipolar disorder, or cyclothymic disorder.

A person who suffers from a severe mood disturbance may behave differently from usual. For instance, a depressed person may neglect work duties or be unable to perform the work (resulting in occupational negligence), and a manic person may become daring in behavior, even performing unlawful actions, such as making threats to others or carrying out sexual assaults.

When the person with a mood disorder develops delusions, the disorder becomes more complicated. An individual could develop grandiose delusions when experiencing a severe manic episode or could develop a depressive delusion when suffering from major depression. By definition, such delusional thoughts are grossly detached from reality and are psychotic in nature. For instance, a depressed person under the influence of a depressive delusion, such as believing that he or she is guilty of a serious crime, may injure self or others. Affected by grandiose delusions, a manic person may behave carelessly, resulting in legal problems. However, besides having delusional thoughts, the patient may be suffering from a severe mood disorder and still tend not to be regarded as insane in the mind of a layperson, because of the absence of obvious strange thoughts or peculiar behaviors, such as those exhibited by schizophrenic patients. Under such circumstances demonstrating to the jury that a person's mood disorder is psychotic in nature, and his or her mental ability is grossly impaired, may be difficult.

Cultural Variations of Clinical Manifestations

Most psychiatrists recognize that mood disorders, like other mental conditions, clinically manifest differently among persons of different ages. For example, a young child who suffers from depression often is not able to describe the symptoms of his or her depressed mood, in contrast to an adult. Clinicians instead make a diagnosis after finding the child has lost interest in daily activities, becomes irritable, or fails to thrive. The elderly person may make somatic complaints rather than express feelings of depression. In a similar way the presentation of a clinical picture of depression can be different because of the ethnic or cultural background of a patient. Patients of many ethnic groups tend to make somatic complaints rather than directly state they feel down. On the basis of religious beliefs and attitudes, Muslim patients seldom reveal their suicidal ideas, even when they are psychotically depressed, because self-killing is not accepted by their religion. Catholic patients may have a similar tendency to not reveal suicidal ideation even when it is present.

Postpartum Psychosis
Postpartum psychosis is a mental condition that has generated controversy in the legal context. It refers to a psychotic condition (usually in the context of severe depression) that occurs shortly after the delivery of a baby. Scholars consider it to be predominantly of biological and hormonal etiology. Under the influence of a psychotic depression, often associated with depressive delusions or even auditory hallucinations, the mother may attempt or commit homicide actions against her newborn baby or young children. In many societies, such as China (Li, 2000) and Japan (Fukushima, 1985, pp. 188–199), this kind of criminal action is viewed as the result of a psychotic condition (predominantly influenced by delusions or mental confusion) and the legal penalty often is waived. However, in the United States juries in different states sometimes take a different attitude. For example, in the case of Andrea Yates in Texas, her insanity defense plea was not accepted and the jury found her guilty of the murder of her children, which occurred during a postpartum psychotic depression. In other states that may have a different insanity standard, her behavior might have been viewed and judged differently.

DISSOCIATION, POSSESSION, AND MULTIPLE
PERSONALITY DISORDERS

Dissociation refers to mental conditions in which a person is in an altered state of consciousness and possibly behavior, as if in a dream or twilight state. In possession disorder a person behaves and talks as if possessed by another person or spiritual being. During a dissociated or possessed state, the person may commit criminal acts, including homicide. After the event occurs, and the person recovers from the dissociated or possessed state, the person may claim that he or she was not aware of performing the behavior.

Cross-cultural studies indicate that a dissociated or possessed state is becoming increasingly rare in most Western societies, but it is still prevalent in the East and other parts of the world. In contrast multiple personality disorders are more frequently reported in European and American societies but are reported less in other parts of the world. Scholars are not sure of the reason behind this phenomenon (Tseng, 2001, pp. 317–334). Whatever the reason, forensic psychiatrics will be called on to assess the mental state of a defendant after criminal acts occur in the context of altered consciousness.

Although trance, dissociation, possession, and altered personality states differ in certain ways, they share several common characteristics. They are related to some extent to the basic mechanism of the alteration of the state of consciousness and the awareness of self-identification. They are related to the verification of mental integration and involve change of personality and awareness and identity of self. Based on these mental mechanisms, different mental conditions emerge that may occur as normal life conditions, on special daily life occasions, or as morbid states. Thus, they are found on a spectrum ranging between the normal and the pathological states (Tseng, 2001, p. 318).

Another unique feature of these mental conditions is that they can be induced by the self and can occur rather suddenly, and the individual experiencing them can return to his or her original state within a certain time. These conditions can occur in ordinary daily life situations, such as meditation and daydreaming, or as part of a religious or healing ceremony or professional practice, such as hypnosis. They also can occur in reaction to emotional stress. If they occur as pathological conditions, psychological therapy becomes the main approach for treatment.

Dissociation Disorders

States of dissociation or possession can be mild or severe. In mild conditions the altered consciousness state is not far from normal, and the person can easily enter and leave the condition without too many complications. In contrast, a severe condition can involve grave changes of consciousness or a profound possession by an alternative being, and the condition may last several days or even several weeks. Clinically, this is called possession psychosis. The legal implications may be different for different degrees of detachment from reality.

For instance, the *latah* phenomenon, described as a culture-related special mental phenomenon in Malay, is recognized and distinguished by local people as either ordinary or malignant *latah*. The person suffering from malignant *latah* will lose complete control of his or her behavior during the episode and will be considered by laypersons as not responsible for any unlawful actions he or she undertakes (for more information see the section "Culture-Related Specific Disorders" in this chapter).

Possession Disorders

The mental state described by possession disorders may occur merely as a reaction to emotional stress, without relation to religious or healing practices. Possession disorders are believed to occur in many parts of the world. Possession and possession disorders tend to be reported more in psychiatric literature from Asian regions. This may reflect that such phenomena are still prevalent in Asia and have therefore caught the interest of cultural psychiatrists for investigation and report.

In Japan the orthodox religion of *Shinto* is animistic. Japanese traditionally believe that animals (such as foxes, raccoons, dogs, and snakes), trees, mountains, stones, and other objects are associated with spirits. Japanese folk legends are full of stories about animal spirits, particularly the fox spirit. The spirit of the cunning fox can disguise itself into any human form, often a young lady, and play tricks on people. The Japanese commonly say *kitsune-ni-bakasareru*, literally meaning to be fooled by the spirit of a fox (*kitsune*). Perhaps related to this idea is the tendency of people to interpret a possessed person as being possessed by an animal spirit, mostly a fox and occasionally a dog or a cat. According to

Kitanishi (1993) the spirit of the animal that possesses people is believed to stay in certain households. The household with *tsukinomo-suji* (spirit lineage) tends to be looked down on by others and is kept at a distance socially. It is speculated that such households may have originally been those of migrant families that wandered into the established village. Another explanation is that the possessing spirit was brought by a shaman to inhabit the household. It is generally believed that the animal spirits are transmitted through marriage and kept within a family.

In Thailand, although most possessing beings are believed to be the spirits of animals or deceased persons, there is a unique phenomenon in which a person can be possessed by the spirit of another living person. According to Suwanlert (1976) Thai people believe that *phii pob* is the soul of a living person that may come and go among people. When *phii pob* possesses a person, it takes the role of that person. This kind of possession is observed mainly in northern Thailand.

In the south of Taiwan, Wen (1996) conducted a community survey of a selected area and estimated that the people who had had possession experiences (both ordinary and morbid conditions) were not less than 1% of the adult population. He pointed out that the traditional beliefs of pantheism and ancestor worship—close relations and interaction with deceased ancestors—served as the common ground for the frequent occurrence of possessed states. However, he speculated that, in contrast to Japan, the belief in the possibility of interference from an ancestor spirit was more intense among people in Taiwan.

In mainland China, according to the available literature, possession disorders are reported more frequently in the northeastern region, including the areas previously known as Manchuria and internal Mongolia. These areas are geographically close to Siberia, where anthropologists believe the practice of shamanism (in a narrow sense) originated.

According to Zhang (1992), a psychiatrist from Liaoning Province Mental Hospital located in the northeastern region of China, a total of 4,714 cases had been brought to the hospital for forensic psychiatric evaluation. Of those cases 52 (1.1%) had committed murder while suffering from possession disorders. Interestingly, among them were six groups of patients (with more than one person in each group) that committed murder together. Most of them were family members or relatives who were in a collective trance state or in a "shared" possession state.

In this state they killed their victims with the conviction that the person was possessed by an evil that needed to be exorcized.

Mr. and Mrs. Wang, a middle-aged couple in their 50s, had two sons. Mrs. Wang had a past history of possession episodes, claiming that she often was possessed by the spirit of her deceased mother-in-law. Their 24-year-old eldest son, after cohabiting with his girlfriend (which was illegal at that time), began to behave seclusively and strangely, claiming that he was a "headless evil" and intended to kill all of his family members. One night, hearing a noise on the roof, the mother suddenly fell into a possessed state, claiming that she was possessed by a shaman who had come to expel the headless evil from her son. She induced her husband and her 18-year-old son to fall into trance states. In their trance states they together pounded 43 nails into the eldest son's body and stabbed him in the abdomen with a knife. As a result the eldest son died. After the event Mrs. Wang remained in a trance state for 10 days, claiming that she had expelled and killed the dangerous headless evil. After she recovered from her trance state and learned that she had killed her son, she began to cry loudly. (The legal decision in this case was not mentioned in this psychiatric report.)

Dynamically, a tempting interpretation is that the mother, who psychologically lost her son to his girlfriend, reacted with the belief that her son was evil. Her possessed state gave her an excuse to act out her wish to punish the unfilial (or emotionally betraying) son. Clinically, it was a case of associated or collective mental disorder among members of a family. The common belief in the possibility of a person being possessed by evil and the need to conduct an exorcism was the basis for the family's group psychiatric disorder. This case makes clear that the distinction between possession disorder (of a hysterical nature) and possession psychosis (of a psychotic nature) is not merely a clinical matter but also a forensic challenge, when the patient is involved in a crime.

Possession Psychosis

Possession psychosis is a psychotic condition characterized by the delusion of being possessed, in addition to other psychotic pictures, including hallucinations, bizarre behavior, and thought disorders. This condition, even though manifested as a possession state, is different from possession disorder of a hysterical nature in that its onset is not necessarily sudden or in reaction to external stress; it may last a relatively long time, more than several weeks or months; and it does not respond favorably to any psychological treatment for underlying psychological stress. The term *invocation psychosis* is still used by psychiatrists in some societies, including Japan, to describe possession psychosis. From a forensic point of view, this condition may be considered an exculpatory or at least mitigating factor at trial and sentencing.

Dissociative Identity Disorder

Dissociative identity disorder (also called multiple personality disorder) describes the condition in which a person, usually without observable alteration in conscious state, will shift into another personality. Multiple personality disorder is identified more frequently in Western societies than are dissociation or possession disorders, which are rare in Western societies. It is rarely identified in Eastern societies. When a person performs criminal acts in association with multiple personality disorder, as exemplified by the well-known story *Dr. Jekyll and Mr. Hyde*, there is often debate among experts as to how the legal system should determine responsibility.

Characteristically different from possession disorder is the multiple personality disorder. In the latter there is no interpretation by either the patient or other people that the patient is possessed by "others." The person is understood to alternate between (or among) different personalities, either in or out of a trance state. In other words a psychological explanation and not a supernatural interpretation for the phenomena is given. Therefore, the multiple personality disorder is observed mainly in modernized societies, where folk beliefs of a supernatural nature have more or less diminished. Psychiatrists commonly believe that in traditional societies, where trance and possession states are more frequent, the phenomena of altered personality and multiple personality disorders are seldom found. In contrast, in modern societies possessed disorders are rare or diminishing, and double or multiple personality disorders are becoming more prevalent.

According to Ross (1991), the frequency of diagnosed multiple personality disorders in clinical populations increased exponentially during the 1980s. Reviewing the entire world literature, Greaves (1980) pointed out that not more than a couple of hundred cases (mainly in Western societies) have been reported since the beginning of the twentieth century. However, according to Ross, P. Coons in 1986 estimated that 6,000 cases of multiple personality disorder had been diagnosed in North America. In contrast Adityanjee, Raju, and Khandelwal (1989) in India reported that only two cases of multiple personality disorder had been reported in India in the past. They claimed that there was a frequent diagnosis of possession disorder, but the diagnosis of multiple personality disorder was rare. A similar situation has been observed in Japan (Takahashi, 1990).

Beyond the influence of diagnostic practice patterns in different societies, there is good reason to speculate that, in association with the level of modernization or the degree of belief in supernatural powers, there is a trend away from the possessed state to the altered personality state. If we think carefully, we will realize that the possession state and the altered personality state are similar, except that the former is interpreted as the takeover of the self by an "external (supernatural) being," whereas the latter is the takeover of the self by an "internal (psychological) being," or another part of the self. Both offer mechanisms for avoiding taking responsibility for one's actions, but in different ways, based on the common beliefs shared by the people in the society.

In our society forensic psychiatrists continue to debate whether a person who commits a wrongful act while experiencing a dissociated state or while an alter personality is in charge should be legally culpable. Many take the view that they should take legal responsibility and be punished for unlawful behaviors that are undertaken.

SUBSTANCE-RELATED MENTAL DISTURBANCES

Substance Abuse: General Issues

The usage of alcohol and other psychoactive substances by human beings began in prehistory. The people of Africa, Asia, and Europe, in addition to preparing alcohol, also grew opium, cannabis, and some stimulant plant compounds (Westermeyer, 1999). Substances that have been abused have varied in different societies and even in the same societies at different times. Abuse of substances generally depends on their availability, as well as on economic conditions, social controls, and cultural fashions. Proscribed or taboo use of certain chemical substances exists in many societies. Some substances are totally forbidden under any circumstances, such as alcohol in Saudi Arabia, coffee among Mormons, and heroin in the United States (Westermeyer, 1987).

Substances take on symbolic meaning, in some instances representing certain values, attitudes, and identities related to ethnicity. For instance, alcoholism or drunkenness is considered as non-Jewish behavior by many Jewish people and sinful by many Muslims. In contrast, in Eastern Asia being able to drink a lot, particularly on social occasions, is viewed as manly behavior. In China, as a result of the Opium War, opium was regarded as a substance of national shame, associated with severe punishment for abuse.

Obviously, substances that are psychoactive affect a person's mind and behavior, which includes affecting the person's cognitive judgments, emotional regulation, and behavior control. A significant amount of criminal behavior or legally related problems occur in the context of substance abuse.

Cross-Societal Variations in Frequency of Substance Abuse

Alcohol

Available data indicates clearly that alcohol consumption and alcohol-related problems vary significantly among different societies around the world (Tseng, 2001, pp. 351–365). In terms of annual consumption, measured by liter per person, the variation of consumption is observed to be remarkably different: highest in France (16.2), Argentina, and Italy (both 12.6), and lowest in Libya, Egypt, and India (all 0.1). The United States is in the middle range (8.4). Most Muslim societies have very low rates of consumption of alcohol, because it is associated with religious prohibition.

Even in the same society, a change in alcohol consumption can be observed over time. For instance, in Japan it has increased from 5.9 in 1965 to 8.7 in 1995, and it is believed to be even higher at present. This significant increase in the national total consumption has been attributed in part to the remarkable increase of drinking among women after World War II. In Korea alcohol consumption has increased from 8.3 in 1975 to 11.0 in 1995 and is associated with the remarkable improvement in the national economy.

Substances Other Than Alcohol

To assist countries seeking to implement prevention programs, the WHO established the project of Development of Strategies and Guidelines for the Prevention of Drug-Related Problems. By reviewing the reports prepared by countries around the world for this WHO project, Smart, Murray, and Arif (1988) pointed out that although the pattern and degree of drug abuse varied from country to country, some general patterns exist. Clearly the typical abuser of most illegal drugs was a young male, unemployed, relatively unskilled, and living in lower class circumstances. This pattern, with few exceptions, fit most of the countries that submitted reports. In several countries, such as India, Kenya, Mauritius, Nigeria, and Togo, drug abuse was not yet considered an important problem. In others, such as Canada, Finland, France, Ireland, and the United Kingdom, drug abuse was dwarfed by concerns with more serious alcohol problems. Experts from several countries saw drug abuse as an important problem that could not be addressed because more pressing concerns took priority; for example, economic concerns in Bangladesh and Peru. Many countries, at the government level, clearly saw drug abuse as a major national concern that demanded action. Those countries were Australia, Germany, Hong Kong, Indonesia, Japan, Malaysia, Mexico, Pakistan, the Philippines, Singapore, and the United States. Thus, it was a worldwide concern, not related merely to economic and health problems but often associated with serious unlawful behavior.

When abuse involves illegal substances, abuse becomes easy to associate with various kinds of unlawful behavior, including serious criminal action. From a public mental health perspective, substance abuse calls not only for management but also for prevention.

Substance Abuse and Legal Responsibility

From a legal point of view, if a person uses or abuses substances voluntarily and engages in criminal behavior, the influence of the substance is generally not considered an excuse for the criminal behavior in court. The substance may affect a person's mind, but the law will not allow voluntary intoxication to negate the person's general *mens rea* (guilty mind) needed for the crime. It may, however, negate a person's ability to form the specific *mens rea* needed to accomplish certain crimes, such as "assault with intent to commit severe bodily harm."

Many societies take into consideration the extent to which the mental condition is disturbed by the substance. For instance, Binder in 1965 categorized drunkenness into simple and compound drunkenness. Such distinctions among various kinds of drunkenness have been made by forensic psychiatrists in different countries in the West as well as in the East, such as Japan (Fukushima, 1985, pp. 21–71; Hayashi, 2001) and China (Li, 2000, pp. 193–206). In contrast to a person who abuses a substance, if a person takes psychotropic medicine primarily for medical reasons but commits a crime as a result, losing his or her judgment, memory, emotional or behavioral control, or developing other drug-induced impairment, the influence of the psychotropic substance is often considered at least mitigating factor.

CASE 2: WEALTHY HOUSEWIFE IS CAUGHT SHOPLIFTING

Police apprehended a college-educated woman in her 50s, the mother of two grown children, after the security guard of a department store reported her for shoplifting. Her husband, a successful and affluent businessman, was astonished that his wife had taken a cheap, on-sale watch (about $10 in value), while she carried several credit cards and several hundreds of dollars in cash in her wallet. An attorney was hired and a psychiatric evaluation was arranged for her "unusual" behavior.

Psychiatric evaluation revealed that the defendant and her family had immigrated to the United States from Europe several years before. She suffered from headaches, and medication was prescribed by her family physician. The defendant reported that on the day she went shopping, intending to buy an expensive watch for her husband's birthday gift, she experienced a headache. She found the medication she had been carrying in her handbag and took it before she entered the department store. She claimed that she did not remember what happened until she discovered that she had been apprehended and kept in a cell at the police station. While gathering information the forensic psychiatrist learned the woman had taken a sleeping pill no longer available because it may cause amnesia (Rohypnol), instead of a pill for her headache.

After the psychiatric report was submitted to the court, the judge decided that the defendant carried out her unlawful behavior without being fully aware of it. The judge found her guilty but released her with 1 year of probation (and the suggestion that she not take the medication again).

CONDUCT DISORDER AND JUVENILE DELINQUENCY

Basic Concepts

According to the American psychiatric diagnostic classification system, the *DSM-IV*, a "conduct disorder" is a repetitive and persistent pattern of behavior in which the basic rights of others or major age-appropriate societal norms or rules are violated, as manifested by aggression toward people and animals (such as threatening others, initiating fights, cruelty to animals, forcing someone into sexual activity), destruction of property, deceitfulness or theft (such as breaking into another's house, lying to obtain goods or favors, stealing items), and serious violations of rules (such as running away from home, being truant from school).

Psychiatrically recognized conduct disorders rely on a listing of behaviors that describes young people who violate social norms within their community, home, or school (therefore are subject to sociocultural definition). If a law violation has occurred, it is considered and categorized as "juvenile delinquency" (based on legal definition). Not all youths with a diagnosis of conduct disorder are included in the juvenile delinquency category, because they may not have literally violated a law or been apprehended. For instance, a child or adolescent who persistently engages in bullying behavior or is repetitively cruel to animals is not technically labeled a juvenile delinquent (Malmquist, 1997, p. 413).

Epidemiological Data

It is rather difficult to assess epidemiological data on the behavior disorders of children and adolescents, simply because the definition of conduct disorders has been changed considerably over time by professionals, and the frequency rate of juvenile delinquency is greatly subject to how the law defines the delinquency of young people, how the law is enforced, and how the frequency of occurrences is reported.

In the United States the prevalence of delinquency was examined in a collaborative longitudinal study in several places, including Devern, CO, Pittsburgh, PA, and Rochester, NY (Huzings, Loeber, & Thornberry, 1993). The results indicated that delinquency increased with age, from 6 to 17 years, and the prevalence of conduct disorder was greater in males than in females, but decreased between the ages of 10 and 20 years (Cohen et al., 1993). In the United Kingdom, studying one location, the prevalence of conduct disorder in the general population was reported to be 4.5% among 10- to 11-year-olds, with the rate for boys 10 times higher than that for girls (Rutter, Graham, & Rule, 1970). In New Zealand a 13-year follow-up study confirmed that parental discord was a key antecedent variable and confirmed the existence of a linear relationship between rates of offense and intensity of discord. Boys with high exposure to parental conflict and early conduct problems had a 90% probability of becoming early legal offenders (Fergusson, Horwood, & Lynskey, 1992).

Ethnicity and Delinquency

From a cultural perspective, we may generally assert that any ethnic group that values the family and has a cohesive structure, functional authority, and emotional care and support will have a lower occurrence of conduct disorder and juvenile delinquency. From a theoretical perspective, a disturbed personality was considered in the past to be the primary base for developing delinquent behavior. Recently, however, sociocultural conditions or stressors have been considered as factors contributing to delinquent behavior. A more integrated, dynamic understanding of the disturbed personality incorporating sociocultural views may be the best perspective.

Using data collected on nearly 4,000 Anglo-American, Hispanic American, and African American male youths processed at the Juvenile Assessment Center at Hillsborough County, FL, Dembo and colleagues (1998) examined the cross-ethnic differences. They reported that the Hispanic American youths, compared with the Anglo-American youths, tended to reside in households of lower socioeconomic status, reported lower substance misuse and mental health treatment rates, and had a greater lag between their school grades and their chronological ages. Compared with Hispanic American youths, African American youths tended to live in mother-headed households; have a higher rate of referral to juvenile court for property, violence, and public disorder offenses and for drug offenses; and have higher rates of recidivism. On the basis of these findings, the authors pointed out that non-African American (predominantly Anglo-American) youths are experiencing more behavioral problems (based indirectly on personality disorder), whereas African American youths are subject to more environmental stressors.

Concerning ethnic differences in the effect of parenting on gang involvement and gang delinquency, Walker-Barnes and Mason (2001) carried out a longitudinal study of ninth-grade students from an urban, southeastern city with an ethnically diverse sample of Hispanic, African, and Caucasian Americans. In general, they reported that the adolescents decreased their level of gang involvement over the course of the school year, whereas the average of level of gang delinquency remained constant over time. As predicted, the gang involvement and gang-related delinquency were most strongly predicted by peer involvement; nevertheless, parenting behavior continued to significantly predict change in gang involvement and gang delinquency. A significant interaction between parenting and ethnic and cultural heritage found the effect of parenting to be particularly salient for African American students, for whom higher levels of "behavioral control" and lower levels of "lax parental control" were related to better behavioral outcomes over time, whereas higher levels of "psychological control" predicted worse behavioral outcomes.

Sociocultural aspects of family bonding have been said to have a more powerful influence on delinquency in Hispanic adolescents than in the more mainstream American youths (Rodriguez & Weisburd, 1991). However, by examining the data from a longitudinal survey of male Puerto Rican adolescents residing in the South Bronx, New York City, one of the lowest income districts in the United States with the greatest Puerto Rican concentration, Pabon (1998) pointed out that the only significant difference for family bonding variables was found for family involvement on the individual's subsequent involvement in delinquent behavior. Time spent on weekends and evening with family members reduces the opportunity for delinquency, especially at the prime times for delinquent behavior.

Brody and colleagues (2001) were concerned about the potential influence of neighborhood disadvantage, collective socialization, and parenting on the affiliation of African American children with deviant peers. They investigated children ages 10 to 12 years living in Georgia and Iowa, and they reported that the effects of nurturant and involving parenting and collective socialization were most pronounced for children residing in the most disadvantaged neighborhoods.

Samaniego and Gonzales (1999) pointed out research showing that more acculturated Latino adolescents are at increased risk for delinquent behavior relative to their less acculturated counterparts. They examined a sample of Mexican American adolescents and revealed that family conflict, maternal monitoring, inconsistent discipline, and negative peer hassles are the putative mediators that increase in the process of acculturation and tend to contribute to the increase of juvenile delinquency within the immigrant family. Pfefferbaum, Lfefferbaum, Strickland, and Brandt (1999) pointed out the need to develop more culturally sensitive clinical assessments and interventions for adolescents of various ethnic minority groups, including American Indian youths.

SEXUAL DISORDERS

Sexual behavior and sexual disorders, as private personal matters for most people, are relatively difficult to investigate systematically and formally. However, there are sufficient ethological studies among primate societies and anthropological reports of tribal human societies indicating how sexual behavior varies among different societies (Castillo, 1997, pp. 114–119). Most of the information regarding sexual disorders is based on data derived from the West, regarding European American individuals (Laws & O'Donohue, 1997). Literature on non-Western individuals is very scarce. Thus, cross-cultural examination of sexual behavior and disorders is limited. Medical anthropologist Castillo (1997, pp. 124–134), after examining various types of paraphilias defined in the *DSM-IV-TR*, pointed out that there is a need for caution in recognizing and defining various kinds of sexual disorders. We elaborate briefly on the various kinds in the following paragraphs.

Exhibitionism. From an anthropological perspective, this pathological behavior (a man exhibiting his penis to females for sexual excitement) has meaning only in societies where the genitals are normally covered in public. In many tribal societies in tropical areas, traditionally no clothing is worn. Consequently, exposure of the genitals to a stranger of the opposite sex is not considered to be a sexual act as it is in other societies, such as Western societies.

Fetishism. Fetishism refers to the use of inanimate objects for sexual arousal. It is usually a disorder of males. Commonly used fetishes are objects associated with females, such as women's undergarments, stockings, shoes, or other articles. Fetishism tends to occur in a sexually conservative society where encounters between young males and females are rather strictly limited. Under such cultural circumstances, sexual objects are used as substitutes for sexual arousal. This substitution may tend to induce the occurrence of fetishism as a pathological condition.

Frotteurism. Frotteurism is characterized by a person's rubbing against or touching a nonconsenting person in a sexual way. It usually occurs in crowded public spaces, such as on buses or in subway cars. Frotteurism is obviously related to culture in that it occurs in large cities with crowded public transportation vehicles in societies that restrict the sexuality of young people. It also is indicated that it tends to occur in urban areas in societies with high levels of male dominance over females, such as in Japan or India (Castillo, 1997, p. 128).

Transsexualism. Transsexualism is the strong and persistent desire to change sexual identity. There is little literature from Southeast Asian societies for cross-cultural comparison (Heiman & Le, 1975; Tsoi, Kok, & Long, 1977). Tsoi and Kok (1995) reported that the number of transsexuals appearing in medical settings increased significantly with the availability and publicity of sex-change operations in Singapore in the 1970s, correcting the myth held previously that such sexual disorders were rare among the Chinese. As a part of the preoperation psychiatric screening, Tsoi and Kok examined male transsexuals seeking surgical treatment. They reported that there was no difference regarding personal backgrounds or histories of psycho-

sexual development among the Chinese, Malay, and Indian ethnic groups in Singapore. Their view was that if ethnic or cultural factors had any impact on the development of this disorder, it was minor and peripheral.

Homosexuality. Medical professionals from European and
American societies have radically revised their views about
homosexuality over the past half-century, no longer regarding
homosexuality as a disorder. However, social recognition and
cultural attitudes toward this sexual orientation still vary greatly
among different cultures. Some are very liberal, whereas many
remain negative. Even in the United States, homosexual intercourse was until recently illegal in some states, such as Texas.

Despite the shortage of formal and systematic cross-cultural
studies of sexual disorders, it is the general view of scholars
and clinicians that not only sexual behavior but also sexual disorders are subject to social and cultural influences. Culture shapes
the definition of disorder (pathodiscriminating effect), possibly
affects the prevalence of disorders (pathofacilitating effect), and
most obviously affects reaction to the disorders (pathoreactive
effect).

CULTURE-RELATED SPECIFIC DISORDERS

Culture-related specific syndromes are psychiatric syndromes whose occurrence or manifestation is closely related to
cultural factors and thus warrant understanding and management primarily from a cultural perspective (Tseng, 2001,
pp. 211–263). Because the clinical presentation of these syndromes is usually unique and not easily categorized according
to existing psychiatric classifications, they are called specific
syndromes. This group of disorders was referred to as culture-
bound syndromes in the past. However, because it was found
that the disorders are not necessarily bound to a particular ethnic group or cultural unit, but often appear in different ethnic
groups in different geographic areas, the term culture-related
specific syndromes was considered more accurate.

Although culture-related specific syndromes are rarely
encountered in daily clinical practice or in court cases, when
they are, the criminal responsibility associated with them is
often debated. Thus, from a forensic psychiatric point of view,
it is necessary to be aware of and to recognize the existence of

these syndromes. Following are some syndromes that may be encountered in forensic work and deserve attention.

Amok (Indiscriminate Mass Homicidal Behavior)

Amok is a unique homicidal behavior observed in Malaysia and in many other societies in Southeast Asia (such as Laos, Thailand, and the Philippines), in which a person, after encountering emotional stress, suddenly tries to kill people in the street indiscriminately with a dangerous weapon. The person who runs amok will eventually be killed by others or arrested. A person who survives the event often claims that he cannot recall his behavior, and was not aware of what he was doing. Determining legal responsibility for such criminal behavior is a challenge for the law (Hatta, 1996).

Amoklike massacre behavior has become more common in the United States over the past decade and is spreading to European societies as well, inducing profound social concern. The person who runs amok may or may not suffer from a conventional psychiatric disorder. He may be an ordinary person who bursts into anger, someone in a dissociated or possessed state who commits mass murder, or a psychotic patient whose behavior becomes violent while in a delusional state. From a phenomenological perspective, those who carry out sudden mass assaults are similar across cultures. They are often young males who suffer from social isolation, loss, depression, anger, delusion, and so on (Hempel, Levine, Meloy, & Westermeyer, 2000). However, the social reasons for such mass, indiscriminately homicidal behavior can be different from culture to culture. They may include dealing with shame, reacting to anger against authority, or wanting revenge, and so on. Most important is that this phenomenon can become a fashion, imitated by others, illustrating that it is the result of cultural impact by "psychoselective effect"; that is, it is one of many culturally influenced ways that people tend to select to cope with their frustrations and stress.

Latah (Startle-Induced Dissociative Reaction)

Latah is a Malay word that refers to the altered state of consciousness into which a person suddenly falls after being startled by external stimuli or tickled by another. The person goes into a transient, dissociated state, exhibiting unusual behavior, such as echolalia (imitating others' speech), echopraxia (imitating others' actions), command automatism (following others' suggestions), and brisk, explosive, verbal outbursts, usually uttering erotic words that are not permitted in ordinary life. The phenomenon has been observed in other places around the globe and has been given various folk names: in Burma (where it is called *yaun*), Indonesia, Thailand (*bah-tsche*), the Philippines (*mali-mali*), indigenous tribes in Siberia, Russia (*myriachit*), and among the Ainu in Japan (*imu*).

The latah reaction is found predominantly among women, although men may occasionally be involved. Most cases in Malay are found in rural areas. Some people develop latah reactions insidiously, without any precipitating events, whereas, in others it occurs after the person endures psychologically stressful events. The loss of a significant person usually occurs shortly before the first experience of latah reaction. Once such a reaction is experienced, it becomes habitual, and, thereafter, any sudden stimulation may provoke its occurrence. Any sudden noise or being suddenly touched or poked by others might induce an attack of latah. Throwing a rope or other snakelike object in front of the person or simply shouting "snake!" might sufficiently startle the person to start a latah reaction. The condition may last for several minutes or several hours, if the person is continuously provoked. After the dissociative reaction is over, the individual usually claims amnesia and is often puzzled by what had happened. The individual is often very apologetic and embarrassed for the (socially) inappropriate things she or he may have said (sexually colored "dirty" words) or done (such as touching members of the opposite gender) during the attack (Tseng, 2001, pp. 245–250).

In contrast to altered states of consciousness (as observed in meditation or in shaman performances) that are induced through the mental mechanisms of monotonous stimulation (such as quiet chanting or repetitive, simple rhymes) or intensive concentration (meditation), latah's dissociated state is induced (or conditioned) by sudden stimulation.

Among scholars, there is a debate as to whether the latah condition should be regarded possibly as a culture-related mental disorder or as merely an unusual behavior response found in some cultures. According to Malay psychiatrist Woon Tai-Hwang (personal communication, 1982), the majority of individuals who experience the latah condition are considered ordinary people. Except during their latah reaction, they function effectively and adapt well in the community. However, there have been a few cases in which persons have had difficulty controlling (or terminating) their dissociated condition after being startled and have been involved in self-injury or aggressive or homicidal behavior toward others. Such reactions have been labeled malignant latah, as opposed to regular latah.

Although individuals are seldom involved in criminal acts during the latah condition, they do occasionally injure others by using nearby weapons through a startled reflex or at others' criminal suggestions. In such cases whether the person was criminally responsible became a forensic issue as early as the beginning of the 20th century (Fletcher, 1908). Determining whether a person who performs a criminal act (such as picking up a nearby knife and injuring another) during a malignant latah episode should face legal responsibility certainly challenges the legal system.

Family Suicide (Children's Homicide and Parents' Suicide)

Family suicide is a unique suicide behavior observed in Japan. It occurs when parents decide to commit suicide together and take their young children with them in death. Therefore, it actually takes the form of adults' suicide and children's homicide. The parents' desire to have their children die with them is based on the cultural belief that the life of an orphan is miserable (Tseng, 2001, pp. 234–235). Strictly speaking, family suicide can be categorized as a behavior problem rather than as a psychiatric disorder, unless one of the parents suffers from a severe mental disorder (such as schizophrenia, delusional disorder, or psychotic depression) and engages in homicidal and suicidal behavior as a consequence.

A case of family suicide by a Japanese national living in the United States was reported about a decade ago (see the discussion in chapter 9, "A Japanese American Mother Who Drowned Her Two Children," for a detailed discussion). A mother, after being deserted by her husband, was angry and depressed, and tried to drown her two young children and kill herself. The mother was rescued and pleaded cultural justification for her behavior in court, which was verified by a culture expert. The judge took this into consideration and imposed a sentence of 1 year in prison and probation for 5 years. This outcome is in contrast to the situation in Japan, where parent-suicidal–children-homicidal behavior has been regarded as criminal since the Meiji era. This is an example of how cultural excuses may be overapplied in foreign countries when the same behavior is regarded as criminal in the person's home country.

Voodoo Death (Magic Fear–Induced Death)

Voodoo death is a rather peculiar medical-psychological phenomenon that is unfamiliar to most people in modern Western societies. In many undeveloped societies, however, some people still strongly believe that if a person breaks a taboo, or does something very wrong and is cursed by another, usually by a magically powerful person, the person will be punished by death. The person breaking the taboo or being cursed suddenly dies. Voodoo death is based on a belief in witchcraft—the punitive power to bring about misfortune, disability, and even death through "spiritual" mechanisms.

Working in Central Zaire (formerly the Belgian Congo) in Central Africa, Watson (1973) described about four cases of death by curses observed at the hospital every year. In other words the phenomenon was not such a rare occurrence. Watson reported one typical case in which a young adult Bantu woman was admitted to a hospital. Her husband informed the physician that as a result of a serious interfamily quarrel, the services of the local witchdoctor had been sought to put a death curse on her. She understood fully that, as a result, she would die shortly. Her general condition on admission was satisfactory, except for acute depression, but within 2 days she died quietly.

Instead of accepting the notion of psychogenic death, modern medicine has speculated that the mechanism of death is coincidental natural causes; for example, death from dehydration or an existing physical illness, secondary to excessive fear reaction. Because most cases have not been examined thoroughly prior to or after death, there is no way to prove the actual cause of death.

Watson suggested that the role of the curse clearly depends on a receptive state of mind among the tribespeople concerned.

Even though many curses are made in daily life in many societies—such as "drop dead!" in vulgar English—no one takes them very seriously. However, a curse becomes a powerful suggestion when tribespeople believe a witchdoctor or village elder who practices the art of the occult and has strong magic powers over an individual has cursed them. In those circumstances the curse will activate an intense, deep-seated fear based on tradition, superstition, and an innate respect for harmful spirits.

According to Cannon (1957), voodoo death is widely observed among the natives of Africa, South America, Australia, New Zealand, and the islands of the Pacific. From a forensic point of view, the possible occurrence of death through magic fear, particularly among those tribespeople who strongly believe in supernatural power, deserves attention. It also raises an interesting forensic question. If a person places a death curse on another person, and the other person actually dies, should the curser shoulder legal responsibility for the act? A search of the literature yielded no information on how this matter is handled in courts in areas where voodoo is practiced.

REFERENCES

Adityanjee, Raju, G. S. P., & Khandelwal, S. K. (1989). Current status of multiple personality disorder in India. *American Journal of Psychiatry, 146*(12), 1607–1610.

Alarcón, R., & Foulks, E. (1995). Personality disorders and culture: Contemporary clinical views, Part A. *Cultural Diversity and Mental Health, 1*, 3–17.

American Psychiatric Association (2000). *Diagnostic and statistical manual of mental disorders* (4th ed., Text rev.). Washington, DC: Author.

Berrios, G. E. (1994). The history of descriptive psychopathology. In J. E. Mezzich, M. R. Jorge, & I. M. Salloum (Eds.), *Psychiatric epidemiology: Assessment concepts and method*. Baltimore: Johns Hopkins University Press, pp. 47–68.

Brody, G. H., Ge, X. J., Conger, R., Gibbons, F. X., Murry, V. M., Gerrard, M., & Simons, R. L. (2001). The influence of neighborhood disadvantage, collective socialization, and parenting on African American children's affiliation with deviant peers. *Child Development, 72*, 1231–1246.

Cannon, W. B. (1957). "Voodoo" death. *Psychosomatic Medicine, 19*, 182–190.

Castillo, R. J. (1997). *Culture and mental illness: A client-centered approach*. Pacific Grove, CA: Brooks/Cole.

Cohen, P., Cohen, J., Kasen, S., Velez, C. N., Hartmark, C., Johnson, J., Rojas, M., Brook, J., & Streuning, E. L. (1993). An epidemiological study of disorders in late childhood and adolescence, in age- and gender-specific prevalence. *Journal of Child Psychology and Psychiatry, 34*, 851–867.

Comton, W. M., Helzer, J. E., Hwu, H. G., Yeh, E. K., McEvoy, L., Topp, I. E., & Spiztnagel, E. L. (1991). New methods in cross-cultural psychiatry: Psychiatric illness in Taiwan and the U.S. *American Journal of Psychiatry, 148,* 1697–1704.

Cooke, D. J., & Michie, C. (1999). Psychopathy across cultures: North America and Scotland compared. *Journal of Abnormal Psychology, 108*(1), 58–68.

Dembo, R., Schmeidler, J., Sue, C. C., Bordern, P., Manning, D., & Rollie, M. (1998). Psychosocial, substance use, and delinquency differences among Anglo, Hispanic White, and African-American male youths entering a juvenile assessment center. *Substance Use and Misuse, 33*(7), 1481–1510.

Fergusson, D. M., Horwood, L. J., & Lynskey, M. T. (1992). Family change, parental discord, and early offending. *Journal of Child Psychology and Psychiatry, 33,* 1059–1075.

Fletcher, W. (1908). *Latah* and crime. *Lancet, 2,* 254–255.

Foulks, E. F. (1996). Culture and personality disorders. In J. E. Mezzich, A. Kleinman, H. Fabrega, Jr., & L. Parron (Eds.), *Culture and psychiatric diagnosis: A DSM-IV perspective* (pp. 243–252). Washington, DC: American Psychiatric Press.

Fukushima, A. (1985). *Sheishin-kantei: Hanzai-shinli to sekinin-norioku* [Psychiatric examination: Criminal psychology and responsible ability]. Tokyo: Youikaku. (In Japanese).

Greaves, G. B. (1980). Multiple personality disorder: 165 years after Mary Reynolds. *Journal of Nervous and Mental Disease, 168,* 577–596.

Hare, R. D. (1991). *The Hare Psychopathy Checklist–Revised.* Toronto, ON: Multi-Health Systems.

Hare, R. D., Hart, S. D., & Harpur, T. J. (1991). Psychopathy and the DSM IV criteria for antisocial personality disorder. *Journal of Abnormal Psychology, 100,* 391–398.

Hatta, S. M. (1996). A Malay cross-cultural worldview and forensic review of amok. *Australian and New Zealand Journal of Psychiatry, 30,* 505–510.

Hayashi, K. (2001). *Manual for the practice of forensic examination: From clinic to the court.* Tokyo: Kinko Publisher. (In Japanese).

Heiman, E. M., & Le, C. V. (1975). Transsexualism in Vietnam. *Archives of Sexual Behavior, 4*(1), 89–95.

Hempel, A. G., Levine, R. E., Meloy, J. R., & Westermeyer, J. (2000). A cross-cultural review of sudden mass assault by a single individual in the Oriental and Occidental cultures. *Journal of Forensic Sciences, 45*(3), 582–588.

Huzings, D., Loeber, R., & Thornberry, T. P. (1993). Longitudinal study of delinquency, drug use, sexual activity, and pregnancy among children and youth in three cities. *Public Health Report, 108,* Supplement 1, 90–96.

Hwu, H. G., Yeh, E. K., & Chang, L. Y. (1989). Prevalence of psychiatric disorders in Taiwan defined by the Chinese Diagnostic Interview Schedule. *Acta Psychiatrica Scandinavica, 79,* 136–147.

Jablensky, A., Sartorius, N., Ernberg, G., Anker, M., Korten, A., Cooper, J. E., Day, R., & Bertelsen, A. (1991). Schizophrenia: Manifestations, incidence and course in different cultures: A World Health Organization ten-country study. In *Psychological Medicine, Monograph Supplement 20.* Cambridge, UK: Cambridge University Press.

Kitanishi, K. (1993). Possession phenomena in Japan. In *The Proceedings of the Fourth Cultural Psychiatric Symposium: Possession phenomena in East Asia* (pp. 34–50). Seoul, South Korea: East Asian Academy of Cultural Psychiatry.

Kosson, D. S., Smith, S. S., & Newman, J. P. (1990). Evaluating the construct validity of psychopathy in Black and White male inmates: Three preliminary studies. *Journal of Abnormal Psychology, 99*(3), 250–259.

Laws, D. R., & O'Donohue, W. (Eds.). (1997). *Sexual deviance: Theory, assessment, and treatment.* New York: Guilford.

Levy, A. (1996). Forensic implications of the difficulties of defining delusions. *Medicine and Law, 15*(2), 257–260.

Li, C. P. (2000). *Practice and theory of forensic psychiatric assessment: Including analysis and discussion of 97 forensic cases.* Beijing, China: Beijing Medical University Publisher. (In Chinese)

Lopez, S. R. (1989). Patient variable biases in clinical judgment: Conceptual overview and methodological considerations. *Psychological Bulletin, 106,* 184–203.

Lynn, R. (2002). Racial and ethnic differences in psychopathic personality. *Personality and Individual Differences, 32*(2), 273–316.

Malmquist, C. P. (1997). Conduct disorder: Diagnostic and conceptual issues. In J. M. Wiener (Ed.), *Textbook of child and adolescent psychiatry* (2nd ed., pp. 411–425). Washington, DC: American Psychiatric Press.

Moran, P. (1999). The epidemiology of antisocial personality disorder. *Social Psychiatry and Psychiatric Epidemiology, 34,* 231–242.

Pabon, E. (1998). Hispanic adolescent delinquency and the family: A discussion of sociocultural influences. *Adolescence, 33*(132), 941–955.

Pfefferbaum, B., Lfefferbaum, R. L., Strickland, R. J., & Brandt, E. N., Jr. (1999). Juvenile delinquency in American Indian youths: Historical and cultural factors. *Journal of Oklahoma State Medical Association, 92*(3), 121–125.

Robins, L. N., Tipp, J., & Pryzbeck, T. (1991). Antisocial personality. In L. N. Robins & D. A. Rogers (Eds.), *Psychiatric disorders in America: The Epidemiologic Catchment Area study* (pp. 258–290). New York: Free Press.

Rodriguez, O., & Weisburd, D. (1991). The integrated social control model and delinquency. *Criminal Justice and Behavior, 18,* 464–479.

Ross, C. A. (1991). Epidemiology of multiple personality disorder and dissociation. *Psychiatric Clinics of North American, 14*(3), 503–517.

Rutter, M., Graham, P., & Yule, W. A. (1970). *A neuropsychiatric study in childhood.* London: Spastus International Medical Publications.

Samaniego, R. Y., & Gonzales, N. A. (1999). Multiple mediators of the effects of acculturation status on delinquency for Mexican American adolescents. *American Journal of Community Psychology, 27*(2), 189–210.

Smart, R., Murray, G. F., & Arif, A. (1988). Drug abuse and prevention programs in 29 countries. *International Journal of the Addictions, 23,* 1–17.

Suwanlert, S. (1976). *Phii pob*: Spirit possession in rural Thailand. In W. P. Lebra (Ed.), *Culture-bound syndrome, ethnopsychiatry, and alternate therapies* (pp. 68–87). Honolulu: University Press of Hawaii.

Takahashi, Y. (1990). Is multiple personality really rare in Japan? *Dissociation, 3*(2), 57–59.

Tseng, W. S. (2001). *Handbook of cultural psychiatry.* San Diego, CA: Academic Press.

Tsoi, Y. F., & Kok, L. P. (1995). Mental disorders in Singapore. In T. Y. Lin, W. S. Tseng, & E. K. Yeh (Eds.), *Chinese societies and mental health* (pp. 266–278). Hong Kong: Oxford University Press.

Tsoi, Y. F., Kok, L. P., & Long, F. Y. (1977). Male transsexualism in Singapore: A description of 56 cases. *British Journal of Psychiatry, 131*, 405–409.

Walker-Barnes, C. J., & Mason, C. A. (2001). Ethnic differences in the effect of parenting on gang involvement and gang delinquency: A longitudinal, hierarchical linear modeling perspective. *Child Development, 72*(6), 1814–1831.

Watson, A. A. (1973). Death by cursing: A problem for forensic psychiatry. *Medicine, Science, and the Law, 13*(3), 192–194.

Wen, J. K. (1996). Possession phenomena and psychotherapy. In W. S. Tseng (Ed.), *Chinese mind and therapy* (pp. 295–330). Taipei, Taiwan: Laureate Publisher. (In Chinese).

Westermeyer, J. (1987). Cultural patterns of drug and alcohol use: An analysis of host and agent in the cultural environment. *United Nations Bulletin of Narcotics, 39*, 11–27.

Westermeyer, J. (1999). Cross-cultural aspects of substance abuse. In M. Galanter & H. D. Kleber (Eds.), *Textbook of substance abuse treatment.* Washington, DC: American Psychiatric Press.

World Health Organization. (1973). *The international study of schizophrenia.* Geneva, Switzerland: Author.

Zhang, X. F. (1992). A report of 32 cases in hysteria involved in homicide. *Chinese Mental Health Journal, 6*(4), 175–76. (In Chinese).

5

Cultural Dimensions of Various Crimes and Behavioral Problems

In the previous chapter we discussed from a cultural perspective the various psychiatric disorders that often are seen in the forensic context. In this chapter we focus, in contrast, on conduct that our society criminalizes. The behaviors, by themselves, do not constitute mental illnesses, although mentally ill persons may engage in them. Furthermore, the behaviors may be influenced by cultural factors in how the act is defined, viewed, or managed by a society. In general, by professional education and training, clinical psychologists pay more attention to behavioral and psychological problems observed in daily life, whereas psychiatrists tend to focus less on these subjects. However, from both a cultural and forensic perspective, culturally competent forensic experts must have adequate cultural knowledge and reasonable familiarity with various kinds of behavioral problems beyond psychiatric disorders in order to achieve a culturally relevant understanding and formulate an informed opinion. We aim to accomplish this purpose in this chapter. Although it is impossible to review all criminal conduct or psychological and behavioral problems inclusively, we elaborate on many that are commonly encountered in forensic work. We discuss some behaviors that are criminalized but require specialized forensic assessment (such as child abuse) in the next chapter.

SPOUSE ABUSE

Spouse abuse refers to the abusive treatment that occurs between mates. The abuse can be physical (including sexual), verbal, mental, or emotional. Physical abuse, such as violent assault, is easier to recognize than psychological or emotional abuse, such as verbal assaults on a person's character, humiliation, or threats to one's life. Statistics show that the husband generally perpetrates physical abuse toward the wife, although it can be the other way around.

Anthropological and Cross-Cultural Information

Reviewing archived data about family violence in underdeveloped, small-scale, peasant societies that were included in the Human Relations Area Files, Levinson (1988) reported that wife beating was the most common form of family violence, occurring in 84.5% of the 90 societies examined. Lester (1981) found that wife beating was more common in societies in which women were perceived as inferior and that were characterized by high divorce rates. Societies that experienced high rates of alcohol use as well as high rates of alcohol-related aggression also had a higher prevalence of wife beating.

In developing and developed societies, the occurrence of wife beating tends to be underreported, making it difficult to obtain actual figures of prevalence. O'Leary and Curley (1986) predicted that at least half of all married adults in the United States, male and female, would experience one or more acts of physical aggression by their marriage partners. Straus, Gelles, and Steinmetz (1980) estimated that approximately 10% to 15% of women in the United States would be victims of repeated, serious physical aggression by their partners.

In spite of a cultural background emphasizing harmony within a family as a virtue, Asia is not immune to the abuse of wives by husbands. In Japan, according to a mail questionnaire survey conducted by Yoshihama and Sorenson (1994), more than three fourths of women reported physical, sexual, or emotional abuse, perpetrated by their intimate male partners. Perhaps this is not surprising if we understand that the male holds a superior position over women in Japanese culture, even though some changes have occurred since World War II.

Hicks (2003) conducted an interview survey of Chinese Americans in the Boston area and found that about 15% of women studied experienced partner violence. He also discovered that a history of partner violence was associated with a higher rate of major depression and with a dose-response effect; that is, a worse lifetime major depressive episode was associated with the severity of lifetime partner violence.

Comparing the United States, Canada, Finland, Israel, Puerto Rico, and Belize, Steinmetz (1981) reported the interesting finding that the percentage of husbands and wives who claimed they used violence was apparently not an accurate predictor of the severity and frequency of violent acts. For example, in Finland, 60% of married couples reported using violence, but they had the lowest mean frequency scores of actual violent acts; whereas the kibbutz sample from Israel had the fewest number of husbands and wives claiming the use of violence, but those who did use violence were extremely violent.

Causal Factors for Spouse Abuse

Much theoretical speculations has surrounded spouse abuse, particularly wife beating. After reviewing the available literature, Barnes (1999) listed several issues that have been raised by scholars, especially those that are culturally related, with special reference to African Americans. According to Barnes, spouse abuse is the result of social learning, through imitative behavior and modeling from the parents. African Americans learn to use violence during childhood to meet their needs when other methods fail. This is related to cultural norms within families regarding how violence is used. Among African Americans, violence can be viewed as a resource of control to compensate for a lack of other resources, such as money, respect, prestige, power, or knowledge. This is based on cultural values regarding male and female roles. In general boys are taught to be aggressive and dominant and that violence is an acceptable problem-solving strategy, whereas girls are taught to be subservient family caretakers, with a subordinate status.

Concerning the interplay between ethnicity and alcohol-related assaults against wives among different ethnic groups, Kantor (1997) demonstrated that the linkages between drinking and wife beating were not just a problem of economically poor ethnic minorities. Heavy drinking per se was associated similarly in Hispanic American and Anglo-American families. However, there was little or no effect of drinking by African American men on wife assaults. Furthermore, they found that cultural differences in attitudes about alcohol were consistent with greater legitimation of alcohol-related misbehavior and the acceptance of "machismo" drinking by Hispanic Americans compared with Anglo-Americans.

After reviewing societies such as India, where bride burning and dowry death still occur because the laws against such crimes are poorly enforced, and Chile, where wife beating is prevalent because the husband is constitutionally granted marital authority over his wife, Heise (1990) pointed out that the underlying factor for such "crimes of gender" is the unequal power balance between men and women.

Legal Intervention and Its Implications

Historically, spouse abuse has not been viewed as a criminal offense but rather often has been seen as a family problem (Guyer, 2000). Domestic abuse complaints are often handled by social agencies, not law-enforcement agencies. However, intervening in and preventing physical spousal assaults are not merely social concerns but legal matters, particularly concerning incidents that tend to occur repeatedly and to a severe degree.

Different societies use different approaches to deal with spouse abuse. Providing marital counseling is one approach. Using available support from family and relatives to inhibit the husband's misbehavior is another approach. One basic approach is to establish laws protecting women from being abused by their husbands. Establishing shelters for the protection of abused women is another social measure that is commonly used. In the United States most women know that if her husband physically abuses her, she can call law-enforcement officers for protection. The husband will then be subject to the law for his abusive behavior. This may include the issuance of a restraining order to restrict him from coming physically close to his wife. However, many abused women may not notify police, for a variety of reasons, including the fact that husbands may react strongly and negatively to being reported and dealt with legally, which may affect the future of the marital relationship.

INFANTICIDE AND FILICIDE

General Issues and Classification

Filicide is a general term describing the murder of a child by the child's parents. The murder of a baby younger than 24 hours is termed neonaticide, of a child younger than 12 months is called infanticide, and of a child older than 1 year but younger than 5 years is called filicide. From the point of view of contemporary society, when parents kill their infants or small children their behavior is considered homicide, is regarded as criminal, and is subject to severe legal punishment. However, from an anthropological point of view, the intentional killing of infants or children by their parents has been practiced for different reasons in various societies historically and continues to be practiced in many undeveloped societies. As pointed out by Spinelli (2003, p. xv), the murder of a small child is a subject that is both compelling and repulsive. The killing of an innocent elicits sorrow, anger, and horror. It is a crime. It demands retribution. That is the law. Yet the perpetrator of this act is often a victim too, and that recognition makes for a more paradoxical response.

Forensic psychiatry has classified filicide into different categories on the basis of clinical and forensic aspects of the case. On the basis of a review of 131 case reports from the English-language literature (mainly from Western societies), Resnick (1969) proposed five categories, with a percentage distribution from cases he reviewed, namely, altruistic filicide (48.9%), acutely psychotic filicide (21.4%), unwanted child filicide (13.7%), accidental filicide (12.2%), and spouse revenge filicide (3.8%). Including child murder by fathers, Bourget and Bradford (1990) suggested the categories of pathological filicide (relating to a mental disorder), accidental filicide, retaliating filicide, neonaticide, and paternal filicide.

From a cultural point of view, we may subdivide the killing of a baby or small child by a parent or parents into three different groups for discussion: (a) intentional killing for sociocultural reasons, (b) killing under the influence of a mental disorder or emotional problems of the parent(s), and (c) accidental killing of a baby or small children by adults. These three groups are distinctly different from the perspective of the mental condition of the parent when the homicidal action occurred. Let us focus on the intentional killing for sociocultural reasons (rather than because of insanity) first, and then elaborate on killing due to mental illness or emotional problems later.

Various Reasons for the Intentional Killing of Children

The reasons that parents intentionally take the lives of their infants or small children vary. The reasons can be subgrouped further, which we discuss in the following paragraphs.

Born with physical malformation. One common reason for neonaticide is that the baby is born with a severe physical handicap or defect, so it is difficult for the youngster to survive. The parent regards it as more humane to put the baby to death. In some societies such babies are regarded as "witch babies," "fairy children," or "spirit children," and putting them to death may be permitted (Scheper-Hughes, 2003). In West African Bariba of Benin, people believed witches present themselves at birth in the form of various physical anomalies, and those infants were traditionally exposed, poisoned, or starved (Sargent, 1987). In many Pacific islands, in the past, the parents would put (severely) handicapped babies into the ocean, believing that returning them to nature was a more "natural" course to follow, rather then letting them suffer in life because of their defects.

Supernatural belief or superstition. Supernatural belief about a baby may occur even in the absence of a physical malformation. Sometimes it is simply associated with cultural interpretation or belief. Allotey and Reidpath (2001), noting that the mortality rate for children younger than age 5 years was highest in Ghana (with a rate of 23.9 per 1,000 children per year), higher than other countries in West Africa, conducted a field examination there. They reported that almost 15% of the deaths of infants younger than 3 months of age were due to a belief in a spirit child (called chichuru locally). The high mortality rate indicated that babies were not necessarily killed because of severe physical malformations or handicaps. Beyond physical abnormalities, children of mothers who engaged in intercourse in an open place, who had very difficult pregnancies, or who died in childbirth were all considered signs of the delivery of a spirit child. Constant crying and becoming particularly upset if stared at were other indications that the baby was a spirit child and needed to be exterminated.

In Canada the sex ratios of children in certain Eskimo populations have suggested a female infanticide rate of approximately 66%. These groups were said to practice female infanticide because of the belief that the time spent suckling a girl could delay the possible conception of a boy. Sons were preferred to daughters, presumably because sons would grow up to become providers of food in a hunting economy, whereas daughters might constitute an economic burden on the family (Chapman, 1980; Lomis, 1986).

In modern Japan some people still strongly hold the superstitious belief that women born in the year of *hinoe-uma* (firehorse) are ill fated. According to the old Chinese almanac, every 60 years is the year of the "fire and horse," based on the combination of 5 heavenly stems and 12 animals in Chinese astrology. According to this superstition, women born in this year will bring bad luck to their families and future husbands. Families that believe this do not want a man to marry a woman born in this year. Kaku (1975) speculated that because of this stigma, some female babies born in that year might be subject to infanticide. He examined records about pregnancy rates, induced abortions, and infant mortality for the year 1966 (the most recent year of the fire-horse) in Japan and found that compared with the previous years, 1961 to 1965, and the following year, 1967, there was a considerable decrease in pregnancy rates, increased abortions, and a remarkable increase in the mortality rate of girl babies (but not boy babies) in 1966. This supports the idea that many people avoided bearing children (because they were concerned with having a female baby) in that particular year, and, if a female baby was born, the baby was permitted to die through negligence. These data illustrate how female infanticide may be associated with folk superstition.

Unwanted babies. Another reason that parents kill their infants in some cultures is because the mother has given birth to a child out of wedlock, which is considered a terrible and shameful thing. This practice is illustrated in a report from Japan (Ikeda, 1987). With no perceived alternative choice, including the possibility of giving away the babies after they are born, some mothers hide their pregnancies and, when the babies are born, abandon them on the street or somewhere outside, hoping that someone will find and raise the babies. However, in extremely cold weather, the babies die if they are not found quickly. This behavior is condemned by society on one hand, yet is still practiced. Although times are changing, Japan is one society in which this kind of child abandonment may still be observed; for a woman to bear a child without being married has traditionally been unthinkable, which leaves the unmarried mother no other choice but to abandon it. A newborn baby is thought of as still a fetus, rather than a child, and abandoning it is considered the last opportunity to terminate the unwanted birth. Minturn and Stashak (1982) suggested this form of infanticide might be viewed as a terminal abortion procedure, practiced when other abortion attempts fail.

Gender discrimination. In a society where boys are preferred strongly over girls, either for socioeconomical reasons or for cultural attitudes, the practice of killing female children may occur. In India female infanticide or the elimination of girl children ages 1 to 3 years was suspected from 19th-century documents containing official discussions over the matter (Kasturi, 2000). Because of discrimination against female children, the sex ratio of infant mortality in India runs counter to that in the developed world (Ghosh, 1991). In most developed societies, the male infant death rate is always greater than that for female infants because male babies are medically considered to be more vulnerable than female babies. However, in India the female infant death rate is only lower during the first week of life, after which it surpasses that of male infant deaths. This suggests that although female infanticide does occur, the discrimination manifests itself more commonly through the neglect of female children, resulting in death from malnutrition or sickness.

Coale and Banister (1994) pointed out through population research in China that from the late 1930s there were incidences of excessive female mortality (probably infanticide), but that it declined precipitously in the early communist period, around the 1950s. However, there has recently been an escalation in the proportion of young females missing in China. The national policy of one child per one couple started in the 1970s, coupled with the traditional value of a male child, is thought to have contributed to the phenomenon.

Using data obtained from the World Health Statistical Annual published in 1973 on the murder rates by gender and age for all nations of the world, Lester (1991) found that the sex ratio for the murder of babies was more egalitarian in nations with a higher gross national product per capita and more female equality.

As a part of family suicide. Family suicide, most frequently observed in Japan in the past, is rather a unique, culture-related suicidal behavior that we discussed previously (see the section "Family Suicide (Children's Homicide and Parents' Suicide)" in chapter 4). When parents decide to commit double suicide, they force their children to die with them. The age of the children joining parent-suicide and child-homicide action varies, with some children even older than age 5 years.

Thus, certain baby-killing behaviors are observed in various societies. They are associated with cultural issues and, in a broad way, can be regarded as culture-related, specific behavioral problems that may have legal consequences. Evaluation of cases of infant or child murder may require special consideration of cultural and ethical issues involved.

Killing Children While Under the Influence of a Mental Disorder or Emotional Problems

In this situation, in contrast to the previous category, parents undertake homicidal action against their babies or small children while under the influence of a mental disorder.

Postpartum psychosis. A small percentage of women may become psychotic after delivery of their child and, in this state, kill the newborn baby or small child. The psychosis, usually manifested in the form of severe depression, may be associated with the psychotic features of hallucinations or delusions and is considered by psychiatrists to be a mental disorder that occurs predominantly because of biological and hormonal etiologies. (For an expanded discussion of these issues, see chapter 4, "Postpartum Psychosis.")

Psychotic disorders not related to postpartum psychosis. Sometimes a parent, either the father or the mother, kills a child while under the influence of a psychotic condition other than postpartum psychosis. The most common causative mental disorders are schizophrenia, organic mental disorders, or delusional disorders. The parent carries out the murder often while under the influence of a delusion (believing the child to be the devil, for instance) or an auditory hallucination (commanding the parent to kill the child). Researchers refer to this category, including postpartum psychosis, as acute psychotic filicide (Resnick, 1969) or pathological filicide (Bourget & Bradford, 1990). Rarely, child homicide will take place while the parent is under the influence of a dissociation or possession disorder (see the section "Possession Psychosis" in chapter 4). The legal responsibility becomes more controversial if the killing of a child occurs at the hand of a parent with a nonpsychotic mental disorder, such as possession disorder, which is not regarded as psychotic (unless it is a possession psychosis).

Personal emotional problems related to marriage. In a rather small percentage of cases, the murder of children by a parent occurs out of revenge or retaliation against the other parent. This particularly tends to occur when one parent discovers that the other parent is being unfaithful or is neglecting the care of the spouse and children, and he or she feels cheated or rejected. This type of murder is categorized as retaliating filicide (Bourget & Bradford, 1990) or spouse-revenge filicide (Resnick, 1969). This type of child killing tends to occur impulsively, without premeditation. (See the discussion in chapter 9, "Japanese American Mother Drowns Her Two Children.")

McKee and Shea (1998) compared data from an American sample with that from other English-speaking societies, namely, Britain (d'Orban, 1979) and Canada (Bourget & Bradford, 1990). They pointed out that there are remarkable similarities among the women who committed filicide in these (Caucasian) societies. The women appeared to have been experiencing high levels of stress and lack of resources, often raising their children alone, and the majority of them suffered from diagnosable mental disorders that they were attempting to manage without psychiatric treatment or assistance from others.

Accidental Killing of Babies or Children

Sometimes babies or small children may die suddenly by accident or mishap. Death can occur as a purely accidental occurrence, such as a baby or small child falling into a pool and drowning, being burned by fire, falling from a high place, being asphyxiated by a heavy quilt or pillow, and so on. When a baby's death appears accidental, careful examination is warranted to determine whether the baby or child was murdered by the parent. For instance, in some cultures, such as the Far East, a small baby sleeps in the same bed as the parents, using the same quilt. This action is based on the cultural assumption that a small baby can be better protected and cared for by the parents if they are nearby. However, during a sound sleep, a small baby might be covered by a heavy quilt and die from asphyxia. Although rare, this kind of accidental death (associated with negligence) might occur and should be treated differently from killing a baby by purposely obstructing his or her airway. Finally, the sudden death of a baby or a small child may occur unrelated to killing by adults. Medically, the socalled sudden infant death syndrome exists, even though its etiology is still unknown. A careful autopsy is needed where cause of death is in question.

Legal Implications and Debate

Determining whether the behavior of child killing is criminal, especially when undertaken intentionally for the sociocultural reasons elaborated previously, can be quite a legal challenge. This is particularly true when the client comes from a society in which the child-killing behavior is accepted or tolerated to some extent, but the homicidal behavior occurs in a host society in which the intentional killing of babies for any reason is regarded as a criminal act. The extent to which the court will or should consider the sociocultural beliefs and customs practiced in the defendant's society of origin is a matter of considerable debate.

When child-killing behavior occurs in association with a clearly recognized, severe mental disorder (psychosis), the legal implications of the severity of the mental disorder and the extent to which the individual deserves punishment for it are critical issues still being evaluated and debated in our society (see the section "Cultural Perspective on the Defense of Insanity and Diminished Capacity" in chapter 6). However, as we pointed out previously, this is not necessarily true in some states in our society and in many other societies (Oberman, 2003). As long as it is proved that the patient is suffering from a severe mental disorder at the time the incident occurred, the patient's legal responsibility is waived and he or she is subject to psychiatric treatment only.

CHILD ABDUCTION AND KIDNAPPING

Child abduction. Child abduction describes the taking by one parent of a child from where the child is living without the consent of the other parent. Abduction typically occurs when there is an unsettled dispute over child custody and when one parent decides to take possession of the child without the agreement of the other parent. Legislation outlawing this practice has been passed in the United States, as in other countries. The divorce rate is increasing, and there are an increasing number of cases in which parents have difficulty settling child custody disputes.

Child kidnapping. Child kidnapping describes the taking of a child from where he or she lives by a stranger (other than the parent). The resulting harm from kidnapping to the child, due to separating the child from his or her parents and family, the other possible harms, such as sexual abuse, and the terrible emotional pain of the parents and the family over the loss of a beloved child, leads our society to regard child kidnapping as one of the most heinous of crimes.

The reasons for kidnapping may vary. In the past, in undeveloped societies children were kidnapped to be sold elsewhere for child labor or child prostitution. Occasionally, a child, particularly one from an affluent family, may be kidnapped and held hostage for ransom. A child may be kidnapped by a mentally ill person, who takes the child under the delusion that the child is his or her own or with the religious belief that the child should belong (or be wed) to him or her. Recently, associated with the increase of sexual crimes in our society, child kidnapping has been closely related to child sexual molestation. Often the child is kidnapped, molested, and, tragically, murdered afterward.

VIOLENCE AGAINST OTHERS

Causes of Violent Behavior

The cause of violent behavior tends to be analyzed from three aspects, namely, dispositional factors, clinical factors, and contextual factors. Among dispositional factors, the tendencies to become impulsive, to be angry, and to have the trait of psychopathy are considered important. Clinical factors include mental disorders, substance abuse, and personality disorders. Social network and support often are included in contextual factors (Monahan & Steadman, 1994).

We limit the discussion to violent behavior against others, such as assault, although we elaborate on rape or homicide in a separate section.

International Comparisons

Rates of violent crime against others vary among different societies and are subject to change in association with changes in society. For instance, Japan historically has been regarded as a safe place, with a low crime rate. However, according to the official White Paper on Crime for the year 2001 (Comprehensive Research Institute of Justice, 2002), the rate of violent crime (including threats, aggravated assaults, rape, homicide, and so on) has increased remarkably in the past two decades. There were fewer than 100,000 annual reported cases previously, but in the past several years, they have suddenly increased to 263,000 annual reported cases, an increase of almost three times. Noticeably contributing to this is an increase in juvenile delinquency. Crimes committed by foreigners have increased remarkably in the past several years as well. In the year 1987 the rate for crimes committed by foreigners comprised only 0.6% of the total national crimes, but that figure increased to 7.5% in 2003. Although the rate of violent crime is still relatively lower in Japan than in many other societies, the Japanese themselves consider that, associated with socioeconomic and cultural changes, Japan is a much less safe society now. The weakening of parental authority, loss of parental control in urban settings, and exposure to Western culture are some of the factors causing the increase in crime in contemporary Japan.

In China, during the early period of the communist regime, the crime rate was so extremely low that few people felt the need to lock their doors, even when going out. This was associated with tight security controls and a well-organized neighborhood system. After the turmoil of the Cultural Revolution, however, crime increased, and, associated with the open-door policy adopted more than two decades ago, the crime rate increased even more.

Cross-Ethnic Comparison in the United States

In the United States the rate of violent crime is unevenly distributed among different ethnic groups. According to the data on arrests for aggravated assault for the year 1991 (Gall & Gall, 1993), adjusted by the data available for the population (U.S. Department of Commerce, 1997), the number of cases arrested for aggravated assault per 100,000 population was 103.6 for Caucasian Americans, 448.2 for African Americans, 150.9 for American Indians and Native Alaskans, and 38.3 for Asians and Pacific Islanders. (Hispanic Americans were not recorded as a separate ethnic group.) The results illustrate that violent crime varies greatly among different ethnic groups. One decade later, data (Sourcebook of Criminal Justice Statistics Online, 2003) for the year 2001 showed that the number of cases arrested for aggravated assault per 100,000 population was 99.6 for Caucasian Americans, 320.0 for African Americans, 144.6 for American Indians and Native Alaskans, and 37.5 for Asians and Pacific Islanders. In general, rates for arrests for aggravated assault declined for all ethnic groups, but did so more for African Americans. However, the range among the ethnic groups was still the same, with the number of cases being much higher for African Americans and lower for Asian Americans and Pacific Islanders, with Caucasian Americans in between.

Combining this cross-ethnic data on violence with the information about death due to homicide yields interesting results. According to Keppel, Pearcy and Wagener (2002), concerning the trend in the United States for the period of 1990-1998, the age-adjusted death rate per 100,000 population due to homicide was 4.1 for Caucasian Americans, 39.6 for African Americans, 11.1 for American Indians and Native Alaskans, 5.2 for Asians and Pacific Islanders, and 17.5 for Hispanic Americans. That pattern of distribution was relatively maintained in 1998, showing no gross changes for almost a decade (with the exception that the rate for Hispanic Americans dropped significantly to 9.9). In other words, as reflected by these statistical data, violence against others is relatively high for African Americans (associated with a relatively high rate of death due to homicide) and relatively low for Asian Americans or Pacific Islanders.

Legal Implications

As we explained previously, the nature and cause of violent behavior needs to be understood broadly from three dimensions, namely, individual dispositional factors, clinical factors, and contextual factors. In addition to individual factors (whether associated with anger, impulsiveness, poor emotional control, and so on), clinical factors (whether associated with mental disorders, substance abuse, and so on), and contextual factors (such as socioeconomic environment, level of living, social network, and so on), cultural factors need to be considered. How violent behavior is viewed by people (whether seen as adaptive or coping behavior for external stress or as a failure to control behavior) and is accepted or tolerated in the surrounding environment are issues that deserve consideration by the legal system before deciding the extent of punishment deserved for the violent behavior.

HOMICIDE

General Information

Homicide refers to the unlawful taking of the life of another. It can happen with or without a violent act, it can occur accidentally or intentionally, with or without a weapon, or by other means, including poisoning, drowning, hanging, and so on. Jurisdictions in the United States generally further classify homicide as either murder (which may be divided into first-degree premeditated murder and other degrees of murder) or manslaughter (which may be divided into voluntary and involuntary manslaughter). Forensic psychiatry becomes involved in murder cases in a variety of contexts, such as assessing whether the accused carried out the homicidal action under the influence of a psychotic condition, substance abuse, or another mental condition. Forensic psychiatry may also be involved at sentencing, and in a variety of competency matters.

International Comparisons

From an epidemiological point of view, data about murder is relatively easy to obtain for international comparison. This is because homicide is a gross crime that is always reported to the law enforcement system. By relying on the data from the International Crime Statistics for 1989–1990 collected and published by Interpol in 1990, Rushton (1995) tabulated the rate of murder, rape, and serious assault per 100,000 members of the population for 76 countries. Furthermore, the data were grouped into three groups of countries, Asian, Caucasian, and African, for comparison. It was reported that, regarding murder, the mean rates by macropopulation are 2.5 (SD = 2.5), 4.9 (SD = 5.1), and 12.8 (SD = 19.8), respectively, indicating that there were rather consistent and considerable differences among the three groups examined. The data were parallel to the data on serious assault and rape: following the trend that Asian countries tended to have lower rates, Caucasian countries were in the middle, and African countries had higher rates. According to this information, the rate of murder was 9.4 for the United States, 10.3 for the United Kingdom, and 14.8 for the Netherlands in the Caucasian group, and 1.0 for Japan and 1.5 for Korea in the Asian group.

According to the White Paper on Crime published by the Comprehensive Research Institute of Justice of Japan (2002, p. 88), from 1988 to 2000 the incidence of murder per 100,000 population among five developed countries, namely, France, Germany, Japan, the United Kingdom, and the United States, was considerably different, showing a different trend during the 12-year period examined. Japan maintained a flat curve, roughly 1.0, without change; the United Kingdom slightly increased, from 2.0 to 2.9; France decreased, from 4.5 to 3.7; Germany started at 4.0, increased to slightly more than 5.0 in between, and later declined to 3.5; the United States started at 8.5, raised to between 9.0 and 9.5 from 1990 to 1993, and gradually declined to 5.5 in 2000, still being the highest among the five countries compared.

From a social point of view, as with non-lethal violence against others, the rate of homicide will increase when there is instability in the society, with increased stress and loss of organization and rule. An increase in substance abuse will naturally increase the rate of homicide.

Cross-Ethnic Comparison in the United States

Available data (Gall & Gall, 1993) illustrate that in 1991 the number of people arrested for murder and nonnegligent manslaughter per 100,000 population was 3.7 for Caucasian Americans, 31.9 for African Americans, 2.1 for Asians and Pacific Islanders, and 6.8 for American Indians and Native Alaskans (Hispanic American were not calculated as a separate ethnic group). Ten years later the data available for the year 2001 (Sourcebook of Criminal Justice Statistics Online, 2003) showed the number of cases arrested for murder and nonnegligent manslaughter per 100,000 population to be 2.2 for Caucasian Americans, 13.2 for African Americans, 4.9 for American Indians and Native Alaskans, and 1.4 for Asians and Pacific Islanders. The data for 1991 and 2001 illustrate that arrests for homicide considerably decreased for all ethnic groups, particularly for African Americans, but the data still show a wide range of homicidal behavior among these ethnic groups. These rates are parallel to the rates given previously on aggravated assault.

Legal and Cultural Issues

From a legal point of view, homicide is considered a serious crime, and severe punishment is sought. Capital punishment, life in prison without parole, or a long prison sentence are common legal consequences, depending on the nature of the homicide. The severity of the penalty not only is associated with the gravity of the crime but also is related to the legal system involved, which, in turn, is determined by the society and the culture. As we elaborated previously (see the section "Law in Various Cultures" in chapter 1), the severity of legal punishment will be subject to cultural influences and varies among different societies. The death penalty, for example, is carried out in almost all Arab societies but not in European societies, while Asian societies are in between.

When a person commits a homicide under the influence of a psychotic condition, the extent to which an insanity defense will be accepted will vary in different societies, depending on people's attitudes toward murder and how they understand mental disorders. (See also the section "Punitiveness, Including the Death Penalty" in chapter 6.)

MASS HOMICIDE

Mass Homicide in Southeast Asian Societies

For some time, cultural anthropologists and cultural psychiatrists have paid attention to the unique phenomenon of indiscriminate, mass homicidal behavior that has been observed in Southeast Asia. In Malaysia a man, after encountering emotional stress, such as being insulted in public or learning that his wife is not faithful to him, often suddenly kills many people in the street indiscriminately with a dangerous weapon. Locally this is called *amok*, and has been regarded by scholars as a culture-bound syndrome frequently occurring in Malaysia. The person who runs amok will eventually be killed by others or be arrested. This phenomenon occurs so often that a specially designed, fork-shaped weapon was kept in police stations in the past to catch the dangerous men who ran amok (Tseng, 2001, pp. 230–233). (See also the section "Amok (Indiscriminate Mass Homicidal Behavior)" in chapter 4.)

Reviewing past episodes in Malaysia, Teoh (1972) pointed out that the amok syndrome has shown a historical evolution from a deliberate, conscious, frenzied, socially tolerated attack to an unconsciously motivated psychiatric disorder. Murphy (1973) also suggested that over the past several centuries the nature of amok has changed. Initially, the amok person initiated his actions as political terrorism, attacking only identified, religion-related "enemy-subjects" and avoiding injuring his own relatives and friends. There was no sign of mental illness before or after the attack. Later, amok episodes became sudden and unpremeditated and occurred in a dissociated state, with subsequent amnesia (not remembering what had happened), and the amok person killed people indiscriminately. Recently, people who have run amok have tended to have a history of mental illness and have undertaken the mass homicidal action in a psychotic state.

Amoklike massacre behavior has been observed in many other societies in Southeast Asia beyond Malaysia. Referred to by different local names, it is observed in Laos, Thailand, and the Philippines. There are reports of amok behavior from Indonesia and Papua New Guinea as well. This points out that amok is not a culture-bound behavior occurring endemically only in Malaysia; it can occur any place (Westermeyer, 1973).

Recent Mass Homicide in European and American Societies

Mass homicide attack has become more common in the United States over the past few decades and is spreading to European societies as well, inducing profound social concern. The person who carries out mass murder may suffer from a psychiatric disorder. Mass murderers range from non-mentally ill persons who burst into anger, to persons in dissociated or possessed states, to a psychotic individual in a delusional state. The behavior may take place in school, in the workplace, or on the streets.

After studying recent cases in various societies, Hempel, Levine, Meloy, and Westermeyer (2000) revealed that those individuals who carry out sudden mass assaults are similar; namely, they found such individuals are often young males who suffer from social isolation, loss, depression, anger, or delusion. Mass homicide may occur as a fashion, imitated by people who have heard about such mass murders in media reports. This is particularly true of incidents that have occurred in schools, committed by students who are resentful of their teachers or feeling rejected or discriminated against by their schoolmates. Their motivation is multiple, often a combination of anger and revenge, on one hand, and sadness or hopelessness on the other.

After reviewing various incidents of mass murder, Dietz (1993) pointed out a number of warning signs. These signs include repeatedly accusing other people of causing one's problems, making threats and intimidating comments to others, and intimidating or frightening others with a weapon.

It should be noticed that the profile for those who commit mass homicide is different from that of serial killers, who may be associated with a basic personality disorder or psychotic delusion. Mass homicide undertaken by an individual or a small group of people is also entirely different from politically related genocidal behavior that is carried out by a group, often occurring in wartime, and associated with hateful relations with other ethnic groups on a social level.

RAPE

The Nature and the Variety

Rape generally refers to unlawful sexual intercourse with a woman without her consent, often through the use of force. If rape is carried out in a habitual and preferable way for sexual gratification, the behavior may be considered a kind of sexual disorder, because the sexual act deviates from the normal. Men also may be victims of rape, often perpetrated by other men. Rape forces a sexual act involuntarily, violating another's privacy and individuality and causing psychological and even physical damage to the victim.

Hudson and Ward (1997) have correctly asserted that sexual aggression toward others is a heterogeneous phenomenon. Sexually assaultive behavior toward adult women range from the relatively minor to the severe; that is, from unwanted sexual gestures and verbal behavior to the opposite extreme, when a savage sexual assault leads to mutilation and death. Furthermore, men who perpetrate rape vary from those who are essentially no different from nonoffenders to those who have sadistic fantasies and marked delusions. Therefore, caution is needed when we discuss the prevalence of rape and factors associated with it.

Muir, Lonsway, and Payne (1996) found that the rates for reporting sexual assault in Scotland and the United States differ, namely, 30 per 100,000 population in Scotland and 42.3 per 100,000 population in the United States. They interpreted the difference according to cultural theory, which suggested that rape is an expression of power and aggression rather than of sexuality and that sexual assault is supported and encouraged by "rape myths."

Lonsway and Fitzgerald (1994) explained that rape myths are attitudes and beliefs that are generally false but are widely and persistently held and serve to deny and justify male sexual aggression against women. They further described some commonly held myths, such as women routinely lie about rape and only "certain women" are raped, primarily women with bad reputations and those from socially marginal or minority groups.

On the basis of this hypothesis, Muir and colleagues (1996) speculated that greater rape myth acceptance (RMA) is seen in societies plagued by a higher incidence of sexual assault. By surveying undergraduate students in a Scottish university and in an American university about RMA, they found that, overall, male participants reported greater RMA than did the female participants from both universities, indicating gender differences across cultures. However, the American students exhibited higher scores of RMA than did the Scottish students, which is parallel with the finding that rape rates are higher in the United States than in Scotland.

Reviewing studies carried out in the United States regarding RMA among different ethnic college students, Lonsway and Fitzgerald (1994) reported that African American students and

Hispanic American students were more accepting of rape myths than were Caucasian American students. Using vignettes of situations that meet the legal definition for rape, they found that African American students were less likely than Caucasian American students to define the situation as a rape, were more likely to blame the victims, and were less willing to prosecute the rapist.

Cultural definitions of what constitutes rape may affect the victims' self-perception, assessment of the event, and decision to seek treatment (Thompson & West, 1992). On the basis of the hypothesis that victims with the cultural belief that women may contribute to rape through their dress or behavior and that women should control not only their sexuality but also that of males would show more adverse psychological impact from sexual assault, Lefley, Scott, Llabre, and Hicks (1993) assessed African American, Hispanic, and non-Hispanic European American female rape victims and nonvictims matched for ethnicity, age, marital status, and socioeconomic status. They found that Hispanics scored highest and non-Hispanic European Americans scored the lowest, both in perceived community victim blaming and in victims' psychological distress. This result supported the notion that there was remarkable consistency between the respondents' perceptions of public attitudes toward rape in their culture and rape victims' personal psychological responses.

Scott, Lefley, and Hicks (1993) examined rape victims treated at a rape treatment center and found that 51% of them had no observable risk factors, whereas 49% fell into categories of variables that previous research had associated with increased vulnerability, such as impaired ability to evaluate potential threat, prior psychiatric history, and history of previous rape or sexual abuse. They found that among all victims presenting for treatment, 27.5% had a history of prior rape or incest, 14% had a history of psychiatric hospitalization, 7% were mentally retarded, and 7% were tourists or visitors when they were raped. When they divided the victims into ethnic groups, the authors found that African American victims were significantly more likely than Hispanics or non-Hispanic Caucasian Americans to have reported prior rape or incest. Hispanic victims had significantly more psychiatric hospitalization. A significantly greater percentage of the tourists and visitor rape victims were non-Hispanic Caucasian Americans, which illustrated that the different ethnic groups compared experienced different risk factors.

Further Cross-Ethnic and Cultural Data

In the United States in 1991, according to Gall and Gall (1993), the number of people arrested for rape per 100,000 population was 7.7 for Caucasian Americans, 41.7 for African Americans, 3.1 for Asian Americans and Pacific Islanders, and 12.3 for American Indians or Native Alaskans. (Hispanic Americans were not recorded as a separate ethnic group for comparison at the time.) These numbers show a great deal of difference among different ethnic groups in the same society. One decade later, according to the official information available for 2001 (Sourcebook of Criminal Justice Statistics Online, 2003), the number of people arrested for forcible rape per 100,000 population was 5.5 for Caucasian Americans, 18.6 for African Americans, 2.5 for Asian Americans and Pacific Islanders, and 8.3 for American Indians or Native Alaskans. A considerable decrease in rate was noted for all ethnic groups, especially for the African American group. Nevertheless, proportionally, it was high for African Americans and low for Asian Americans and Pacific Islanders, with the others in between.

These statistics describe only those rapes that were reported. The actual statistics are likely to be much higher. According to Koss (1992), the Federal Bureau of Investigation's Uniform Crime Reports recorded 102,555 rapes in 1990, which accounted for 6% of all violent crimes reported. To understand the actual occurrence of experiencing unwelcome sexual experiences, Russell (1984) conducted a community study in San Francisco involving a large random sample of women. As a result, Russell reported a 24% figure for rape. This was comparable to the finding made by Koss, Gidycz, and Wisniewski (1987), who performed a survey of a national sample of university women, reporting that 27.5% women had experienced rape or attempted rape since the age of 14. Gavey (1991) carried out a similar survey of university students in New Zealand and found out that 25.3% of female students reported experiences of rape and attempted rape. In Japan, according to the official White Book on Crime published by the Comprehensive Research Institute of Justice (2002, p. 5), in 2001 the number of reported rape cases was 2,228, with an annual incidence rate of 18 per 100,000 population, accounting for 2.8% of all violent crimes reported. On the basis of these figures, researchers can say that many rape victims do not make official reports and, even when a report is made, only a relatively small number of rapists are arrested.

Legal Implications

The occurrence of rape is subject to various psychological and sociocultural factors, affected by the rape myths held by people in the society, the risk factors that make the victim vulnerable, the trend for reporting the incident once it has happened, and how the victim and her family react to the incident. Cultural sensitivity is greatly needed in assessing both the perpetrator and the rape victim.

For various reasons, not all victims who are subject to sexual assault will take action and report the rape to authorities or the legal system. Neville and Pugh (1997) examined the post–sexual assault behavior among African American women and reported that both general and ethnic-specific factors contributed to the women's decision not to report the assault to police. General factors included the victim's relationship to the assailant, the degree of physical force used, the level of self-blaming for the incident, and the perceived outcome of reporting the incident. Social expectations also may contribute to a women's decision about whether to report the crime. Ethnic-specific factors include the strained relationship between the police and African American communities across the nation, making them reluctant to report to the police. Instead, they may disclose the assault to someone in their family or among their friends and receive support and comfort from them. Therefore, this ethnic-related, post-sexual assault behavior needs to be taken into consideration when the case is assessed from a forensic point of view, and presented in court when relevant.

In court, similar to the trend observed in sexual harassment, in the case of rape the ethnic or racial background of the rapist, the victim, and the jury, coupled with their genders, will interact in such a way to influence the jurors' decision. Racial bias becomes more evident, especially in trials in which the evidence is ambiguous (Landwehr et al., 2002). However, as pointed out by Hymes, Leinart, Rowe, and

Rogers (1993), the interaction of the race of the victim and defendant has not been consistent across studies. The authors pointed out that racial bias appears to lead jurors in trials of stranger rape, such as convicting African American defendants more readily and sentencing them more harshly than European American defendants, but that acquaintance rape may demonstrate a different pattern. They conducted a study with American undergraduate students, reading a trial transcript that established defendant–victim familiarity and sexual contact but was ambiguous about the victim's consent. The race of the defendant and of the victim was manipulated by design. The authors found that both African American and European American defendants were rated as more guilty when the victim's race differed from that of the alleged assailant. Hymes and colleagues pointed out that racial bias in jurors' decision making does not automatically place African Americans at a disadvantage. The (college-educated) jurors appeared to consider the racial relationship between the victim and the defendant and what they thought this relationship implied about the victim's willingness. As a result both African American defendants and European American defendants were more likely to be convicted if their race differed from that of the alleged victim.

RELIGION-RELATED WRONGFUL BEHAVIOR

Religious Behavior May Be Harmful

From an anthropological perspective, religion is defined as "belief and ritual concerned with supernatural beings, powers, and forces" (Wallace, 1966, p. 5). Regarding the purpose of religion, it "offers explanations, answering existential questions, such as how the world came to be, how humans are related to natural species and forces, why humans die, what happens after their death," and so on (Keesing, 1976, pp. 386–387). In a layperson's mind religion is generally regarded as a good thing that teaches people how to be good and behave well, and religious people are viewed as people who provide good models for others to follow. However, some religious people engage, in the name of religion, behaviors that are harmful to the members or to others.

For example, recent memory recalls the collective suicide of 39 members of the Heaven's Gate cult, who, following their leader, Marshall Applewhite, a former mental patient, ended their lives in a planned, organized way when the comet Hale-Bopp appeared in the sky in March 1997. The members believed they were escaping a revamping of Earth by hitching a cosmic ride to heaven. Another tragic incident of religious group behavior was the massive suicide of the members of the People's Temple in late 1978. Following the Reverend Jim Jones, their religious leader, more than 900 members moved from California to Guyana, South America, to establish a new life in the jungle. At their leader's order, as part of a religious ritual, all of them (including 200 or more children) swallowed cyanide and perished together.

History yields no shortage of examples of cult leaders predicting the end of the world and persuading their believers to prepare for salvation. Many believers sell their properties, quit their jobs, and make all necessary preparations for the end of the world. These kinds of religious episodes have occurred in the East as well. In Korea in 1997 a cult leader predicted the end of the world and caused social turmoil. In Taiwan in 1999 several hundred people sold their property and followed their leader to the United States to await the appearance of God on television on a certain day for His instructions on how to deal with the end of the world.

As part of its religious rituals, some groups believe that sexual acts among members or with the leader will enhance the blessings of God (Kim, 1972). It was suspected that the leader of the Branch Davidians had sexual relations with the female children of cult members. However, the most terrifying aspect of the Branch Davidians was their plan to start an antigovernment military movement. They purchased and stored a massive number of weapons in their attempt to achieve their religious goal, a plan that ended in tragedy in Waco, Texas, in 1993.

What are the common characteristics of those religious groups that are easily labeled pathological or sinister? Usually there is a powerful and convincing charismatic leader who demands absolute obedience from the members. The cult is often tightly organized and members' behavior is strictly controlled. The goal of the religion is rationalized in such a way that it is convincing to the members, who have a strong faith in their leader. As a result, the members lose their ego functions and their rational judgment and are willing to blindly follow the leader's orders.

Aside from extremely deviant religious groups, there is a borderline normality in many religious groups. For instance, a cult leader matching marital partners (as in the Unification Church or so-called Moonies) raises a question from a modern mental health perspective. A religious group fighting with different sects of the same religion, with other religious believers, or with nonbelievers, whether in occasional physical fights or formal wars institutionalized at a national level, poses questions from humanistic and religious points of view. Religions involved in politics, politicized religious movements, or religious organizations that seek economic gain are some examples.

Legal Implications

When religious people show pathological behavior, manifest unlawful acts or even harmful behavior to others, including their believers, there is a need for legal intervention. It is relatively easy to carry out legal action if it involves a small deviant religion. When a large, socially recognized, and respected established religion is involved this may become rather complicated and challenging. People may hesitate and refuse to admit that religious people can commit unlawful and harmful behavior toward others.

If the legal persons or professionals who are asked to work on the case happen to be faithful members of the particular religion, countertransference may create problems in the performance of their professional jobs. Countertransference is a psychological mechanism that has been recognized and described in psychiatric work. It means that the professionals, because of their personal views and feelings toward the persons involved—the patients or defendants—will lose their neutrality and professionalism in working on the case. In an opposite way, if the religion happens to be one toward which the professionals have a preexisting negative view and feeling, their professional work may be hindered by negative countertransference. In other words the professionals' own background and attitude, as a part of their culture, will affect their professional work. This reaction is particularly true in a case involving religion, and it needs careful self-examination and management.

CONFLICT BETWEEN RELIGIOUS BELIEF
AND SOCIETAL LAW

Some Examples

Examples abound of how religious beliefs, as a part of culture, may conflict with social expectations, rules, or demands, leading to legal involvement. For example, a Muslim woman refuses to remove her veil to take the photograph for her driver's license; parents, insisting on following their religious beliefs, refuse to let their child receive a blood transfusion, even when one is necessary to save the child's life; a young man uses his religious beliefs of nonviolence as an excuse to refuse to be drafted for war; despite the legal rule of monogamy, a man marries several wives, because of his religious belief in polygamy. These are all situations in which religious beliefs or rights clash with social expectations or requirements, and require legal intervention.

Possible Solutions for Such Conflict

There are no easy solutions, but, from a forensic point of view, there is a need to distinguish first whether the behavior in question occurs as a part of an individual's sincere religious beliefs and long practiced religious behavior or is simply being used as an excuse to obtain what the person wants or to avoid what he or she does not want, shirking social responsibility or duty. The professional must try to understand, with cultural empathy, from the person's perspective and not be biased and influenced by his or her own religious background.

REFERENCES

Allotey, P., & Reidpath, D. (2001). Establishing the causes of childhood mortality in Ghana: The "spirit child." *Social Science and Medicine, 52*(7), 1007–1012.

Barnes, S. Y. (1999). Theories of spouse abuse: Relevance to African Americans. *Issues in Mental Health Nursing, 20*(4), 357–371.

Bourget, D., & Bradford, J. M. W. (1990). Homicidal parents. *Canadian Journal of Psychiatry, 35*, 233–237.

Chapman, M. (1980). Infanticide and fertility among Eskimo: A computer simulation. *American Journal of Physical Anthropology, 53*, 317–327.

Coale, A. J., & Banister, J. (1994). Five decades of missing females in China. *Demography, 31*(3), 459–479.

Comprehensive Research Institute of Justice. (2002). *Hanzai hakushio* [White paper on crime]. Tokyo: Homu-shio-homu-sogo-kenkiujio [Comprehensive Research Institute of Justice, Justice Ministry].

Dietz, P. (1993, December). *Work place violence: Myths, facts, and corporate prevention.* Workplace violence prevention courses, Newport Beach, CA.

D'Orban, P. (1979). Women who kill their children. *British Journal of Psychiatry, 134*, 560–571.

Gall, S. B., & Gall, T. L. (1993). *Statistical record of Asian Americans.* Detroit, MI: Gale Research.

Gavey, N. (1991). Sexual victimization prevalence among New Zealand university students. *Journal of Consulting and Clinical Psychology, 59*, 464–466.

Ghosh, S. (1991). Discrimination all the way. *Health Millions, 17*(2), 19–23.

Guyer, C. G., II. (2000). Spouse abuse. In F. Kaslow (Ed.), *Handbook of couple and family forensics: A sourcebook for mental health and legal professionals* (pp. 206–234). New York: Wiley.

Heise, L. (1990). Crimes of gender. *Women's Health Journal, 17*, 3–11.

Hempel, A. G., Levine, R. E., Meloy, J. R., & Westermeyer, J. (2000). A cross-cultural review of sudden mass assault by a single individual in the Oriental and Occidental cultures. *Journal of Forensic Science, 45*(3), 582–588.

Hicks, M. H. R. (2003). Partner violence and major depression in women: A community study of Chinese Americans. *Journal of Nervous and Mental Disease, 191*(11), 722–729.

Hudson, S. M., & Ward, T. (1997). Rape: Psychopathology and theory. In D. R. Law & W. O'Donohue (Eds.), *Sexual deviance: Theory, assessment, and treatment* (pp. 332–355). New York: Guilford.

Hymes, R. W., Leinart, M., Rowe, S., & Rogers, W. (1993). Acquaintance rape: The effect of race of defendant and race of victim on White juror decisions. *Journal of Social Psychology, 133*(5), 627–634.

Ikeda, Y. (1987). *Jido-giakutai: Yuganda oyako-kankei* [Child abuse: Distorted parent-child relations]. Tokyo: Chuokoronsha. (In Japanese).

Kaku, K. (1975). Were girl babies sacrificed to a folk superstition in 1966 in Japan? *Annals of Human Biology, 2*(4), 391–393.

Kantor, G. K. (1997). Alcohol and spouse abuse: Ethnic differences. *Recent Development in Alcoholism, 13*, 57–79.

Kasturi, M. (2000). Female infanticide: Selections from the records of the government of the North-Western provinces, Second Series, Volume VIII, Allahabd, 1981. *Indian Journal of General Study, 7*(1), 125–133.

Keesing, R. M. (1976). *Cultural anthropology: A contemporary perspective.* New York: Holt, Rinehart & Winston.

Keppel, K. G., Pearcy, J. N., & Wagener, D. K. (January 2002). Trends in racial and ethnic-specific rates for the health status indicators: United States, 1990–98. Healthy People 2000 Statistical Notes. No. 23. pp 1–12. Department of Health and Human Services.

Kim, K. I. (1972). New religions in Korea: The sociocultural consideration. *Korean Neuropsychiatric Association, 11*(1), 31–36. (In Korean).

Koss, M. P. (1992). The underdetection of rape: Methodological choice influence incidence estimates. *Journal of Social Issues, 48*, 61–75.

Koss, M. P., Gidycz, C. A., & Wisniewski, N. (1987). The scope of rape: Incidence and prevalence of sexual aggression and victimization in a national sample of higher education students. *Journal of Consulting and Clinical Psychology, 55,* 162–170.
Landwehr, P. H., Bothwell, R. K., Jeanmard, M., Luque, L. R., Brown, R. L., III, & Breaux, M. A. (2002). Racism in rape trials. *Journal of Social Psychology, 142*(5), 667–669.
Lefley, H. P., Scott, C. S., Llabre, M., & Hicks, D. (1993). Cultural beliefs about rape and victim's response in three ethnic groups. *American Journal of Orthopsychiatry, 63*(4), 623–632.
Lester, D. (1981). A cross-cultural study of wife abuse. *Aggressive Behavior, 6,* 361–364.
Lester, D. (1991). Murdering babies: A cross-national study. *Social Psychiatry and Psychiatric Epidemiology, 26*(2), 83–85.
Levinson, D. (1988). Family violence in cross-cultural perspective. In V. B. Van Hasselt, R. L. Morrison, A. S. Bellack, & M. Hersen (Eds.), *Handbook of family violence.* New York: Plenum Press.
Lomis, M. J. (1986). Maternal filicide: A preliminary examination of culture and victim sex. *International Journal of Law and Psychiatry, 9*(4), 503–506.
Lonsway, K. A., & Fitzgerald, L. F. (1994). Rape myths: In review. *Psychology of Women Quarterly, 18,* 133–164.
McKee, G. R., & Shea, S. J. (1998). Maternal filicide: A cross-national comparison. *Journal of Clinical Psychology, 54*(5), 679–687.
Minturn, L., & Stashak, J. (1982). Infanticide as a terminal abortion procedure. *Behavior Science Research, 17*(1–2), 70–90.
Monahan, J., & Steadman, H. J. (Eds.). (1994). *Violence and mental disorder: Development in risk assessment.* Chicago: University of Chicago Press.
Muir, G., Lonsway, K. A., & Payne, D. L. (1996). Rape myth acceptance among Scottish and American students. *Journal of Social Psychology, 136*(2), 261–262.
Murphy, H. B. M. (1973). History and evolution of syndromes: The striking case of *latah* and *amok.* In M. Hammer, K. Salzinger, & S. Sutton (Eds.), *Psychopathology.* New York: Wiley.
Neville, H. A., & Pugh, A. O. (1997). General and culture-specific factors influencing African American women's reporting patterns and perceived support following sexual assault: An exploratory investigation. *Violence Against Women, 3*(4), 361–381.
Oberman, M. (2003). A brief history of infanticide and the law. In M. G. Spinelli (Ed.), *Infanticide: Psychological and legal perspectives on mothers who kill* (pp. 3–18). Washington, DC: American Psychiatric Publishing.
O'Leary, K. D., & Curley, A. D. (1986). Assertion and family violence: Correlates of spouse abuse. *Journal of Marital and Family Therapy, 12,* 281–290.
Resnick, P. J. (1969). Child murder by parents: A psychiatric review of filicide. *American Journal of Psychiatry, 126*(3), 325–334.
Rushton, J. P. (1995). Race and crime: International data for 1989–1990. *Psychological Reports, 76*(1), 307–312.
Russell, D. E. H. (1984). *Sexual exploitation: Rape, child sexual abuse, and workplace harassment.* Thousand Oaks, CA: Sage.
Sargent, C. F. (1987). Born to die: The fate of extraordinary children in Bariba culture. *Ethnology, 23,* 79–96.

Scheper-Hughes, N. (2003). Culture, scarcity, and maternal thinking. In M. G. Spinelli (Ed.), *Infanticide: Psychological and legal perspectives on mothers who kill* (pp. 119–130). Washington, DC: American Psychiatric Publishing.

Scott, C. S., Lefley, H. P., & Hicks, D. (1993). Potential risk factors for rape in three ethnic groups. *Community Mental Health Journal, 29*(2), 133–134.

Sourcebook of Criminal Justice Statistics Online. (2003). *Arrest by offense charged, age group, race, United States, 2001.* Retrieved from http://www.albany.edu/ sourcebook/1995/pdf/t410.pdf; accessed March 3, 2004.

Spinelli, M. G. (2003). *Infanticide: Psychosocial and legal perspectives on mothers who kill.* Washington, DC: American Psychiatric Publishing.

Steinmetz, S. K. (1981). Cross-cultural marital abuse. *Journal of Sociology and Social Welfare, 8,* 404–414.

Straus, M. A., Gelles, R. J., & Steinmetz, S. K. (1980). *Behind closed doors: Violence in the American family.* New York: Doubleday.

Teoh, J. I. (1972). The changing psychopathology of *amok. Psychiatry, 35,* 345–351.

Thompson, V. L. S., & West, S. D. (1992). Attitudes of African American adults toward treatment in cases of rape. *Community Mental Health Journal, 28,* 531–536.

Tseng, W. S. (2001). *Handbook of cultural psychiatry.* San Diego, CA: Academic Press.

U.S. Department of Commerce. (1997). *Statistical abstract of the United States* (117th ed.). Washington, DC: U.S. Government Printing Office.

Wallace, A. F. C. (1966). *Religion: An anthropological view.* New York: McGraw-Hill.

Westermeyer, J. (1973). On the epidemicy of *amok* violence. *Archives of General Psychiatry, 28,* 873–876.

Yoshihama, M., & Sorenson, S. B. (1994). Physical, sexual, and emotional abuse by male intimates: Experiences of women in Japan. *Violence and Victims, 9*(1), 63–77.

6

Cultural Considerations in Specific Types of Forensic Evaluation

Cultural considerations apply broadly to various aspects of forensic psychiatric work. In this chapter we focus on the practical application of cultural competencey to legal situations the forensic evaluator may face. First, we review the cultural considerations at each phase of the legal process. In the process we discuss the important cultural aspects to consider when working with various professionals in the legal system, such as the parties to a lawsuit and the attorney. Finally, we explore cultural issues that may arise when forensically evaluating criminal, civil, or family-related cases. Forensic psychiatrists and psychologists in particular may find this chapter to be of interest.

CULTURAL INPUT IN VARIOUS PHASES OF THE LEGAL PROCESS

Initial Phase

Working With Attorneys on Cultural Issues
Forensic psychiatrists will spend a good part of their working lives in contact with attorneys as well as with judges. When

working with legal professionals, psychiatrists would do well to remember that the attorney or judge differs not only in professional training but also in belonging to a different "professional culture." As we discussed previously, the legal system operates on a distinctly different professional model than the psychiatric or medical system (see the section "The Culture of the Legal System" in chapter 1). Psychiatrists and psychologists should recognize that there is great ambiguity and abstractness in matters of culture, which may contrast with the perceived needs and expectations of legal professionals. Forensic mental health professionals are well situated to assist the attorney and judge in recognizing and comprehending the cultural aspects of behavior in the case at hand.

When working with an attorney, assessing his or her knowledge of and experiences with cultural issues in general and with the particular culture(s) involved in the current case may be helpful. If the attorney is aware of pertinent cultural issues, learning the exact nature of the cultural questions(s) the attorney wants answered will be part of the process of case evaluation. After performing a culturally informed forensic evaluation, the forensic psychiatrist may then discuss with the attorney his or her own opinions regarding the cultural issues that deserve consideration, and how to bring them to the court's attention. Pitfalls to avoid include overemphasizing culture, ignoring basic clinical and forensic principles, minimizing problems related to language issues, and ignoring important demographic factors and the degree of acculturation in cases involving immigrants (Boehnlein, 2003). Finally, recognizing and addressing any ethnic or cultural countertransference or related feelings that the attorney may have toward the parties in the suit may be important.

Working with the Parties to the Suit

When a forensic psychiatrist comes into contact with a party to the lawsuit, he or she should consider the person's ethnic or cultural background, in addition to personal factors such as age, gender, educational level, or personality. Such an awareness will assist the examiner in understanding how to relate to the person in a culturally relevant way, including how to communicate and elicit the needed information. Special efforts may be required to understand and communicate with certain populations, such as if the person is a foreigner, an immigrant, a racial or ethnic minority, a child, or a woman or if the person has an oral communication disability. When there are language differences, properly selecting and training a translator becomes a key issue (see chapter 2).

When the examinee differs from the examiner ethnically, racially, or even religiously, the examiner should consider and manage, if necessary, the possible impact of such factors in establishing a professional relationship. The examiner should recognize ethnic or racial transference and countertransference that might occur between the examinee and the examiner, particularly when negative or intense.

Conducting a Psychiatric Assessment of Mental Condition

Initially, after the forensic psychiatrist has been retained in a case, he or she will begin preparations for performing the assessment, such as conducting a document review. The psychiatrist will meet with the examinee at some point in this process and perform a professional assessment of the mental status and psychological condition of the examinee. We covered previously important cultural aspects of interviewing and assessing examinees (see chapter 2).

Assessment of Competency for Legal Decision Making

The forensic psychiatrist may need to assess in the initial interview whether the examinee is mentally competent for the legal purpose at hand. Because no psychiatric diagnosis is synonymous with incompetence, the psychiatrist cannot make the determination of competence by knowing simply if the examinee is suffering from a mental disorder. Rather, the relevant issue will be if the individual has the mental capacity to deal with the particular legal functions and challenges in question. In many cases this will include the ability to communicate a choice, understand relevant information, appreciate the situation and its likely consequences, and manipulate information rationally and relevantly (Gerbasi, 2002, p. 181). Besides the level of education, intelligence, cognitive function, and social knowledge, including familiarity with the legal system, cultural influences may be important. Naturally, any recent immigrant or ethnic minority member with language problems who is unfamiliar with the local legal system may need especially careful assessment in this regard.

Weinstock, Leong, and Silva (2003) pointed out that value judgments are an inevitable part of capacity and competence determinations. Value judgments may be involved in establishing the cutoff line for competency abilities. Forensic psychiatrists must be aware of this and distinguish value judgments from scientific data, particularly in the cultural realm when data may be sparse and cultural stereotypes may dominate one's thinking.

Working with a Clinical Psychologist

Forensic psychiatrists may benefit from communicating and discussing with a psychologist whether ethnicity, culture, and language might affect the process and results of psychological testing. Suggestions may be made regarding how to minimize such cultural impact. Topics that might be relevant include how to adequately prepare and provide explanation to the examinee, how to select proper instruments for measurement, and how to interpret the data obtained in a culturally meaningful way. (For details see chapter 3 and the section "A Chinese Student Suspects His Korean Professor of Persecuting Him" in chapter 9).

Pretrial Phase

Completing the Total Assessment

Before trial, the forensic psychiatrist will have completed the evaluation of a case, including completing the formal mental examination, incorporating the results of psychological measurements, and, most important from a cultural perspective, having adequately assessed the individual's personal past history, family background, and social environment. On the basis of this comprehensively gathered information, the examiner in a criminal case may gain a more relevant understanding of the person's motive and of the nature of the wrongful behavior, particularly from a cultural perspective. The culturally competent forensic assessment may require interviews of the person's family members, friends, or even neighbors to obtain adequate third-party information.

The Cultural Formulation

Culturally competent forensic psychiatry may require cultural consideration when performing a psychiatric assessment, cultural formulation when developing an opinion from all the gathered information, and, finally, proposing cultural strategies to the attorney working for the court. After eliciting the needed cultural information, in addition to the usually considered psychiatric and forensic factors, the examiner may need to analyze, integrate, and formulate the impact of culture on the diagnosis and medicolegal issue at hand in a comprehensive way for presentation to the court and attorneys. This will mean understanding the person's lifestyle, stresses, social supports, and coping style as culturally shaped. Skill is required to integrate these results and formulate an opinion on the cultural aspects of a forensic case that is accurate, simple, reliable, and understandable.

The Culturally Relevant Forensic Report

After competing the clinical assessment and cultural formulation of the case, the forensic examiner should consider preparing a report in a culturally competent way. Several issues deserve attention when cultural issues are going to be incorporated, in addition to following the general rules and basic guidelines for preparing a forensic report.

When the clinician is writing a forensic report, the terms *race, ethnicity, minority,* and *culture* should be used properly and accurately because they have specific meanings and definitions. Using these terms interchangeably invites confusion. (We covered these terms in the section "Culture, Race, Ethnicity, and Minority" in chapter 1.)

The examiner may need to distinguish between traditional beliefs, customs, and value systems of a culture and those that are currently followed by a cultural group, as they may not be the same. For immigrants, the length of time spent in the host society and level of acculturation to it may need to be considered. The report should provide, when relevant, the sources of the cultural information relied on (the examinee, his or her family or friends, people of the same ethnic group in the community, etc.) or should refer to published articles or books that formally deal with cultural issues.

Explaining dynamically the ways culture affects the situation may be important. Even though culture is an abstract concept, its impact on human behavior can be presented in a clear manner, such as how culture may induce stress, shape coping patterns, and influence the choice of resolution. In the legal process, culture can influence the process and results of case assessment and shape the opinions formed and presented by experts. It can be dynamically and thoroughly described and explained in the forensic report, making it be more easily comprehensible by legal professionals as well as by laypersons.

Trial Phase

Preparing to Testify About Ethnic and Cultural Issues
A skillful cross-examination has the potential to change the outcome of a case. Manarin (2002) listed suggestions for mental health experts on how to deal with cross-examination in court. These general hints can be applied to the cultural dimension. For example, these hints include knowing the details of the defendant's personal history from a cultural perspective, being aware of the "examiner effect" (due to the examiner's gender, race, or other particular characteristics, such as religious background) on the process of examination, and avoiding confirmatory bias associated with tunnel vision (paying attention to cultural evidence that supports the examiner's beliefs and dismissing or misinterpreting nonsupportive data).

Because culture is an abstract issue, presenting and discussing it in a simple and understandable way is very important during testimony. A jury may have little education or training about cultural issues. Opposing counsel and the judge will also need simple, salient, and clear explanations about culture and the role it plays in understanding the case, particularly regarding motive in committing the unlawful behavior and the nature and degree of his or her understanding of its "wrongfulness" from a legal perspective.

The Ethnic and Cultural Backgrounds of Courtroom Personnel
The forensic mental health specialist may wish to consider the ethnic and cultural backgrounds of the court personnel, including the attorneys, judge, experts, and, most important the jury. The first step will be to assess as best one can the extent to which the personnel are familiar with the particular ethnic or cultural issues in the case. Next, the forensic professional will need to adequately prepare them for dealing with these issues. One must be careful to not offend any ethnicity

or cultural group when describing or making comments about an ethnicity or cultural system, particularly when others in the court share that ethnicity or culture. Ethnic or cultural neutrality should be maintained, avoiding personally subjective (and ethnic-biased) comments, particularly negative ones.

Ethnic or cultural transference means the displacement of pre-existing knowledge, attitudes, and biases toward any particular ethnic or cultural group, with or without knowing it. Anticipation of the ethnic or cultural transference that might occur may need consideration, including transference toward (and among) the parties in the suit, the attorneys (on both sides), the experts, and, most important, the jurors. This ethnic or cultural transference may occur toward any person present in the court, including the plaintiff, the victim, the defendant, the attorneys, or the experts. Ethnic or cultural transference occurs interactionally among the persons involved in a courtroom situation in different directions and will affect the legal process and outcome.

Sentencing Phase

The Impact of Ethnicity, Race, and Culture on the Legal Decision

Ethnic, racial, and cultural factors may influence the outcome of a trial and, in criminal trials, the sentence that is imposed. This may be particularly true for certain kinds of offenses, such as sexual harassment or sexual assault (see the section "Sexual Harassment," infra, and the section "Rape" in chapter 5). However, the impact of ethnic, racial, and cultural factors on the legal process and decisions deserve attention, as it is broadly observed in various kinds of criminal cases.

The effect of race on outcome in criminal trials has been studied in the United States. Using data from Supplemental Homicide Reports and Trial Judge Reports, Sorensen and Wallace (1995) examined the issue of racial disparity in Missouri's capital process from 1977 through 1991. They found that Blacks killing Whites are most likely to be convicted of capital murder overall, whereas Whites killing Blacks are least likely to result in charges or convictions.

Many simulation studies have been carried out in the past to determine possible effects of race on sentencing. Sweeney and Haney (1992) carried out a meta-analytic review of these experimental studies and revealed that racial bias did influence sentencing decisions and that Black defendants were punished significantly more harshly than their White counterparts. These findings were not occasional, and were not confined to the southern United States or to trials for the crime of rape. Also, this racism-related effect does not now appear to be a thing of the past, even though overt acts of racism may have declined recently.

Mazzella and Feingold (1994) carried out a meta-analysis of experimental research on mock juror judgments related to various factors, including physical attractiveness, race, social status, and gender of the defendants and victims. They discovered that there were no notable effects of race on the punishment for robbery, assault, or rape, but (mock) jurors recommended greater punishment for Blacks than for Whites for negligent homicide and greater punishment for Whites than for Blacks for fraud. Racial factors have different effects on sentencing, depending on the nature of the crime.

These studies examined racial factors of Caucasian Americans (Whites) and African Americans (Blacks) only, who have been historically affected by racism, but not of other racial or ethnic groups. Furthermore, they focused on concrete and identifiable ethnicity or race, without examining abstract cultural dimensions. Some people criticize that experimental studies are far from the reality that takes place in court. There is no way to deal with or actively manipulate the variables (ethnic or racial factors) in court, except through the process of jury and expert witness selection.

Pfeifer and Ogloff's (1991) experimental study found that sufficient jury instructions specifying the conditions required to find a defendant guilty may serve to dissipate the jurors' prejudices over racial factors. Forensic experts should be aware of the effects of ethnic, racial, and cultural factors on the results in court and try to minimize any bias or prejudice that originates from such factors to further fairness in legal decision making.

Culture and Mitigation in Sentencing

After a guilty verdict is rendered but before a sentence is passed there may be an opportunity for the defense attorney to raise factors that might mitigate a harsh penalty. The defending attorney can properly use the professional opinion of the forensic psychiatrist even at this final stage; indeed in many cases this would be the principle use of forensic psychiatric evidence. Based on all the gathered information, including cultural information, the forensic psychiatrist's opinion can be helpful in explaining to the court the cultural aspects of the defendant's motive and intent.

CULTURAL DEFENSE STRATEGY

Past Trends

In recent years American criminal courts have seen a rise in the use of cultural defense strategies; that is, arguing that the defendant's cultural background should excuse his or her crimes, mitigate responsibility, or reduce the penalty for criminal behavior, as we described previously (Reddy, 2002). Although courts commonly hear cultural evidence in those trials where cultural group rights are under dispute, cultural defense cases are unique in their focus on the cultural identity of the defendant and on diminishing individual responsibility for the criminal act (Torry, 1999). Courts have permitted the incorporation of cultural factors into existing, legally recognized defenses, especially the category of defense known as "excuse," which regards the act itself as wrongful but forgives the actor, or defendant, because he or she lacks the requisite culpability (Winkelman, 1996). Magnarella (1991) indicated that in the past courts in the United States have repeatedly rejected cultural background as a defense for native-born minorities but have been far more tolerant of the cultural defense for foreign-born aliens with markedly different cultural practices from those in the United States.

According to Reddy (2002), over the past one or two decades, American criminal courts have heard a string of diverse cases that have relied on the cultural defense strategy. Examples of this include Laotians charged with rape (*People v. Kong Moua*, 1985) who claim they were engaged in traditional bridal capture (*zij po niam*); a Japanese woman charged with murder (*People v. Kimura*, 1985) for her practice of parent-child suicide (*oyako-shinju*); and Chinese and Hmong men whose murder of their adulterous wives was excused as a culturally legitimate response (*People v. Chen*, 1989; *People v. Moua*, 1985). Reddy, however, argued that in many cases cultural differences are increasingly "problematized" or "medicalized." so that they slide more easily into the realm of a psychological disorder. For instance, in a murder trial of an Iranian Jew, who killed his wife after years of psychological abuse, the defense attorney went so far as to argue, "It was being a Persian Jew that determined his personality. Culture is what he was suffering from. It was almost like an illness" (*People v. Hanoukai*, 1994). Culture moved from being the cause to clearly becoming the problem, pathologizing cultural differences.

Comments: The Need for Adequate Cultural Knowledge and Insight

The courts may be commended for recognizing the importance of cultural factors in the legal process. However, because of the possibility of misuse or abuse, the application of a cultural defense strategy deserves careful consideration (Coleman, 1996; Torry, 2000; Woo, 1989). First, the forensic expert may need to clarify to what extent the culture concerned (as a set of beliefs, attitudes, and value systems, manifested as custom, etiquette, ritual, or other cultural behaviors) still exists and is faithfully practiced by the people of that culture and particularly by the person concerned. That is, the expert must inquire into whether the culture represents merely a traditional or ideal culture that existed in the past or if it is still actively practiced by most of the people of that cultural group. Misidentification of culture should be avoided (Volpp, 1994). The next question is to what extent cultural factors relate to the unlawful behavior undertaken.

The actual and original nature of the custom or ritual performed in the traditional culture also needs to be known. For example, the "bride capture" practiced by some ethnic groups in South Asia is a "game" played culturally so that a man, accompanied and assisted by his fellow men, tries to capture (or kidnap) a woman from her home to his home to become his wife. The woman usually has already consented to marry him. The game is played with joy and excitement, and no one complains (or brings criminal charges) that the woman has been kidnapped. This behavior differs from the actual kidnap or forced rape of a woman unknown to the assailant. To differentiate between these two, and minimize the use of cultural custom to justify criminal conduct, the evaluator must raise a number of questions. The evaluator should ask who is the woman in the case (does she know about the game of bride capture), did she consent (either directly or indirectly) to marry the man, and why does she allege that she was raped.

Collateral information may be valuable in sorting out whether the people of the same ethnic or cultural group share the same view. Checking with Laotians who currently live in the United States (where the alleged crime occurred) about how they would interpret facts in the case may be helpful. One might further ask to what extent this alleged traditional custom of bride capture is still practiced in the United States by other Laotians.

Finally, inquiring about the legal attitude toward culture-rooted behaviors or customs in the home country may be useful. For example, parent suicide coupled with child homicide may still occur in contemporary Japan when parents are in extreme distress, and such an event usually receives a sympathetic reaction from people in general. However, such behavior was officially criminalized in Japan more than a century ago. Courts in Japan do not allow this culture defense for child homicide. (For further discussion, see the section "Japanese American Mother Drowns Her Two Children" in chapter 9.)

Suggestions: Suitable and Appropriate Cultural Considerations

Criminal responsibility requires the presence of a wrongful act (*actus reus*), a criminal intent (*mens rea*), concurrence between these two, and the causation of some harm (Slovenko, 2002, p. 211). A court will be concerned with whether the unlawful action was undertaken voluntarily and what the defendant's state of mind was in carrying out the criminal action. These factors will influence the outcome of a case, as well as any resulting punishment. For example, in situations where there is much judicial discretion in sentencing, a lawyer who commits a crime may receive a more severe punishment than others, in part based on the theory that the lawyer would have a more probing understanding of the wrongdoing involved.

Cultural considerations of how a person comprehends and interprets his or her behavior from his or her own cultural perspective also should be incorporated. The forensic expert should be aware that the unlawful act as defined legally by the society may be different from the wrongful act as perceived culturally by the person concerned. In other words culture may affect the criminal intent for the crime. Individual and cultural considerations apply to all persons, regardless of ethnic or cultural background. Every person is shaped by cultural views, beliefs, and values, whether belonging to a minority ethnic group or not, whether immigrant or original resident. To state it simply, everyone deserves cultural consideration but no one should be entitled to claim a cultural defense unless there is a strong connection between the claimed culture and the legally defined wrongful behavior. Even persons from an ethnic majority should be allowed to use a cultural defense in these circumstances. In any ethnic or racial group, there exist subethnic or subcultural differences that warrant attention. When the cultural system of such a group is vastly different from that of mainstream society it may deserve extra consideration. At all times caution may be needed to avoid overplaying or distorting the use of culture as an excuse.

CRIMINAL CASES

Assessment of Competency to Stand Trial

Forensic psychiatrists and psychologists often are asked to assess mental competence for persons involved in criminal or civil cases. Of these cases, the assessment of competency for criminal trials is the most frequently adjudicated issue, and we elaborate on that next.

Basic Considerations

Competence to stand trial, according to Miller (2003, p. 187), historically finds roots in the English common law requirement that a criminal cannot be tried in absentia. Originally interpreted to mean that defendants must be permitted to be physically present at their trials, the concept was ultimately extended to include mental presence as well as physical. This means that the defendant who is present in court should be in a mental condition sound enough to appreciate how he or she is to be judged and to participate in defending himself or herself.

The U.S. Supreme Court's definition of competence to stand trial (provided in *Dusky v. United States*, 1960) has been pervasive and enduring (Grisso, 1996). The Court established the standard as to whether the defendant "has sufficient present ability to consult with his attorney with a reasonable degree of rational understanding and a rational as well as factual understanding of the proceedings against him." There are two main components of competence to stand trial (Miller, 2003, p. 187): (a) cognitive—the capacity to comprehend relevant legal concepts and procedures, and (b) volitional—the capacity to use information appropriately in one's own defense and to function effectively in the legal environment.

Cultural Attention

To assess competency the evaluator will need to assess the defendant's responses to probing questions. Whatever questions one asks, care must be exercised to select questions that adequately assess cultural factors that may be involved. For example, the Group for the Advancement of Psychiatry devised a list of questions to be used in assessing trial competency. Of the 21 items listed (Melton, Petrila, Poythress, & Slobogin, 1997, p. 124), several deserve discussion from a cultural perspective: item 1, Understanding his current legal situation; item 4, Understanding the legal issues and procedures in his case; and item 8, Appraising the roles of the defense counsel, the prosecuting attorney, the judge, the jury, the witnesses, and the defendant. These items inquire about capacity to comprehend relevant legal concepts and procedures, which are cognitive aspects of competency. They will be subject to the defendant's level of intelligence, mental capacity, and familiarity with the legal system experienced in the past through social learning. From a cultural point of view, the latter may be limited if the person concerned does not speak the language of the mainstream and does not have the proper means to learn socially about the legal system that operates in the society. If the person is an immigrant from another society with a different legal system, the person may have difficulty comprehending the legal system operating in the host society. To what extent such individuals can learn about and comprehend the legal situation needs careful evaluation.

The examiner clearly should not carry out the assessment by asking only simple questions requiring yes or no answers. People from certain cultures may give a "yes" answer that simply acknowledges they are listening to the question and not that they understand what is being asked. In other words, they are merely complying with the questions out of concern for not offending the questioner (an authority figure), even though they may not understand what is being asked. These are culturally shaped behaviors that manifest through communication patterns. The skillful examiner should determine to what extent the person actually comprehends and is not simply answering yes or no for cultural reasons.

Two items—item 11, Trusting and communicating relevantly with his counsel, and item 14, Maintain a collaborative relationship with his attorney and helping to plan a legal strategy—also will be heavily subject to social and cultural influences. If a person originally comes from a society where past experience with the law has taught him or her to be wary of trusting anyone, particularly someone involved in the legal system, trust and the ability to communicate relevantly and collaborate with counsel may be limited. Whether this is a question of mental capacity or cultural impact, it needs careful consideration.

Finally, three items—item 15, Following testimony for contradictions or errors; item 16, Testifying relevantly and being cross-examined if necessary; and item 17, Challenging prosecution witnesses—are volitional aspects of competence that will be subject to the person's personality and social experience in interactions with others, including authority figures. These items also will be influenced by culturally rooted behavior patterns. Persons coming originally from an (autocratic) society that discourages them from voicing their opinions in public, who are not used to challenging their opponents (as is encouraged in a democratic society), and who have not learned to debate with others verbally may be less competent in these areas, which are crucial in court.

In summary, many questions an examiner asks to assess competency may be influenced by cultural factors, placing the culturally naive defendant at a disadvantage. This disadvantage cannot be remedied by defense counsel or a competency restoration program unless it is recognized.

Instruments Commonly Used

To perform a comprehensive assessment of competence to stand trial, several instruments have been developed, such as the MacArthur Competency Assessment Tool–Criminal Adjudication and the Competency to Stand Trial Assessment Instrument. We previously addressed the use of psychological instruments to assess competency (see the section "Competence to Stand Trial" in chapter 3).

Assessment of Mental Condition at the Time of the Offense

Assessing mental state at the time of the offense is one of the more challenging tasks in forensic psychiatry. The evaluation must be done retrospectively and the evaluator may be without direct information to use as the basis for making a conclusion. Furthermore, the evaluations require the application of a complex legal framework (Foote, 2000). Therefore, the assessment of criminal responsibility must be thorough and thoughtful, incorporating all relevant background information available. This includes the personal history, psychiatric history, and social and cultural history of the defendant.

The assessment of mental state will typically include assigning a psychiatric diagnosis to the examinee's condition. In making a psychiatric diagnosis, the forensic examiner will rely on an official classification system and its associated criteria. In the United States the *Diagnostic and Statistical Manual of Mental Disorders–Fourth Edition–Text Revision (DSM-IV-TR)*, published by the American Psychiatric Association (2000), is the currently used classification system. This classification system, however, is based primarily on clinical information obtained from European Americans who form the majority ethnic group. The *DSM-IV-TR* resembles the *International Statistical Classification of Diseases and Related Health Problems–Tenth Revision* published by the World Health Organization (1992), but it is not entirely similar to other psychiatric classification systems used by many other countries around the world. For example, acute paranoid disorder is recognized in the Chinese classification system, but not in the *DSM-IV-TR*. Sensitive paranoia is included in the German classification system, but not in the American one. Although this latest version of the *DSM-IV-TR* has made considerable effort to attend to cross-ethnic and cultural considerations necessary in making diagnoses, some limitations remain in making assessments and diagnoses of culturally diverse populations, even in our own society, not to mention among immigrants.

If a psychiatrist, even one who is clinically competent in general, is not familiar with certain mental disorders that tend to be observed in the relevant cultural group, he or she may miss the correct diagnosis (Tseng, 2001, pp. 435–461). For instance, in a cross-cultural context, the clinician may not make the distinction between a mild form of dissociative disorder and a severe form of possession psychosis if he or she has no experience with mental disorders characterized by alternate states of consciousness. Such disorders are not usually observed in the United States, but are still prevalent in other societies.

Cultural psychiatrists know that some people in non-Western societies tend to suffer from acute psychotic episodes and to recover within a short period of time. The diagnosis of a psychotic condition at the time of an offense may be missed, because a psychiatrist does not usually examine a defendant immediately after the unlawful behavior occurs and a defendant suffering from an acute psychotic episode might have recovered without a noticeable trace of it by the time of the examination. Most psychiatrists used to working in Western societies tend to deal with psychotic patients whose psychoses often run relatively long or chronic clinical courses. Therefore, even clinically competent American psychiatrists may not be familiar with acute psychotic cases involving rather brief episodes. Understanding and recognizing this clinical condition will certainly present a challenge for forensic psychiatrists. If undetected or ignored, the opportunity to pursue an insanity defense may be missed.

In a parallel manner, the forensic examiner must carefully evaluate the purported presence of such a psychosis to determine that it actually occurred, because in such an instance the forensic examiner must place considerable reliance on collateral source information because of the present absence of signs and symptoms of present illness.

Cultural Perspectives on the Defenses of Insanity and Diminished Capacity

For a defendant to be found responsible for a crime, the state must prove, beyond a reasonable doubt, that he or she committed a wrongful act and possessed the necessary intent to commit the crime. If both cannot be established beyond a reasonable doubt, then the verdict must be not guilty, and the defendant must be released (Miller, 2003, p. 213). If the court finds that the defendant was suffering from a severe mental disorder at the time of the crime and lacked the mental ability to know whether his or her behavior was wrong or right, the effects of the mental disorder will justify the conclusion that a criminal intent was not present. This is called an insanity defense, which seeks a decision of "not guilty by reason of insanity" (or a related term). The insanity defense results in complete exculpation on the criminal charge, but the defendant typically faces subsequent commitment to a mental health facility for treatment.

Even if a wrongful act and a criminal intent can be proved, resulting in a criminal conviction, a mentally disordered defendant may have his or her degree of criminal responsibility reduced and the sentence mitigated because of the disorder. This occurrence is called diminished capacity, which is another approach to protect mentally disordered defendants that is used in some jurisdictions in the United States (Miller, 2003, p. 221).

Insanity defense. To examine patterns of utilization of this defense in our society, Blau and McGinley (1995) surveyed attorneys in the state of Wyoming about their use of the insanity defense during the preceding 5 years. The attorneys reported using the insanity defense throughout the various stages preceding trial, with more use and benefit to the defendant being reported than previously suggested. This was particularly true in the earlier stages in the criminal justice process. Regarding their views and attitudes toward the insanity defense, defense lawyers were more in favor of it, whereas prosecuting attorneys were relatively more opposed. Janofsky, Dunn, Roskes, Briskin, and Rudolph (1996) studied all defendants in Baltimore City's circuit and district court who pleaded not guilty by reason of insanity in the year 1991. Of 60,432 indictments filed, 190 defendants (0.31%) entered a plea of not criminally responsible by reason of insanity. They pointed out that the data does not bear out popular perceptions of the insanity defense being overused and misused.

Katoh (1994) reported that in Japan in 1991, among the total penal code offenders, 0.6% was found to be suffering from certain mental disorders. For the period 1987 to 1991, the percentage of defendants suffering from mental disorders varied among different offenses committed. Homicide was remarkably high (19.8%), as was arson (17.9%), but percentages were much less for robbery (3.4%) and rape (2.1%). Among the mental disorders, schizophrenia was one of the most frequent (61.1%), alcoholism was next (9.9%), followed by manic-depressive psychoses (bipolar disorder in current *DSM-IV* nosology) (7.1%), and stimulant-induced psychosis (3.5%). These findings are noticeably different from our society, where mental disorders associated with abuse of substances other than alcohol are relatively low, but alcohol-induced mental disturbances are rather high.

The assessment of mental condition at the time of a crime, as we have discussed, can be quite a challenge from a cross-cultural perspective. One reason is that when the offender is suffering from a culturally unique mental disorder or an acute brief psychotic condition, clinical misdiagnosis may occur. Furthermore, the jurors, as laypersons, may or may not accept the mental health expert's diagnosis, depending on how they perceive the disorder. Their attitudes will be influenced by personal knowledge, experiences, and psychiatric knowledge, as well as their (cultural) attitudes toward the disorder. For example, jurors may not understand the severity of the mental impact and disturbance of a delusional disorder and that a delusion can grossly distort a person's cognitive judgment of reality and severely affect criminal intent. Jurors may not be sympathetic toward a defendant who suffers from a substance-induced mental disorder, believing that it was his or her own choice and, therefore, fault for indulging in the substance. In other words it is not merely the professional opinion of the mental health expert but also the perception and attitude of the jurors toward the opinion that may be subject to cultural influences.

Although many defendants may be willing to be considered "insane," if the label will relieve legal responsibility or result in reduced punishment, some offenders may not welcome this approach. Defendants lacking insight (self-awareness of suffering from a mental illness) may refuse to admit that they were under the influence of a mental disorder at the time of the crime. Culturally, some defendants may have strong negative views about mental illness. Consequently, they may not want to be regarded as crazy but prefer to face criminal charges. This raises the question of whether a defense attorney should have the ability to plead insanity even without the defendant's consent.

Diminished capacity defense. The diminished capacity approach focuses on the difference between general and specific intent crimes (Miller, 2003). All crimes, except strict liability offenses, require that the defendant have the general intent to commit a crime. Some crimes require an additional specific intent beyond that identified with the physical act connected with the offense (e.g., premeditated murder, aggravated assault, and assault with intent to rape). A successful diminished capacity defense can reduce a specific intent crime to a general intent crime.

In 1971 Judge David Bazelon stated, "Under *McDonald v. United States*, any abnormal condition that impairs mental or emotional processes and behavior controls may deprive an individual of the freedom of choice that we regarded as a prerequisite to imposing criminal responsibility. The source of that impairment may be physiological, emotional, social or cultural" (Diamond, 1978, p. 196). Diamond pointed out that the law could be "demedicalized" by extending legal exculpation to all those persons who for any reason lack the ability to make a free, rational, responsible decision when faced with the temptation or impulse to commit a crime. Such exculpatory reasons might include poverty, continued unemployment, or chaotic living conditions. Accordingly, Diamond (1978, p. 198) argued that the insanity defense was not a very useful or practical way for the law to cope with the problem of responsibility of the mentally ill offender. He believed that the use of the diminished capacity defense was the most logical and pragmatically useful way of relating the criminal law to the mentally ill offender.

Historically, courts in 31 states have accepted diminished capacity. However, in the early 1980s opposition to the concept of diminished capacity increased, because of a shift in social policy emphasis away from individual rights and toward law and order. For example, in California the legislature repealed diminished capacity in 1982, holding, "As matter of public policy, there shall be no defense of diminished capacity, diminished responsibility, or irresistible impulse in a criminal action" (Miller, 2003, p. 223). Thus, this approach is greatly subject to social policy and the cultural atmosphere.

Finkel and Slobogin (1995) pointed out that traditional insanity tests ask for an all-or-nothing, nonculpability decision and the jury must find the defendant either guilty or not guilty by reason of insanity, which is often a difficult decision to make. Finkel and Slobogin argued that this all-or-nothing approach fails to reflect the complex culpability judgments that jurors often make in insanity cases. They proposed, instead, a relative culpability schema for insanity. This approach, allowing a relative grading of insanity and its corresponding culpability, is well suited to consideration of cultural factors, because, from a cultural perspective, the human mind and behavior, including psychopathology, exist in a broad spectrum, with variations, and are difficult to split into an all-or-nothing, dichotomized judgment.

Anglo-American common law has for centuries recognized that persons under significant psychological stress (as distinguished from mental disease) might bear decreased responsibility for their criminal behavior and receive reduced sentences or even be found not guilty (Miller, 2003, p. 225). Because psychological stress is relative and depends on a variety of individual factors and external influences, there is room for consideration of cultural aspects. In some Asian societies, such as China or Japan, the legal system does not recognize psychological stress at the time of a crime but may recognize diagnosable mental disorders. So long as there is proof that the defendant suffered from a mental disorder, clarification of his or her state of mind during the criminal action may not be required. The judge will take the defendant's diagnosed psychiatric disorder into account when making his or her decision and when sentencing, according to the nature of the mental disorder. The law in these two societies recognizes two levels of mental disturbance: "mental forfeiture" and "mental weakness" (Fukushima, 1985; Li, 2000). The former level refers to severe mental disorders, such as schizophrenia, in which the person loses the mental ability to make proper judgments about reality; the latter level refers to minor mental disorders, such as obsessive-compulsive disorders, which result in a vulnerable mental capacity but not a total loss of mental functioning.

Forensic psychiatrists in China and Japan must make great efforts to reach the correct diagnosis, as the result will affect the categorization of the defendant's level of mental disturbance. If it is mental forfeiture, the defendant's legal responsibility will be completely eliminated; if it is mental weakness, a partial reduction of responsibility is possible. In effect, these countries allow a diminished capacity defense according to the categorization of the mental disorder diagnosed by the psychiatrist. The same goal being pursued in our society is approached with a slightly different legal methodology, because of differences in the legal system and concepts about and attitudes toward mental disorders held by legal and medical professionals.

Punitiveness, Including the Death Penalty

As we elaborated previously (in chapter 1), there are significant differences in the practice of punishment in various cultures around the world, and even within the United States. Researchers have observed that the southern subculture in the United States tends toward assigning severe legal punishments. Borg (1997) analyzed the 1990 General Social Survey and found little overall variation in levels of support for the death penalty between southerners and nonsoutherners. However, he did find regional variations in the effects of racial prejudice, religious fundamentalism, and political conservatism in support of capital punishment. Barnett (1985) proposed a classification system for differentiating homicides in terms of their levels of seriousness, considering three elements: the certainty that the defendant is a deliberate killer, the status of the victim, and the heinousness of the killing. By applying Barnett's scale to the severity of the crime, Keil and Vito (1989) reviewed and analyzed the legal data from the southern state of Kentucky and found that prosecutors were more likely to seek the death penalty in cases in which Blacks killed Whites and that juries were more likely to apply the death sentence to Blacks who killed Whites. This trend supports the notion that legal punishment is affected by race. Using a factorial design approach, Applegate, Wright, Dunaway, Cullen, and Wooldredge (1993) examined college students, asking them to rate a vignette describing a murder involving a White victim and a Black offender, as opposed to other victim-offender racial combinations. Their analysis suggested that the race of the offender, but not that of the victim, has a significant influence on support for capital punishment. Lynch and Haney (2000) examined the jury-eligible participants by randomly assigning one of four versions of a stimulated capital penalty trial in which the race of the defendants and the victims were varied among White or Black. The results revealed that although Black defendants were treated only slightly more punitively than White defendants in general, discriminatory effects were concentrated among participants whose comprehension was poorest, which suggests that providing adequate instruction to the jury is very important in minimizing any possible bias and discriminatory effects, including race-related ones.

When the prosecution seeks the death penalty, they usually make an extra effort to prove that the defendant is guilty, whereas the defense will attempt various mental health approaches, including claiming incompetence to stand trial or to have waived Miranda rights, raising an insanity defense, or using mental health evidence for mitigation of sentencing. Forensic psychiatrists involved in such cases must exercise special care and effort, which will typically include an especially thorough evaluation and the development of a carefully reasoned opinion on the issues in question. Needless to say, all resources should be used, including social and cultural information available about the defendant.

CASE 1: MOTHER WITH POSTPARTUM DEPRESSION KILLS HER FIVE CHILDREN (THE CASE OF ANDREA YATES, ABSTRACTED AND REVISED FROM REGAN & ALDERSON, 2002)

Andrea Yates and her husband, Russell, followed very conservative Christian beliefs. The husband was seen as the head of the household and the wife was to submit herself to her husband and adhere to his decisions. They believed that contraception was wrong and they would "accept as many children as God sends." During the marriage the wife gave birth to five children. The husband strictly followed his religious beliefs and called on his wife to fulfill a number of responsibilities. He required her to home school the children, although he was minimally involved in their day-to-day care.

The wife had a family history of mental illness. Her brothers and sister were treated for depression, and her mother had taken antidepressant medication in the past. The wife suffered from postpartum depression and, after the birth of her third child, received treatment. After giving birth to her fourth child, she became depressed again and attempted suicide, but quickly improved after treatment. When the couple decided to conceive a fifth child, doctors warned them that her illness could return but reassured them that the same medication would likely help her.

During the pregnancy family members and friends of the wife thought the husband had been inattentive to her needs and requested he lighten her workload. He reportedly could not understand why his wife could not keep up with taking care of the children and home schooling them. A friend of the wife noticed that the husband admired other women in the neighborhood who had many children. He was heard saying, "She's got nine kids, teaches her kids tee ball, and does just fine. I don't know why she [Andrea] is having so much trouble." The husband may not have had a good understanding of his wife's illness.

After the birth of their fifth child, the wife's symptoms of depression recurred and she again attempted suicide. The husband took her to a different doctor, who did not agree to hospitalize her. She had stopped taking her medication. Two days later, she murdered all five of her children by drowning them in the bathtub. In court the jury found her guilty of murder because she knew that it was wrong to kill the children. The jury rejected the insanity defense.

The couple's religious beliefs, customs, and attitudes—their religious culture—clearly played a prominent role in their lives, including contributing to the stress the wife experienced and the tragic events that occurred. Her mental condition made her unable to deal with the distress she faced in life. Some have suggested, however, that her husband deserves some blame for the occurrence of the tragedy as well. He knew of his wife's mental problems after the birth of previous children. Had the couple used birth control measures, the repeated occurrence of postpartum depression might have been avoided. Had her spouse assisted more with taking medication and regularly following up with her doctor, the postpartum depression likely could have been treated. The husband's own personality and the couple's religious culture, which determined their views on childbearing and the role the husband should play in the family, all indirectly contributed to the tragedy. Regan and Alderson (2002) pointed out that in the court there was a "lack of (such) cultural awareness," which resulted in blaming only the mentally disordered wife, who actually undertook the action of filicide. This case challenges us to be aware that criminal behavior might best be comprehended with cultural (or subcultural) awareness (even for members of the majority ethnic group).

CASE 2: LET THE SELLER BEWARE (MATTHEWS & TSENG, 2004)

A 24-year-old Pacific Island male, Mr. Lautusi, was stopped by the police and charged with driving without a state auto safety inspection sticker. Upon questioning by the judge, Mr. Lautusi revealed that he had very recently purchased the car from a man who had lied to him about its condition. The seller had represented that the car was able to pass the safety inspection as is, but this was not so. Mr. Lautusi believed this to be a reasonable defense to the charge; his assertion was that the seller was responsible for the car's not passing inspection. The female judge spent some time explaining to Mr. Lautusi the Western concept of *caveat emptor* ("let the buyer beware"). Also, the judge stated that she was showing leniency toward the defendant based on his cultural perspective, and she significantly reduced the fine levied for the offense. Mr. Lautusi, however, remained firm in his assertion that the court was treating him unjustly. The defendant, following the definition from his own (home) culture as to who would be responsible for such a problem, refused to understand and accept the American legal conceptualization. In addition, on a personal level, he had difficulty in accepting a female judge passing judgment on his behavior.

Assessment for Risk of Violence

Mental health professionals are increasingly asked to assess the risk of future violent behavior in a variety of clinical-legal situations. In addition to sentencing defendants, these situations may include civil commitment, bail determination, release decisions from hospitals and prison, and treatment planning for high-risk populations (Heilbrun, Ogloff, & Picarello, 1999). Beyond this, there is increasing demand from private industry for fitness-for-duty evaluations of employees who are thought to be disturbed.

On the basis of past research, researchers have suggested certain components in assessing for dangerousness: risk factors (the variables used to predict aggression), harm (the amount and type of aggression being predicted), and risk level (the probability that harm will occur) (National Research Council, 1989). In contemporary U.S. society, where drugs and firearms may be readily available, the abuse of some substances is a risk factor that increases aggressive and violent behavior and the use of firearms increases the harmfulness of aggressive behavior. In contrast, in a society where substance abuse is rare and firearms are not available for ordinary people, risk factors for aggressive behavior will include mental disorders or personality disorders, and the lethality of method will be relatively less, often involving the use of a knife to kill others. Thus, social environment shapes the nature of risk assessment. Cultural attitudes toward violent behavior will influence the occurrence of aggressive behavior as well.

From clinical experience, confirmed by research studies, psychiatrists realize that predicting violence is quite difficult. Many variables are involved, and we do not have enough knowledge of their differential impact to make highly accurate predictions. Psychologists advocate using structured assessments. Various instruments have been developed for this purpose, which we discussed in chapter 3.

Readiness for Conditional Release

Forensic psychiatrics may be asked to evaluate patients committed to psychiatric hospitals, particularly forensic hospitals, to determine whether and under what conditions they should be released. Major concerns are whether the mental disorder has improved sufficiently for the offender to be returned to the community, what the risk is of dangerous behavior toward self and others, and how the patient will adjust socially and occupationally to the community. Besides focusing on the patient, a thorough assessment may involve the family or friends as supporting resources, and the community to which the person is going to be released. When discharge from the hospital is contemplated, the following basic questions should be answered (Dvoskin & Heilbrun, 2001): Has the mental health system done everything it reasonably can to reduce the subsequent violence risk in the community? Has a plan been developed for living in the community that incorporates future follow-up and crisis intervention? Are there mechanisms for the early detection and prevention of psychiatric, social, and legal problems?

In addition to assessing the patient's mental status, prognosis, degree of likely compliance to follow-up care, and the risk of danger to self and others, one may need to evaluate the attitudes of family, friends, and people in the community toward this mentally ill person who has behaved unlawfully. Certainly these issues will be subject to social and cultural factors and will affect the outcome of adjustment. For example, mental health workers know that when the family and community hold negative attitudes toward a mentally ill person, the outcome for the patient returning to the community is relatively poor. If there is a welcoming attitude toward the patient, tolerance for any residual symptoms, and an ease in accommodating him or her into community life, the prognosis will be much better. Clearly, cultural attitudes toward psychiatric patients should be included in decision making about releasing patients into the community.

CIVIL CASES

Forensic psychiatrists may be called on to perform evaluations in a variety of settings outside of the criminal courts. These evaluations might include, for example, the assessment of competency to execute tasks such as making a will (testamentary capacity) or enter into a contract, disability evaluations, and personal injury actions or other claims of tort liability. Many cases occur in the workplace setting, where differences in culture, race, or ethnicity may give rise to or affect conflicts between individuals.

General Considerations

Civil cases involve disputes between private parties, in contrast with criminal cases where the state is a party to the action. One party (the plaintiff) asserts a complaint against another party (the defendant), usually seeking financial compensation for harm suffered but sometimes seeking "equitable relief," such as an injunction, or declaratory relief. Settlement out of court is common in civil cases, but when agreement cannot be reached, voir dire (literally, "to speak the truth") of the jury venire is conducted and the trial begins (Melton et al., 1997, pp. 36–37). The degree of certainty required for a decision in civil cases is much lower than it is in criminal cases. In most cases the plaintiff must prove the case by a "preponderance of the evidence," showing the plaintiff's version of the facts to be more likely than the defendant's, rather than meet the "beyond a reasonable doubt" standard of proof.

The expert in a civil case will typically be retained by one side or another, rather than being court appointed. In performing evaluations the expert should, just as in criminal cases, consider the relevant cultural dimensions to the case. Because there are numerous kinds of civil cases, we have selected only some representative cases that reveal important ethnic or cultural issues for discussion and illustration of how cultural knowledge and consideration will be useful.

CASE 3: MENTAL ILLNESS OR ANGER?

A 40-year-old Japanese American man in Hawaii, Mr. Tanaka, was fired by his new boss, Ms. Anderson. Ms. Anderson was a Caucasian American woman who had transferred 3 months before from the U.S. mainland to take over the Hawaii office of the company. This was her first experience working in such a culturally diverse environment, encountering staff of many different ethnic backgrounds. Partly because of her own anxiety, and partly to assert her authority, she treated her staff with stiff rules and high demands. She tended to talk down to her staff, including Mr. Tanaka, her assistant chief, which was quite different from the local custom in Hawaii, where people usually try to relate to each other with a warm aloha spirit.

Mr. Tanaka had been working on his job for nearly two decades without any previous problems. He had several supervisors in the past, all of whom were male. He related well with them most of the time, without difficulty. He was praised often by his former bosses as a responsible staff member and was promoted to assistant to the chief.

Mr. Tanaka had great difficulty in getting along with his new female boss. He could not stand to be frequently ordered around and criticized by a woman, particularly because Ms. Anderson was rude in her attitude and the way she talked to him. He felt she looked down on people of minority ethnic groups. He tried to control his resentment, until one day, when she jokingly criticized him as a "dumb Japanese," he could no longer hold back his anger. He pounded the table with his fist and shouted back at Ms. Anderson. Very much astonished by this sudden outburst of wild temper, Ms. Anderson interpreted it to mean that Mr. Tanaka was suffering from a mental illness. She fired Mr. Tanaka immediately, with the explanation that he was "crazy."

Mr. Tanaka was surprised at being fired. He complained to the union and decided to handle the matter through an attorney. His attorney requested a psychiatric examination. The psychiatrist, who was familiar with Asian cultures, interviewed Mr. Tanaka's family, as well as his colleagues in the office. All collateral information gathered indicated that Mr. Tanaka was a quiet, sincere man who had never displayed his temper in public. He did not have any past history of psychiatric disorders. An interview with Mr. Tanaka revealed that he had lost his temper simply because he felt he was being insulted by his female boss because of his ethnicity. He felt proud to be Japanese American and could not tolerate being criticized as a "dumb Japanese." The psychiatric report concluded Mr. Tanaka was fit for duty and was not mentally ill. Ms. Anderson's supervisor transferred Ms. Anderson back to the mainland, and Mr. Tanaka was allowed to resume his job.

CASE 4: SHAME (MATTHEWS & TSENG, 2004)

A 38-year-old Filipino woman employed as a hospital housekeeper was questioned by her supervisor about the disappearance of some items from a patient's room. The supervisor also asked to search her purse, just as she had done with all of the other housekeepers who were on duty at the time of the incident. Although everyone reported that the investigation was cordial and good-natured, the woman subsequently developed a severe depression, multiple somatic symptoms, and spells of moaning and wailing. She filed a workers' compensation claim, and an independent medical examination was conducted. The examiner's initial impression was one of malingering. However, consultation with a Filipino psychiatrist revealed that in this woman's culture the supervisor's suspicion was something that brought great shame and disgrace to the woman. The examiner was able to revise his opinions to reflect these cultural issues.

This case demonstrates that when the examiner is unfamiliar with the culture and behavior of the examinee, he or she should consider seeking cultural consultation. By doing so, proper cultural information can be obtained and cultural empathy for the meaning of shame (in this case) can be fully appreciated and integrated into a culturally appropriate final opinion.

Determination of Psychiatric Disability

Not only forensic psychiatrists or psychologists but also general psychiatrists and clinical psychologists will be involved in the determination of mental disability in employment situations. The examiner's job may be to assess whether the claimant is disabled, whether the disability is related to work, and what is the severity of the disability, including the prognosis. The assessment will be used in making decisions as to whether the plaintiff is entitled to compensation and the amount of compensation that should be awarded. The mental health experts may be retained by either side, such as for an insurance company or a government agency, or for the attorney hired by the plaintiff. In formulating judgments of the nature and severity of the mental disability, examiners should consider social and cultural factors.

Cultural Expectation of Social Support and Compensation

Beyond individual personality characteristics and family beliefs, cultural attitudes toward the social welfare system will significantly influence the use of the public support system and the seeking of compensation. People from some groups have cultural beliefs and attitudes that tend to prize self-reliance for dealing with problems and, unless absolutely necessary, they avoid depending on others or on the public. In contrast, people from other cultural groups may feel that they are entitled to receive help from the public and depend on society at large.

This wide gap in attitudes toward the social system of support is well illustrated in the multiethnic society of Hawaii, where many ethnic groups live together in the same social system. Japanese Americans, for example, are somewhat reluctant to request assistance and depend on the resources of the public welfare system. They are known for taking pride in self-support, working hard, living diligently, and avoiding being dependent on others' resources as much as possible. In contrast, native Hawaiian people may hold a different attitude. Some may feel that the society owes them (because, historically, they lost control over their islands when members of the majority group took over by force). Being taken care of by the society at large may also reflect indigenous cultural attitudes due to the nature of traditional Hawaiian society. These attitudes are coupled with contemporary social factors such as cultural destruction, economic and educational deprivation, and difficulty securing employment. As a result, the proportion of Hawaiian people receiving social welfare is remarkably high. A disproportionately high number of Filipino American people tend to apply for workman's compensation. This is not only because many of them are working in labor-related jobs, but also because of their cultural tendency to seek work-related compensation.

Any person who is injured during work will not hesitate to apply for this beneficial compensation. Therefore, it is important to know that, besides individual factors, cultural factors will significantly affect the pattern of seeking and relying on social welfare and insurance compensation.

Cultural Patterns of Complaining About Problems

The pattern of presenting complaints to the evaluator is a dynamic process that is subject to a variety of influences. These influences include an examinee's own individual personality, his or her perception and understanding of problems, and the nature of the psychopathology from which the person is suffering. This culturally shaped, help-seeking behavior manifests in a particular style of making complaints (Tseng, 2003, pp. 225–246). Some examinees do not know how to present complaints and tend to underreport their problems, overfocusing on a certain kinds of problems (such as somatic complaints) and ignoring other kinds of suffering (such as emotional ones). Others tend to exaggerate their sicknesses. Clinical skill and an understanding of cultural patterns of problem presentation are necessary for the evaluator to assess the nature and severity of the complaints. This is particularly true in cases involving potential compensation.

Sexual Harassment

General Issues

Sexual harassment refers to unwelcome sexual advances, requests for sexual favors, and other verbal or physical conduct of a sexual nature. It can take place in various settings, such as an occupational or military setting, church, or school. Submission to this conduct is made a term or condition of employment or is the basis for employment decisions affecting the person. Alternatively, the conduct has the purpose or effect of unreasonably interfering with an individual's occupational, working, or studying performance, or it creates an intimidating, hostile, or offensive work or study environment. Associated with the increased tendency for men and women to work closely in various work, study, or public settings, and coupled with the rising human rights movement and gender equality in contemporary societies, sexual harassment has recently engendered a great deal of awareness, attention, and concern (Gold, 2003; Heise, 1990; Whitson, 1997).

What constitutes a proper social relationship and what becomes unwelcome behavior between men and women is based on a complex interaction of factors. Individual factors (such as perception, habit, and the personality of the individuals involved), interpersonal factors (roles played and the interaction that occurs reciprocally between them), and cultural matters (how proper social relations between men and women are traditionally defined and what is customarily expected and practiced in a society) all exert an influence. Behavior deemed sexual harassment can occur within the context of an individual and cultural misunderstanding, or it can happen as the result of purposeful and malicious intent.

From a cultural point of view, we might hypothesize that sexual harassment will be more likely to occur when there is a wide gap between the hierarchy and status between men and women. When men occupy more powerful positions and females assume more vulnerable statuses, sexism and the belief that men are superior and females are inferior may result. Sexual advancement toward other sexual subjects may be viewed culturally as generally desirable behavior, without the need for inhibition.

Some Cross-Cultural Issues and Findings

Fitzgerald and colleagues (1988) developed the Sexual Experiences Questionnaire (SEQ) as an instrument for assessing sexual harassment. The original instrument was designed with the majority group of European Americans in mind. To suit Latinas working in the United States, particularly Mexican American women with moderately low acculturation, Cortina (2001) made revisions and developed the SEQ–Latina (SEQ-L). Six new items relevant to Latina experiences are tapped into dimensions already built into the original SEQ. (For details, see the section "Sexual Harassment Assessment: Sexual Experiences Questionnaire" in chapter 3). In contrast to this, Wasti, Bergman, Glomb, and Drasgow (2000) used the SEQ for Turkish samples and claimed that the study demonstrates measurement equivalence for cross-cultural application to Turkish individuals.

Wyatt and Riederle (1994) examined the relationship between sexual harassment in work and sexual abuse in childhood or adulthood, or both, in a community sample of African American and European American women. Those most likely to be sexually harassed in work and social settings were women with sexual abuse histories, regardless of ethnicity. However, a history of childhood sexual abuse was more negatively associated with African American women's well-being than were repeated experiences of sexual violence.

Wasti and Cortina (2002) investigated coping responses by working women to sexual harassment from different cultural groups. They found that avoidance, denial, negotiation, and advocacy seeking are generally used for coping. However, Turkish and Hispanic American women engage in more avoidance than Anglo-American women, and Hispanic women use more denial but less advocacy seeking.

Piotrkowski (1998) conducted a study to test the hypothesis that gender harassment is related to decreased job satisfaction and increased distress and that majority and minority women differ in their responses to it. Examining women office workers, he reported that, as predicted, the frequency of harassment was negatively correlated with job satisfaction and positively associated with an index of distress. However, the minority status was unrelated to frequency of reported harassment or to responses to it.

Legal Implications

Because sexual harassment takes place between two persons, depending on the parties' subjective perceptions, complaints, and accusations, and sometimes without objective evidence or witnesses to support its occurrence, it may be relatively difficult to assess and to judge. Furthermore, the nature of "unwanted" sexual advances is subject not only to individual but also to sociocultural interpretation, which complicates the situation.

Also, researchers have observed that in court the gender and ethnic or racial backgrounds of the jury, matched with that of the parties on either side, tend to influence the result of the judgment. There are some experimental investigations on how racial bias will affect the decision made by mock jurors. For example, Wuensch, Campbell, Kesler, and Moore (2002) used college students of different racial backgrounds, namely, European American and African American, and of different genders for a mock jury. The mock jury, as four groups (namely, Gender x Race) was asked to make a decision based on a simulated civil case in which a female plaintiff accused a male defendant of sexual harassment. The investigators manipulated the racial background of the litigants to examine how the racial factor would affect the jury's decision. They revealed that the mock jurors of both races tended to favor the litigants of their own race and their own gender. Racial bias was highest among European American male jurors and lowest among European American female jurors, in contrast to African American male and female jurors.

FAMILY-RELATED ISSUES

Various family-related problems give rise to the need for forensic assessment, including child custody, child abuse and neglect, and interracial adoption. We elaborate on the cultural aspects of these problems in this section, including how domestic issues should be handled from a legal perspective, through family law, and the cultural considerations needed in dealing with problems in domestic relations.

Child Custody Determination

Historical Considerations and General Issues
When a couple with children decides to divorce and live separately, disposition of their children becomes one of the most critical issues requiring settlement. Divorcing parents who cannot agree on custody arrangements themselves will seek help from the legal system. The current standard for custody determinations most commonly used in the United States is "the best interests of the child" standard. To determine what custody arrangements are in the best interests of the child, courts, or the parties themselves, may retain forensic experts to evaluate the great variety of relevant factors that go into this determination, including cultural factors.

Culture plays a significant role in viewing parenthood. Gindes (2000) described how the high rate of divorce and the increasing diverse lifestyles people choose in our society have highlighted the questions of who should be responsible for the children, where they should live, and who should raise them.

The answers to such questions have changed over time, as have the legal views on parenthood. In the United States, at the turn of the 19th century, fathers bore the responsibility for and the right to the children (Walters & Chapman, 1991). Compelling economic reasons supported this long-standing presumption. However, during the 19th century, associated with changes in sex roles in society, the presumption in favor of fathers began to change. Courts began to recognize the importance of psychological family bonds along with the need for economic security. Rationales for preference for mothers as custodians of children progressed from motherhood as instinct, to the tender-years doctrine, to the standard of best interest of the child.

In the 20th century, social changes gave rise to a legal preference in favor of gender neutrality in custody decisions in the U.S. courts. The yielding of maternal preference held significant implications for divorcing families in the United States, many of whom are from diverse ethnic and cultural groups. Some have retained traditional notions about family and the roles of the father and mother. Some may be unfamiliar with or do not accept the American standard of gender neutrality. These issues may become important in evaluating a divorcing couple with children.

CASE 5: MOTHER NOT PERMITTED BY HER HUSBAND TO VISIT THEIR CHILDREN AFTER THE DIVORCE

The Lums and their two small children had emigrated from Asia to the United States several years before. Mr. Lum spoke a fair amount of English and found a job outside the home, whereas Mrs. Lum spoke very little English and worked as a dishwasher at an Asian restaurant. Mr. Lum became intimate with a young woman at his place of work. Mr. Lum complained that his wife was uneducated, and he divorced her and married the young woman. As an authoritative and dogmatic man, Mr. Lum not only decided to keep their two children but also forbade Mrs. Lum to visit them. Mr. Lum's personal and cultural wish was for his children to become close to his new wife as their "mother," and he believed that a visit by his ex-wife to the children would interfere with the children's relationship with their new "mother." Without knowing her rights as a divorced wife, the ignorant Mrs. Lum obediently followed her ex-husband's command, trying only to catch glimpses of her children from a distance, when they happened to come out and play outside of the house. Mrs. Lum's coworker noticed that Mrs. Lum looked depressed and inquired why. After discovering how she had been mistreated by her ex-husband, Mrs. Lum was encouraged to visit a social service agency. Through a social worker's involvement, Mrs. Lum finally gained the right to visit her children periodically. This case illustrates how immigrants who are unfamiliar with the legal system in the host society may need help in understanding their legal rights or risk of being taken advantage of.

General Aspects of the Assessment

When forensic experts are asked to contribute to the assessment of custody, many issues should be considered, particularly from a cultural perspective. Roll (1998) correctly asserted that children are capable of integrating highly diverse and even contradictory cultural and religious identity fragments. The more distinctly a child's cultural inheritance varies from that of the dominant society, the more it must be taken into account. The more bias or hostility that exists against an aspect of the child's cultural inheritance, the more that cultural component needs to be considered. This applies particularly when the divorcing parents are an interracial couple. In other words the child's ethnic identity should be seriously considered, as in the case of a transracial adoption (Fletchman-Smith, 1984; Griffith, 1995, 2003). If the child's parents were interethnic or interracially married or one of the parents was of an ethnic minority, special consideration is needed regarding the ethnicity and cultural background of the parents and the child (Roll, 1998).

The assessment must examine specific parent–child factors and interactions, such as the socioeconomic stability of the parent, the psychological maturity of the parent, the bond developed between the child and the parent, the wishes of the child's parent or parents as to custody, the wishes of the child, the matching of the gender of the parent and the child (for gender identification), the child's present adjustment to home or school, the parent's past performance in the parental role, and the future implications for the child (Gindes, 2000). These factors are mainly derived from a psychological perspective and focus on the welfare of the child. They are based on the fact that children are young and vulnerable and need the legal system for protection. However, attention needs to be paid to the welfare of the parents as well, because family life is a product of well-adjusted parents and children.

On a practical level, if psychological instruments are to be used in the evaluation process, careful consideration should be given to whether the instruments chosen are suitable given the ethnic, cultural, or racial backgrounds of those involved (see the section "Assessments for Child Custody" in chapter 3).

Technical Aspects of Assessment

The major considerations in child custody disputes involve the process employed to arrive at the custody determination, the criteria used in determining custody, and the types of possible custody arrangements (Gindes, 2000). In the process of assessment for custody determination, the evaluator will pay special attention to one particular area: the relationship, bond, and interaction between the parent and child. This focus is because the relationship developed between parent and child is crucial to the psychological development of the child. As correctly pointed out by Galatzer-Levy and Ostrov (1999), decisions of custody do not depend per se on the general psychological health of the parents, but do depend, in part, on the impact of the parents' psychological functioning on the child. Also, the way in which "facts" about family life are collected often profoundly affects their content and significance. These issues deserve discussion from a cultural perspective.

What constitutes a "normal" or "healthy" relationship and interaction between parent and child may vary considerably among cultures and should therefore not be judged simply from the point of view of the evaluator. The extent to which intimacy is demonstrated, affection shown, and verbal communication carried out and the role and hierarchical relationship that is maintained are all subject to profound cultural influence. A judgment should not be made without adequate cultural knowledge and experience pertinent to the norms of the culture in question or without consulting with cultural experts. People of some cultures tend to have a wide gap in their behavior in private life and in public. In public settings (e.g., during an interview with the examiner), the parents may tend to be polite and formal toward the examiner and less intimate and affectionate toward their family members, including their children.

If such distance is observed, the evaluator must determine if this is culturally prescribed behavior (Azar & Cote, 2002). (See also the section "Assessments for Child Custody" in chapter 3.) The evaluator should not assume that the behavior observed in public reflects the behavior in private family life. Careful inquiry, reliance on collateral information, and proper adjustment of the baseline may be needed to comprehend the actual parent-child relationship and interaction in ordinary life circumstances. Home visits by a mental health worker of the family's culture as an ancillary procedure may be quite helpful.

Particular Issues for Consideration

A broad range of additional factors may need to be considered from a cultural perspective: What is the family structure and system? What kind of support is available from an extended family? What are the cultural implications of a child being raised by certain parents within a particular marriage-family system? In the contemporary multicultural society, we can observe different variations of marriage-family systems that need consideration when an opinion is to be made regarding child custody. The following are some examples of variations associated with a culture or subculture.

Single-parent family. Associated with the frequent occurrence of divorce, many families are headed by a single parent. Whether the child should be awarded to a family headed by a single father or to one with a single mother may be at issue. In addition to considering the age and gender of the child, the evaluator must consider the cultural attitudes and practices of child rearing.

Matrilineal family system. In some cultures, such as in the Pacific Islands of Micronesia, the family operates and is maintained through a matrilineal system (i.e., title and property are inherited through the mother-daughter lineage) rather than a patrilineal system (in which inheritance passes through the father-son lineage) (Tseng, 2001, pp. 39–56). Whether there is a need for special consideration associated with different family systems awaits further study.

Custody by grandparents. In our society, coresidence among grandparents and grandchildren has become increasingly common. The most common reason children are in the care of their grandparents is child maltreatment, typically associated with substance abuse by one or both of the parents (Pruchno, 1999). Goodman and Silverstein (2002) compared the well-being of children raised by African American, Latino, and White custodial grandmothers. They reported that Latino grandmothers produced greater well-being in coparenting families, reflecting a tradition of intergenerational living. Toledo, Hayslip, Emick, Toledom, and Henderson (2000) pointed out that there are cultural differences in the experience of grandparenting and that the personal and role-related difficulties associated with raising a grandchild, especially a problem grandchild, relative to being a traditional grandparent, were universal across American and Mexican samples of grandparents that they studied. However, they reported that Mexican grandparents in their sample, in contrast to the American sample, experienced enhanced meaning in their role, despite the greater financial and parental stress they encountered.

Child Abuse or Neglect

Cross-Cultural Information About Child Abuse
  Child abuse refers to the physical or mental mistreatment of a child by parents or primary caregivers, and it includes physical, emotional, or sexual abuse, as well as neglect. (We cover sexual abuse in detail later.) Child neglect refers to the failure of a parent to fulfill obligations owed to his or her child. Abuse or neglect will significantly affect both a child's physical growth and his or her mental health condition. Of the different kinds of family-related problems, child abuse is relatively easy to compare and discuss cross-culturally, because the concept of abuse is rather explicit, even though its actual definition and clinical recognition are subject to cultural variations. The subject of child abuse and neglect has been extensively reviewed, including reports from beyond European American societies (D'Antonio, Darwish, & McLean, 1993; Korbin, 1981). It helps greatly to understand child abuse from a cross-cultural perspective. Child abuse and neglect are generally considered worldwide problems.
  In sub-Saharan Africa, LeVine and LeVine (1981) reported that "marginal" children—the result of casual unions or of marital breakups—constituted a rapidly increasing high-risk population for abuse or neglect, because they tended to receive inferior care.

LeVine and LeVine commented also that the use of child labor, like many other aspects of African child-rearing practices that have evolved in response to the exigencies of an agricultural economy, might seem harsh or neglectful by Western standards.

Johnson (1981) described that despite a wide range of caretaking practices found in most areas of lowland South America, it was widely acknowledged that throughout Amazonia mothers attended to infants with scrupulous care, nursing them on demand and providing close physical contact. Parents in some cultures became indifferent to a child's needs only when the child reached the crawling or walking stages. Children were left for long periods of time without food and were denied emotional reassurance. Johnson further explained that, similar to other societies, undesirable social and economic conditions—such as insecure resources, social isolation, and lack of support—tended to be associated with child neglect. Mothers lacking support from their husbands and extended kinsmen were more likely to find their children frustrating, were less inclined to consider their needs, and were more harsh and punitive with them.

Concerning child-rearing practices in rural areas of India, Poffenberger (1981) reported the differential treatment of boys and girls within this cultural framework. Young girls had to be obedient and learn to conform in their own homes and in the homes of their in-laws. The difficulty in adjusting to a new family required strength of personality; therefore, the kind of emotional dependence on the mother that was desirable in sons was not encouraged in daughters. Poffenberger described discipline as common in India, but not battering abuse and neglect. He commented that the very social structure in India that required conformity provided parents with a support system of other adults and older children. The presence of others in the household restrained parental temper and reduced the likelihood that frustration would lead to uncontrolled violence toward young children.

Wagatsuma (1981) reported on the different forms of child abuse observed in Japan. He described the phenomenon of child abandonment, in which a parent leaves an infant in a hospital, a clinic, or another public place, such as a railway station or a department store. Common reasons for deserting infants were unwed pregnancy, financial problems, or family conflict. In Japan to give one's baby to an orphanage was associated with feelings of shame, as it was necessary to publicly expose the parents' identity. The secret abandonment of their babies became the choice for young mothers who had difficulty keeping them. Wagatsuma further stated that according to the ministry survey, cases of abandonment were much more frequent than cases of child abuse or neglect. In Japan being an unwed mother and having an illegitimate child was considered very shameful. Having a child from a previous marriage made remarriage very unlikely for a woman. Therefore, the cultural attitudes toward the status and the fates of these women led to child abandonment. Another form of child abuse pointed out by Wagatsuma was associated with the unique phenomenon of children-murder–parents-suicide acts known as family suicide (see the section "Family Suicide (Children's Homicide and Parents' Suicide)" in chapter 4).

Ikeda (1987) reported case material regarding child abuse in Japan based on her clinical observations. She pointed out that when a nuclear family was isolated from extended family ties, because of frequent moves, lived in urban settings, and had a father with drinking problems, child abuse tended to occur. If the child was young, abuse was by the biological parents, whereas older children often suffered abuse by stepparents, particularly stepmothers. The image of the cruel stepmother so common among laypersons appears to be borne out by the research data in Japan.

Regarding China, Wu (1981) indicated that in Taiwan filial piety was one of the oldest of moral virtues. Extensions of traditional filial piety toward parents are certain extraordinary expectations of children, as described in old books or classic children's stories (Tseng & Hsu, 1972). These have many themes, such as sacrificing a child's life for the parents' sake, a child accomplishing an impossible task or suffering self-inflicted pain to fulfill a parent's wishes or demands, or a child supporting his or her parents with difficult circumstances or self-sacrifice. Wu pointed out that such filial concepts and codes express fundamental values in parent-child relations and child abuse-like behavior is practiced within this cultural context.

In Hong Kong, Tang (1998) conducted a telephone survey of nearly 1,000 randomly selected households to gain information on child abuse. The Chinese version of the Conflict Tactics Scale (by Straus) was used for assessment. Tang reported that physical abuse was 526 per 1,000 children for minor violence and 461 per 1,000 children for severe violence. Comparing this with data from U.S. families, he concluded that Chinese families in Hong Kong showed slightly lower rates of minor violence but higher rates of severe violence toward children, as defined by the scale.

Regarding contemporary mainland China, Korbin (1981, pp. 166–185) commented that there were very few cases of child abuse or neglect acknowledged officially. There is good reason to believe that this more or less reflects the actual situation. Associated with the national family policy of "one child per couple" to prevent a potential population explosion, most young couples in urban settings have only one child, whereas nearly half of young parents in rural areas have a second child. A child is viewed as a treasure of the parents and often is indulged by the grandparents. Thus, instead of abuse or neglect, child psychiatrists have witnessed problems associated with child indulgence syndrome.

On the basis of the cross-cultural information available, Korbin (1981, pp. 1–12, 205–210) commented on the cultural aspects of child abuse. He indicated that certain facts in the cultural context can act either to increase the incidence of child abuse and neglect or to diminish the likelihood of their occurrence. The factors were the cultural value of children (whether children were viewed as valuable for future generations), beliefs about the categories of children (whether children were considered inadequate or unacceptable categories by cultural standards), beliefs about child capabilities and developmental stages of children (expecting children to behave in certain ways at certain ages in terms of competence and humanness), and the embeddedness of child rearing in kin and community networks (the existence of a network of concerned individuals beyond the biological parents—a crucial element in the etiology of child abuse). Finally, Korbin pointed out that although children in general might be highly valued by a cultural group, there were categories of children that were more vulnerable to maltreatment. These included illegitimate, adopted, deformed, or retarded children; high birth order; and female children. Vulnerability depended to a large degree on the cultural context.

Forensic Psychiatric Implications

Maitra (1996) questioned whether child abuse falls within a universal diagnostic category. On the basis of his work with

South Asian families in Britain, Maitra pointed out that cultural beliefs about the self, subjective experiences and interpersonal connections, child-rearing patterns, and child abuse could be viewed and defined differently in different societies. Special caution and careful assessment are therefore necessary in transcultural evaluations. Even though, for the sake of universal application, Finkelhor and Korbin (1988, p. 5) have tried to define child maltreatment as "the portion of harm to children that results from human action that is proscribed, proximate, and preventable," cross-cultural variability in child-rearing beliefs and behaviors makes it clear that no universal standard exists for optimal child care or for child maltreatment (Korbin, 1991).

For instance, Pacific Island people, such as the Hawaiians or Samoans, are known to physically discipline their children. Adults may hit the hips or the extremities of a child, but they are very careful not to hit the child's head, which is believed to be where the soul resides. Distinguishing between ordinary, corporal discipline and the physical maltreatment of a child is a forensic challenge (Levesque, 2000). (See case 2 "Child Discipline or Abuse?" in chapter 1.)

Look and Look (1997) warned us that some cultural practices, mainly relating to Eastern medicine, might be misinterpreted as child abuse. In traditional Eastern medicine certain treatment methods were used when a person, including a small child, was ill, such as skin scraping, cupping, and moxibustion. According to the traditional medical concepts of yin and yang, when the skin was scraped (with a coin or another instrument), it helped to elevate the yang element from the feverish patient and cure the sickness. When these treatments were applied to small children, many scratch scars or burned lesions on skin remained, either on the back of the trunk or on the abdomen, on the extremities or around the neck, which could easily be mistaken by health care workers as a sign of child abuse. In such cases careful history taking and a physical examination for a differential diagnosis are warranted.

Clinically, there needs to be a careful distinction between (ordinary) parental discipline of children and (abnormal) parental abuse of children. In drawing this distinction, an evaluator should consider a broad range of factors. It is not merely a matter of the parent's conscious intention or the nature and severity of the corporal punishment given by the parents; it has to be understood from the perspective of what is culturally perceived and customarily practiced and what values are exemplified by the behavior. Considerations include how people of the same cultural background perceive the parental behavior concerned. Finally, the parental behavior needs to be viewed from the standpoint of the society in which it occurred and judged from a legal perspective, in the spirit of child protection. Thus, a comprehensive approach is necessary, rather than merely relying on a single aspect of the whole picture (Levesque, 2000).

CASE 6: "THE HONOR OF MY FAMILY IS WORTH MORE THAN THE LIFE OF MY DAUGHTER" (WALID PEDRO EWEIS, M.D.)

Mr. Nasrallah, a 45-year-old man, emigrated from Jordan to California with his wife and three teenage daughters. The children attended school and adapted to American life faster than their parents. When the eldest daughter, Leila, reached the age of 16, she started to date a boy she had met in high school. Mr. Nasrallah found out about this and became very angry, demanding to know if she had "lost her virginity." When Leila admitted that she engaged in a sexual relationship with her boyfriend, Mr. Nasrallah became even more upset and decided his duty was to save the family honor by killing his daughter. He used his belt, the closest thing he had at hand, and repeatedly battered Leila. Neighbors and the wife summoned the police and an ambulance was called. Leila spent 2 days in a hospital, but did not die. At his trial, Mr. Nasrallah stated that the "honor of [my] family is worth more than the life of my daughter" and, when his daughter disgraced the family name by "losing her virginity without being married," the only way to restore the name and honor was to kill her. Interestingly enough, the battered Leila testified in court in favor of her father, explaining that his culture dictated that kind of behavior. Leila's uncle testified that, traditionally, the duty of carrying that obligation, so-called honor killing, fell first on the eldest brother, then on the father, then on the next closest male relative, such as an uncle. It should be noted that, in Jordan, the law no longer permits honor killings, but the practice continues. In court Mr. Nasrallah stated that he now understood American law and no longer wished to kill his daughter. After hearing this, the judge released him on probation.

This case illustrates the situation in which a custom, although technically forbidden by the law of the defendant's homeland, was nevertheless still practiced. The behavior also was considered to be wrongful behavior according to the laws of the hosting society. The defendant explained the reasons for his behavior and expressed understanding and acceptance of the law in the hosting society. On the basis of this, the culturally sensitive judge made a sensible decision and imposed a reasonable sentence on the defendant.

Assessment of Parental Competence

As Azar and Benjet (1994) insightfully pointed out, the most difficult decision in child custody cases is whether to terminate parental rights and permanently sever the legal bond between a parent and child. Judges have a great deal of discretion in making termination decisions; thus, the potential for bias may be great. Judges' own conceptions of an "adequate" parent, conceptions based on their own ethnic-cultural backgrounds, may influence their findings and judgments. Even if judges look for input in the form of expert testimony, that, too, may be subject to personal and ethnic-cultural bias, as well as professional limitations. Professionals still have a poor psychological knowledge base and skills for assessments regarding parenting. This is simply because parenting behavior varies greatly across different ethnic and cultural groups.

Parenting fitness is commonly brought into question in cases in which severe child abuse or neglect has occurred. Forensic examiners may be asked to evaluate parents for their competence to perform their roles as parents. If the parent(s) is suffering from a severe mental disorder, with obvious mental deterioration and a poor prognosis, making an assessment and formulating an opinion may be relatively easy. However, if the situation is related to behavior problems, without the direct contribution of a mental illness, the determination becomes a delicate and challenging task.

The proper and adequate parental role and performance needs first to be defined. A major concern is whether the person concerned has the ability to care for, support, nurture, protect, and discipline his or her child. The information typically taken into consideration in termination hearings are the nature of the original abuse or neglect report, the mental status of the parent, the degree of parental compliance with service plans, the extent of the parents' cooperation with caregivers (e.g., child protective services), and movement toward improved "parenting skills" (Azar & Benjet, 1994). Conceptualizing the areas and items needing evaluation may be relatively easy, but decision making is more difficult because there is no objective measurement for each item to be assessed.

The outcome in these cases will be influenced by cultural factors as well. Compliance with service plans and cooperation with public caregivers will be subject to ethnic and cultural factors, too, and should not be judged only according to the norms of the mainstream. Many people of minority ethnic groups, based on language problems, lack social knowledge about the role and function of public agencies, mistrust governmental organizations because of their past history and experiences, and may not show compliance and cooperation as expected by the court. There is also a basic philosophical gap: People of many cultural groups hold the fundamental belief that children belong to their parents and family, and they have difficulty accepting the legal reality that government or public organizations have the right to intrude on their natural right to keep their family and to function as parents.

Issues relating to cultural factors deserve careful consideration when professionals assess parental competence. The expert opinion should reflect a broad, careful consideration of the individual's personal style, the family background, and the social circumstances in which the parental role is formed, including a cultural perspective as well. Professionals making decisions about termination of parental rights at times are making rather subjective decisions (introducing possible personal and cultural biases) in a matter of the utmost seriousness—that is, the possible legal severing of a parent-child bond.

CASE 7: MOTHER WHO LOST HER HUSBAND AND DAUGHTER

Mrs. Ho emigrated with her husband and daughter from South Asia. Her husband managed to find a temporary job to support the family but, unfortunately, was killed by a car one day when he was crossing the street. Mrs. Ho became severely depressed from the sudden loss of her husband. She also became paranoid, suspecting that her husband might have been murdered for his anticommunist activities in his home country. Neighbors reported her to child protective services when they found that her 5-year-old daughter was not being properly cared for. The social worker had some difficulty assessing Mrs. Ho because Mrs. Ho hardly spoke English and there was limited communication even when an interpreter was used. Under the impression that Mrs. Ho was suffering from depression and a delusional state, the social worker referred her to a psychiatric hospital. The family court judge decided that Mrs. Ho was not competent as a parent, and arrangements were made for her daughter to stay with foster parents.

Mrs. Ho, after her discharge from the hospital, was puzzled by the disappearance of her little daughter. The social worker tried to explain to her the legal decision that had been made regarding her daughter, but she did not understand the matter and refused to accept what she was told. She wandered the streets searching for her daughter. When she saw a young girl playing in someone's house, she tried to enter and "kidnap" the girl. The police were called and Mrs. Ho was hospitalized again and diagnosed as psychotic. Feeling hopeless in her life, losing her husband in the accident, and having her own daughter taken away by the government, she attempted suicide in the hospital by hanging.

For the professionals involved, finding a way to rescue and protect the young daughter from the mentally disabled mother without completely sacrificing the mother's rights and perhaps her life became quite a challenge. Perhaps a more creative approach could have been tried. For example, psychiatric care could have been provided for the mother and daughter together (as a family unit), in a home-style care setting, under professional supervision, as is done in some societies where the value of the family is strongly emphasized.

Sexual Abuse of Children

Abney and Priest (1995, p. 11) defined sexual abuse of children as "the sexual manipulation and/or coercion of a dependent child or adolescent by a dominant authority figure in which the child or adolescent is unable to give informed consent." Psychiatrists increasingly recognize that the traumatic early childhood experience of sexual abuse may have neuropsychiatric sequelae that can precipitate various kinds of psychopathology on the victim in childhood and in adulthood. Like other forms of child abuse, the sexual abuse of children is of great concern among mental health workers and society at large.

Considerable research on childhood sexual abuse exists; however, few studies have examined the role of ethnicity, race, and culture in abuse (Kenny & McEachern, 2000). Some research exists regarding perpetrators, however. By studying the convicted sex offenders in a men's prison in Indian Spring, Nevada, West and Templer (1994) reported that a disproportionate number of child molesters were Caucasian American and a disproportionate number of rapists were African American. Fontes (1995, p. xiii) stated that cultural issues are relevant to child sexual abuse in how cultural beliefs or attitudes contribute to family climates in which children can be sexually abused, how cultural organization prohibits or hinders disclosure, and how culture plays a role in seeking or accepting social service or mental health assistance.

Cross-Ethnic and Cross-Cultural Information

The yearly incidence report on documented cases of child maltreatment by the U.S. Department of Health and Human Services, National Center on Child Abuse and Neglect (1998) reported that for the year 1996 there were 119,397 victims of sexual abuse. Among them, 63,280 (53%) were (non-Hispanic) European American children, 32,237 (27%) were African American children, 13,134 (11%) were Hispanic American children, and 10,745 (9%) were other ethnic group children (including Asian American and Native American children). When these percentages were adjusted for population differences of each ethnic group (according to data from the U.S. Department of Commerce, 1997), the incidence rate per 100,000 population was 0.33 for (non-Hispanic) European Americans, 0.96 for African Americans, 0.46 for Hispanic Americans, and 0.89 for other ethnic groups. From these figures, it can be said that the number of sexually abused children is relatively high among African American and other ethnic groups (including Asian American and Native American) in contrast to (non-Hispanic) European American and Hispanic American groups.

In a cross-ethnic comparison of sexually abused children, Mennen (1994b) recruited abused cases, ages 6 to 18 years, from Southern California facilities to study Latina (Hispanic American), non-Hispanic Caucasian (European American), and African American girls. All participants were administered a series of standardized instruments for measurement of mental condition and level of functioning. Mennen found that the sexually abused girls of the three ethnic groups examined had similar characteristics of abuse and mental condition; namely, higher levels of depression and anxiety and lower levels of self-esteem than (ordinary) children in a standardization sample. Their symptom levels did not show any significant differences among the three ethnic groups studied. The only difference found was the duration of sexual abuse. The non-Hispanic Caucasian girls experienced longer abuse (an average of 3.99 years) than the Latina (2.16 years) or African American girls (2.23 years) (Mennen, 1994a).

International Information

Although anthropologists have theorized in the past about the universality of the incest taboo, suggesting the rarity of actual incest, DeMause (1991) argued that the real cultural universal has been the presence of widespread incest and child molestation in most places at most times. Through field observation, LeVine and LeVine (1981, pp. 35–55) remarked on the situation in sub-Saharan Africa, where the sexual molestation of girls is a known phenomenon. For instance, they encountered cases of rape of prepubescent girls by adult Gusii men, who, in many instances, were closely related to members of their victims' parents' generation. Actual father-daughter incest occurred occasionally. In addition, the seduction of pubescent girls by male schoolteachers was the occasion for recurrent scandals in Nigeria and Kenya.

After reviewing data from a survey of child sexual abuse in large nonclinical populations of adults that was conducted in 19 countries, Finkelhor (1994) indicated that all rates are in line with comparable North American research, ranging from 7% to 36% for women and 3% to 29% for men. Most studies found females to be abused more than males, 1.5 to 3 times more. On the basis of this comparison, we can see that child sexual abuse is a worldwide phenomenon.

Obtaining epidemiological data from communities regarding the prevalence of sexual abuse for cross-cultural comparison is difficult. This is primarily because the actual occurrence of sexual abuse by adults often is concealed. Instead, many studies rely on retrospective data, examining childhood histories of the sexual abuse of adult participants, particularly college students, even though they often represent a special subpopulation from an epidemiological perspective.

Meston, Heiman, Trapnell, and Carlin (1999) from Austin, Texas, examined university students of Asian and European ancestry regarding their past histories of childhood abuse. The results showed that male and female students of Asian ancestry reported higher levels of physical and emotional abuse and neglect than their European counterparts. However, in contrast, female students of European ancestry reported a higher incidence of sexual abuse than female students of Asian ancestry.

Moghal, Nota, and Hobbs (1995) also carried out a retrospective study concerning Asian ethnic minority populations. They reviewed cases referred to two teaching hospitals in Leeds, United Kingdom, over the 8-year period between 1985 and 1993. A total of 37 cases were identified. Among them, 25 were girls and 12 boys, with ages ranging from 1 to 15 years (mean 7 years, mode 3 years) when they were sexually abused. The perpetrators were identified in 16 of the 37 cases. All of them were male: 7 were fathers, 3 were mothers' partners, 1 was an uncle, 1 a grandfather, 1 a brother, and the remaining 3 were strangers. Moghal and colleagues pointed out that in the United Kingdom professionals as well as laypeople tended to deny the existence of the sexual abuse of children among Asian ethnic minority populations, based on assumptions about the Asian family structure, its culture, and its religion. However, they commented that Asian family members were less likely to initiate concerns and professionals need to be more open to the possibility of sexual abuse.

Clinical and Legal Implications

Forensic examiners, clinicians, social welfare agencies, and law enforcement should know that, as speculated by Okamura, Heras, and Wong-Kernberg (1995), as many as 80% of sexual abuse cases are not reported, and the actual incidence of sexual abuse is much higher than the statistics reflect. This is particularly true for many ethnic groups. Even adults and parents who may know that a child is being sexually abused may not disclose it for fear of disrupting and destroying the family unit (Conte, 1995). This fear is not merely because of cultural influences; it is also related to the pathology of adult parents and family dynamics.

In addition to clinical sensitivity, cultural sensitivity is necessary to investigate the occurrence of child sexual abuse and to provide care. Heras (1992) indicated that one must understand the context of the abuse, the attitude people take toward child sexual abuse, and what is culturally congruent and dysfunctional. Although incest is taboo in most cultures, among people from developing societies, it is not uncommon that family values, such as financial economy or the importance of maintaining extended family ties, take priority over the concern for child molestation.

Without knowing the culturally permitted behavior between adult parents and their children, sometimes any close physical contact or intimate interaction can be misinterpreted as inappropriate sexual behavior. In extreme cases well-intentioned mental health workers may misjudge a situation and wrongfully accuse adults or parents, bringing about harmful or even tragic results to the family.

CASE 8: IS IT A CRIME FOR AN UNCLE TO PET HIS TEENAGE NIECE IN A PARK? (SHAE LOCK, M.D.)

Mr. Lamug is a 34-year-old Filipino man who was arrested for making sexual advances on his 15-year-old niece Marina in a park one evening. Marina was born and raised in the Philippines. When she was 13 years old, she moved to the United States with her mother and siblings. Her father, with whom she was particularly close, stayed behind in the Philippines, pending immigration clearance, because the parents were not yet legally married. Marina seemed to make a good adjustment to life in the United States, making the honor roll at school and helping out at home. Shortly after the move, Mr. Lamug, her uncle, befriended Marina. This relationship eventually became intimate. When the mother found out, she disapproved of their relationship because of the age difference between them, but not because Marina was too young to date. Over time, however, the mother came to accept the relationship, because Mr. Lamug took on some of the responsibilities of Marina's father, driving her to school, making sure that she did her homework, and forbidding the use of tobacco or alcohol. Their relationship continued for nearly a year until the pair was seen kissing in the park by a police officer, who arrested Mr. Lamug. Marina was taken to an emergency shelter where she began a hunger strike in hopes of freeing her "boyfriend." Mr. Lamug claimed that it was rather common and permitted in the Philippines for an older man to date a young girl, as long as he obtained permission from the girl's parent(s). Furthermore, for a man to become intimate with a much younger girl was also not considered wrong. The laws of the host society, however, prohibited such contact and the man could be charged with sexual molestation of an under-age child or even of statutory rape, if he had sexual intercourse with her.

A forensic evaluator in this case will need to study whether adult men date and become intimate with teenage girls in the home country and what is the general attitude held by the Filipino American people in our society. Other useful avenues of inquiry may be how long Mr. Lamug had been in the hosting society, his previous relationship histories, and whether he might actually have known about the legal prohibition (in the hosting society) against becoming sexually involved with a young sexual partner who has not yet attained the legal age of consent. By integrating all of this information, an evaluator can render a proper professional opinion regarding what kind of legal responsibility should be imposed. No one can avoid legal responsibility by simply asserting that such an action is permitted back in his or her home country.

CASE 9: TRAGEDY OF A FATHER SUSPECTED OF BEING A SEXUAL ABUSER (FROM TSENG, 2003)

A couple with a 5-year-old daughter emigrated from Asia to the United States. Their English was very limited, but the wife was able to find a simple labor job outside of the house, leaving the husband to take care of the home. Their daughter developed a skin rash around her private parts and was given some ointment by her doctor for local application. The father, who thought that it was his job to help the daughter apply the ointment, kindly did so, without thinking that it might be perceived as wrong to do so in the host society. At the daughter's kindergarten, as part of a routine exercise, the teacher gave a picture to all the students, inquiring if any person had touched their private places. The teacher was surprised to learn from this particular girl that her father touched her private place "every day." The alarmed teacher reported this to the child protection service, and the social worker, accompanied by a policeman, went to the house, intending to remove the girl for her protection. Without knowing what was going on, the father panicked and tried to stop his daughter from being taken away. He physically struggled with the police. In the middle of the physical conflict, the policeman drew his gun, perhaps trying to stop the father's desperate, violent behavior, but by mistake shot the father. The mother came back from work and was shocked to discover her daughter in a state of panic and her husband dead. The tragedy of this case might have been avoided if there had been greater cultural consideration. The social worker and policeman could have provided an interpreter and given adequate explanation to the father to avoid this unfortunate result.

Abused children will generally be removed from the abusing parents for the sake of protecting the child. Legally, certain social agencies, such as child protection service, are given the authority to carry out child protection. However, there is a need for cultural considerations in carrying out this protection. How the parents view and understand the procedure of child protection needs to be carefully investigated and comprehended. In many cultures it is considered the parents' unconditional right to keep their children, and it is unthinkable for them to have their children forcibly taken away, no matter what the reason. Without attention to such issues, serious reaction may be elicited from the parents, contributing to their dysfunction and diminishing the prospect of reunion.

Fontes (1995) advocated that to perform culturally informed interventions for sexual child abuse, evaluators need to consider several issues. Beyond the possibility of ethnic or cultural matching between professionals and clients, awareness of cultural issues is vital. To have knowledge and be familiar with the family to be served is essential. Furthermore, to have a diverse and high-quality treatment team is very desirable. Not only should staff be recruited that is diverse and of the same ethnic and cultural background of the people to be served in the community but the staff should be well trained and clinically competent. Finally, any specific treatment recommendations by a cultural consultant or expert based on the client's culture should not be seen as rigid prescriptions to be used with clients in all cases but rather as suggestions that are worth considering. A dynamic adjustment is necessary, depending on the individual situation.

REFERENCES

Abney, V. D. & Priest, R. (1995). African American and sexual child abuse. In L. Fontes (Ed.), *Sexual abuse in nine North American cultures* (pp. 11–30). Thousand Oaks, CA: Sage.

American Psychiatric Association. (2000). *Diagnostic and statistical manual of mental disorders* (4th ed., Text rev.). Washington, DC: Author.

Applegate, B., Wright, J., Dunaway, R., Cullen, F., & Wooldredge, J. (1993). Victim-offender race and support for capital punishment: A factorial design approach. *American Journal of Criminal Justice, 18,* 95–115.

Azar, S. T., & Benjet, C. L. (1994). A cognitive perspective on ethnicity, race, and termination of parental rights. *Law and Human Behavior, 18*(3), 249–268.

Azar, S. T., & Cote, L. R. (2002). Sociocultural issues in the evaluation of the needs of children in custody decision-making: What do our current frameworks for evaluating parenting practices have to offer? *International Journal of Law and Psychiatry, 25*(3), 193–217.

Barnett, A. (1985). Some distribution patterns for the Georgia death sentence. *U.C. Davis Law Review, 18,* 1327–1374.

Blau, G. L., & McGinley, H. (1995). Use of the insanity defense: A survey of attorneys in Wyoming. *Behavioral Sciences and the Law, 13,* 517–528.

Boehnlein, J. (2003, October). *Working with attorneys on cultural issues.* Paper presented at the annual meeting of the American Academy of Psychiatry and the Law, San Antonio, TX.

Borg, M. J. (1997). The southern subculture of punitiveness? Regional variation in support for capital punishment. *Journal of Research in Crime and Delinquency, 34*(1), 25–45.

Coleman, D. L. (1996). Individualizing justice through multiculturalism: The liberals' dilemma. *Columbia Law Review, 96,* 1093.

Conte, J. (1995). Assessment of children who may have been abused: The real world context. In T. Ney (Ed.), *True and false allegations of child sexual abuse: Assessment and case management* (pp. 290–302). New York: Brunner/Mazel.

Cortina, L. M. (2001). Assessing sexual harassment among Latinas: Development of an instrument. *Cultural Diversity and Ethnicity Minority Psychology, 7*(2), 164–181.

D'Antonio, I. J., Darwish, A. M., & McLean, M. (1993). Child maltreatment: International perspectives. *Maternal-Child Nursing Journal, 21*(2), 39–52.

DeMause, L. (1991). The universality of incest. *Journal of Psychohistory, 19*(2), 123–164.

Diamond, B. L. (1978). Social and cultural factors as a diminished capacity defense in criminal law. *Bulletin of the American Academy of Psychiatry and the Law, 6*(2), 195–208.

Dusky v. United States, 362 U.S. 402 (1960).

Dvoskin, J. A., & Heilbrun, K. (2001). Risk assessment and release decision-making: Toward resolving the great debate. *Journal of American Academy of Psychiatry and the Law, 29,* 6–10.

Finkel, N. J., & Slobogin, C. (1995). Insanity, justification, and culpability toward a unifying schema. *Law and Human Behavior, 19*(5), 447–464.

Finkelhor, D. (1994). The international epidemiology of child sexual abuse. *Child Abuse and Neglect, 18*(5), 409–417.

Finkelhor, D., & Korbin, J. (1988). Child abuse as an international issue. *Child Abuse and Neglect, 12,* 3–23.

Fitzgerald, L. F., Shullman, S. L., Bailey, N., Richards, M., Swecker, J., Gold, A., Ormerod, A. J., & Weitzman, L. (1988). The incidence and dimensions of sexual harassment in academia and the workplace. *Journal of Vocational Behavior, 32,* 152–175.

Fletchman-Smith, B. (1984). Effects of race on adoption and fostering. *International Journal of Social Psychiatry, 30(1–2), 121–128.

Fontes, L. (1995). Culturally informed interventions for sexual child abuse. In L. A. Fontes (Ed.), *Sexual abuse in nine North American cultures* (pp. 259–266). Thousand Oaks, CA: Sage.

Foote, W. E. (2000). Commentary on "the mental state at the time of the offense measure": Should we ever screen for insanity? *Journal of American Academy of Psychiatry and the Law, 28,* 33–37.

Fukushima, A. (1985). *Sheishin-kantei: Hanzai-shinli to sekinin-norioku* [Psychiatric examination: Criminal psychology and responsible ability]. Tokyo: Youikaku. (In Japanese).

Galatzer-Levy, R. M., & Ostrov, E. (1999). From empirical findings to custody decisions. In R. M. Galatzer-Levy & L. Kraus (Eds.), *The scientific basis of child custody decisions.* New York: John Wiley.

Gerbasi, J. B. (2002). Competency: Civil and criminal. In *Forensic psychiatric review course* (pp. 181–250). Bloomfield, CT: American Academy of Psychiatry and the Law.

Gindes, M. (2000). Child custody. In F. Kaslow (Ed.), *Handbook of couple and family forensics: A sourcebook for mental health and legal professionals* (pp. 258–285). New York: John Wiley.

Gold, L. (2003). Sexual harassment. In R. Rosner (Ed.), *Principles and practice of forensic psychiatry* (2nd ed., pp. 282–289). New York: Oxford University Press.

Goodman, C., & Silverstein, M. (2002). Grandmothers raising grandchildren: Family structure and well-being in culturally diverse families. *Gerontologist, 42*(5), 676–689.

Griffith, E. E. H. (1995). Forensic and policy implications of the transracial adoption debate. *Bulletin of the American Academic Psychiatry and Law, 23*(4), 501–512.

Griffith, E. E. H. (2003, October). *Transracial adoption debate.* Paper presented at the annual meeting of the American Academy of Psychiatry and the Law, San Antonio, TX.

Grisso, T. (1996). Pretrial clinical evaluations in criminal cases: Past trends and future directions. *Criminal Justice and Behavior, 23*(1), 90–106.

Heilbrun, K., Ogloff, J. R. P., & Picarello, K. (1999). Dangerous offender statutes in the United States and Canada: Implications for risk assessment. *International Journal of Law and Psychiatry, 22*(3–4), 393–415.

Heise, L. (1990). Crimes of gender. *Women's Health Journal, 17,* 3–11.

Heras, P. (1992). Cultural considerations in the assessment and treatment of child sexual abuse. *Journal of Child Sexual Abuse, 1,* 119–124.

Ikeda, Y. (1987). *Jido-giakutai: Yuganda oyako-kankei* [Child abuse: Distorted parent-child relations]. Tokyo: Chuokoronsha. (In Japanese).

Janofsky, J. S., Dunn, M. H., Roskes, E. J., Briskin, J., & Rudolph, M. S. (1996). Insanity defense pleas in Baltimore City: An analysis of outcome. *American Journal of Psychiatry, 153*(11), 1464–1468.

Johnson, O. R. (1981). The socioeconomic context of child abuse and neglect in native South America. In J. E. Korbin (Ed.), *Child abuse and neglect: Cross-cultural perspectives* (pp. 56–70). Berkeley: University of California Press.

Katoh, H. (1994). Criminal policy for offenders with mental disorder in Japan. *Japanese Journal of Psychiatry and Neurology, 48*(Suppl.), 19–23.

Keil, T., & Vito, G. (1989). Race, homicide severity, and application of death penalty: A consideration of the Barnett Scale. *Criminology, 27*, 511–535.

Kenny, M. C., & McEachern, A. G. (2000). Racial, ethnic, and cultural factors of childhood sexual abuse: A selected review of the literature. *Clinical Psychological Review, 20*(7), 905–922.

Korbin, J. (Ed.). (1981). *Child abuse and neglect: Cross-cultural perspectives*. Berkeley: University of California Press.

Korbin, J. (1991). Cultural perspectives and research directions for the 21st century. *Child Abuse and Neglect, 15*, 67–77.

Levesque, R. J. R. (2000). Cultural evidence, child maltreatment, and the law. *Child Matreatment, 5*(2), 146–160.

LeVine, S., & LeVine, R. (1981). Child abuse and neglect in sub-Saharan Africa. In J. E. Korbin (Ed.), *Child abuse and neglect: Cross-cultural perspectives* (pp. 35–55). Berkeley: University of California Press.

Li, C. P. (2000). *Practice and theory of forensic psychiatric assessment: Including analysis and discussion of 97 forensic cases*. Beijing, China: Beijing Medical University Publisher. (In Chinese).

Look, K. M., & Look, R. M. (1997). Skin scraping, cupping, and moxibustion that may mimic physical abuse. *Journal of Forensic Science, 42*(1), 103–105.

Lynch, M., & Haney, C. (2000). Discrimination and instructional comprehension: Guided discretion, racial bias, and the death penalty. *Law and Human Behavior, 24*(3), 357–358.

Magnarella, P. J. (1991). Justice in a culturally pluralistic society: The cultural defense on trial. *Journal of Ethnic Studies, 19*(3), 65–84.

Maitra, B. (1996). Child abuse: A universal "diagnostic" category? The implication of culture in definition and assessment. *International Journal of Social Psychiatry, 42*(4), 287–304.

Manarin, B. (2002). Criminal responsibility and mental health experts: The A, B, Cs of cross-examination. *Medicine, Science, and the Law, 42*(2), 135–146.

Matthews, D., & Tseng, W. S. (2004). Culture and forensic psychiatry. In W. S. Tseng & J. Streltzer (Eds.), *Culture competence in clinical psychiatry*. Washington, DC: American Psychiatric Publishing.

Mazzella, R., & Feingold, A. (1994). The effects of physical attractiveness, race, socioeconomic status, and gender of defendants and victims on judgments of mock jurors: A meta-analysis. *Journal of Applied Social Psychology, 24*, 1315–1344.

Melton, G. B., Petrila, J., Poythress, N. G., & Slobogin, C. (1997). *Psychological evaluations for the courts: A handbook for mental health professionals and lawyers* (2nd ed.). New York: Guilford.

Mennen, E. F. (1994a). The relationship of race/ethnicity to symptoms in childhood sexual abuse. *Child Abuse and Neglect, 19*, 115–124.

Mennen, F. (1994b). Sexual abuse in Latina girls: Their functioning and a comparison with White and African American girls. *Hispanic Journal of Behavioral Sciences, 16*, 475–486.

Meston, C. M., Heiman, J. R., Trapnell, P. D., & Carlin, A. S. (1999). Ethnicity, desirable responding, and self-reports of abuse: A comparison of European- and Asian-ancestry undergraduates. *Journal of Consulting and Clinical Psychology, 67*(1), 139–144.

Miller, R. D. (2003). Criminal competence. In R. Rosner (Ed.), *Principles and practice of forensic psychiatry* (2nd ed., pp. 213–232). London: Arnold.

Moghal, N. E., Nota, I. K., & Hobbs, C. J. (1995). A study of sexual abuse in an Asian community. *Archives of Disease in Childhood, 72,* 346–347.

National Research Council. (1989). *Improving risk communications.* Washington, DC: National Academy Press.

Okamura, A., Heras, P., & Wong-Kernberg, L. (1995). Asian, Pacific Island, and Filipino Americans and sexual child abuse. In L. Fontes (Ed.), *Sexual abuse in nine North American cultures* (pp. 67–96). Thousand Oaks, CA: Sage.

People v. Chen, No. 87-7774, N.Y. Super. Ct. (1989).

People v. Hanoukai, No. 56-4533, Van Nuys Super. Ct. (1994).

People v. Kimura, No. A-091133, La. Super. Ct. (1985).

People v. Kong Moua, No. 315972-0, Fresno Super. Ct. (1985).

People v. Moua, No. 328106-0, Fresno Super. Ct. (1985).

Pfeifer, J., & Ogloff, J. (1991). Ambiguity and guilt determinations: A modern racism perspective. *Journal of Applied Social Psychology, 21,* 1713–1725.

Piotrkowski, C. S. (1998). Gender harassment, job satisfaction, and distress among employed White and minority women. *Journal of Occupational Health and Psychology, 3*(1), 33–43.

Poffenberger, T. (1981). Child rearing and social structure in rural India: Toward a cross-cultural definition of child abuse and neglect. In J. E. Korbin (Ed.), *Child abuse and neglect: Cross-cultural perspectives* (pp. 71–95). Berkeley: University of California Press.

Pruchno, R. (1999). Raising grandchildren: The experiences of Black and White grandmothers. *Gerontologist, 39*(2), 209–221.

Reddy, S. (2002). Temporarily insane: Pathologising cultural difference in American criminal courts. *Sociology of Health and Illness, 24*(5), 667–687.

Regan, J., & Alderson, A. (2002, August). Criminal responsibility or lack of cultural awareness? The Andrea Yates story. *Tennessee Medicine,* 337–339.

Roll, S. (1998). Cross-cultural considerations in custody and parenting plans. *Child and Adolescent Psychiatric Clinic in North America, 7*(2), 445–454.

Slovenko, R. (2002). *Psychiatry in law/law in psychiatry.* New York: Brunner-Routledge.

Sorensen, J., & Wallace, D. (1995). Capital punishment in Missouri: Examining the issue of racial disparity. *Behavioral Sciences and the Law, 13,* 61–80.

Sweeney, L., & Haney, C. (1992). The influence of race on sentencing: A meta-analytic review of experimental studies. *Behavioral Science and Law, 10,* 179–195.

Tang, C. S. (1998). The rate of physical child abuse in Chinese family: A community survey in Hong Kong. *Child Abuse and Neglect, 22*(5), 381–391.

Toledo, J. R., Hayslip, B., Jr., Emick, M. A., Toledom, C., & Henderson, C. E. (2000). Cross-cultural differences in custodial grandparenting. In B. Hayslip, Jr., & R. Goldberg-Glen (Eds.), *Grandparents raising grandchildren: Theoretical, empirical, and clinical perspectives.* New York: Springer.

Torry, W. (1999). Multicultural jurisprudence and the culture defense. *Journal of Legal Pluralism, 44,* 127–161.

Torry, W. (2000). Culture and individual responsibility: Touchstones of the culture defense. *Human Organization, 59*(1), 58–71.

Tseng, W. S. (2001). *Handbook of cultural psychiatry.* San Diego, CA: Academic Press.

Tseng, W. S. (2003). *Clinician's guide to cultural psychiatry.* San Diego, CA:

Academic Press.

Tseng, W. S., & Hsu, J. (1972). The Chinese attitude toward parental authority as expressed in Chinese children's stories. *Archives of General Psychiatry, 26,* 28–34.

U.S. Department of Commerce. (1997). *Statistical abstract of the United States*
(117th ed.).Washington, DC: U.S. Government Printing Office.

U.S. Department of Health and Human Services, National Center on Child
Abuse and Neglect. (1998). *Child maltreatment 1996: Reports from the states
to the National Center on Child Abuse and Neglect.* Washington, DC: U.S. Government Printing Office.

Volpp, L. (1994). (Mis)identifying culture: Asian women and the "culture
defense." *Harvard Women's Law Journal, 57,* 57–101.

Wagatsuma, H. (1981). Child abandonment and infanticide: A Japanese case.
In J. E. Korbin (Ed.), *Child abuse and neglect: Cross-cultural perspectives*
(pp. 120–138). Berkeley: University of California Press.

Walters, L. H., & Chapman, S. E. (1991). Changes in legal views of parent-
hood: Implications for fathers in minority culture. In F. W. Bozett & S. M.
H. Hanson (Eds.), *Fatherhood and families in cultural context* (pp. 83–113).
New York: Springer.

Wasti, S. A., Bergman, M. E., Glomb, T. M., & Drasgow, F. (2000). Test of the
cross-cultural generalizability of a model of sexual harassment. *Journal of
Applied Psychology, 85*(5), 766–778.

Wasti, S. A., & Cortina, L. M. (2002). Coping in context: Sociocultural determinants of responses to sexual harassment. *Journal of Personality and Social
Psychology, 83*(2), 394–405.

Weinstock, R., Leong, G. B., & Silva, J. A. (2003). Competence **assessment**. In
R. Rosner (Ed.), *Principles and practice of forensic psychiatry* (2nd ed.,
pp. 85–88). London: Arnold.

West, J., & Templer, D. I. (1994). Child molestation, rape, and ethnicity. *Psychological Report, 75,* 1326.

Whitson, M. H. (1997). Sexism and sexual harassment: Concerns of African
American women of the Christian Methodist Episcopal Church. *Violence
Against Women, 3*(4), 382–400.

Winkelman, M. (1996). Cultural factors in criminal defense proceedings.
Human Organization, 55(2), 154–159.

Woo, D. (1989). The People v. Fumiko Kimura: But which people? *International
Journal of the Sociology of Law, 17,* 403–428.

World Health Organization. (1992). *International statistical classification of diseases and related health problems, Tenth revision (ICD-10).* Geneva, Switzerland: Author.

Wu, D. Y. H. (1981). Child abuse in Taiwan. In J. E. Korbin (Ed.), *Child abuse
and neglect: Cross-cultural perspectives* (pp. 139–165). Berkeley: University of
California Press.

Wuensch, K. L., Campbell, N. W., Kesler, F. C., & Moore, C. H. (2002). Racial
bias in decisions made by mock jurors evaluating a case of sexual harassment. *Journal of Social Psychology, 142*(5), 587–600.

Wyatt, G. E., & Riederle, M. (1994). Sexual harassment and prior sexual
trauma among African-American and White American women. *Violence
Victim, 9*(3), 233–247.

7

Legal Regulation of Psychiatry and Medical Practice: Cultural Considerations

The practice of medicine, psychology, and psychiatry, which belong to a general professional culture, differ considerably in various societies around the world because of differing historical, social, economic, and cultural backgrounds. Most societies legally regulate medical practice to control quality and protect patients. Because legal systems vary in different societies, how the law regulates psychiatric practice also varies remarkably in different cultures. Psychiatric practice may be more tightly regulated than other medical specialties because psychiatrists often deal with patients who lack mental competency, are unable to make proper judgments for themselves, and may heavily rely on the clinician to make decisions for them regarding hospitalization, medication, and psychological therapy. In psychotherapy, we expect patients to reveal their personal lives and emotional matters to the therapist, and through this they often form very intimate relationships with the therapist. They may become dependent on the therapist, who is expected to professionally handle the delicate relationship between them. Regulating relations between patient and therapist to ensure that proper

231

boundaries are observed is a professional, ethical, and legal concern (Slovenko, 2002).

Professional ethics in general and as applied to forensic psychiatry remains an important topic of debate. Some researchers have suggested clearer ethical guidelines are needed. Griffith (1998) has asserted that in discussion about ethics in forensic psychiatry, issues of ethnicity and culture, including ethnic minority issues, should not be ignored.

In this chapter we review the legal and ethical regulation of psychiatric and medical practices primarily from a cultural perspective. The topics covered may be of interest not only to medical and psychiatric professionals, but they also may provide useful background information for nonmedical professionals, such as attorneys and judges, who are intimately involved in the legal process of regulating psychiatry. The regulation of psychological practice, while similar in some ways, has important differences. Comparing such regulatory schemes is beyond the scope of this book.

PSYCHIATRIC CARE OF THE MENTALLY ILL

General Trends in Psychiatric Care: Social and Cultural Perspectives

Beyond the technical aspects of treatment, social and economic considerations very much influence the practice of medicine and psychiatry. The duration of an episode of hospitalization in our society, now driven largely by the "managed care" approach of the medical insurance system, will generally be for less than 2 or 3 weeks. For some private institutions that rely on private medical insurance, the average stay is less than 4 or 5 days. Treating psychiatrists may only have enough time to intervene in an acute crisis; there is not enough time for long-term inpatient treatment and rehabilitative work. This situation contrasts starkly with many other countries, where the government absorbs medical expenses and the average stay in a psychiatric hospital can be several months or more, although the quality of care might be quite variable.

The number of psychiatrists and psychiatric beds available to the community varies greatly in different societies and in different geographic regions, even within the same society. For example, in Asia the number of psychiatrists available per 100,000 population was 0.5 in Malaysia, 0.8 in China, 2.4 in Korea, and 5.2 in Japan, and fewer than 8.0 in the United States (Tseng et al., 2001). Of course, the quality of psychiatric care is to be judged not only by the number of psychiatrists and psychiatric hospitals available but also by the nature and type of care provided and the level of competence of the clinicians. Examining the number of psychiatrists available across a range of communities or societies can give us a rough idea of the tremendous variation in psychiatric service among various societies.

The care of mentally ill persons is also subject to changing medical-sociopolitical policies. For example, a vigorous movement toward deinstitutionalization took place in the United States in the 1970s, based on the professional and political belief that if patients were released into the community from custodial care institutions there would be more opportunity for them to be rehabilitated and recover. As a result, many patients were discharged into the community, where there were no adequate facilities and systems to accommodate and provide care for them. Many mental patients became homeless, wandering in the community. Some have asserted this led to the criminalization of the mentally ill because once they were free from institutionalization many committed crimes of various sorts and ended up in the prison system. As pointed out by Davis (1992), a number of U.S. studies have shown that the proportion of mental patients arrested is greater than that for the general population.

In some societies psychiatry has been used inappropriately as a tool of the state. People may be hospitalized involuntarily not for mental illness but for political reasons. This misuse of psychiatry has been encountered in the past in certain communist countries, such as the former USSR (Yegorov, 1992) and China (Lyons & O'Malley, 2002; Mirsky, 2003).

In our society the frequency of psychiatric malpractice suits brought by patients against psychiatrists has increased tremendously over the past several decades. The probability of a psychiatrist facing a malpractice suit was less than 5% per year in the 1970s and has increased to 20% in this decade. Alarmed by this phenomenon, psychiatrists have changed the way in which they practice. Although some changes may have benefited patient care, other changes may have been made only for the psychiatrist's own protection—so-called defensive medicine— and which increases costs and detracts from the quality of care.

Civil Commitment (Involuntary Hospitalization)

Under certain circumstances, a severely mentally disturbed person may be committed to a hospital without his or her consent. This is often the case when a patient loses rational judgment, lacks insight, and is unwilling to be admitted voluntarily despite the clear indication for it. The criteria under which a person may be civilly committed have become an important concern in contemporary society.

Variations of practice. In many developing societies, particularly in rural areas that lack mental health facilities where there are difficulties in transportation, acutely disturbed mental patients are handled by tradition and local custom (Peszke & Wintrob, 1974), without being committed to psychiatric institutions. Even in developed societies wide gaps often exist between rural and urban areas in the practice of involuntary hospitalization. Involuntary hospitalization occurs much more in urban areas, where alternative ways of handling very disturbed mental patients are quite limited.

Rates of compulsory admission of psychiatric patients vary considerably even among developed countries (Fulop, 1995; Hatling, Krogen, & Ulleberg, 2002; Loue, 2002; Soothill et al., 1981). After examining compulsory admission rates in Europe, Riecher-Rössler and Rössler (1993) reported that between 1980 and 1990 the rates of compulsory admission varied greatly among European countries. The rate (manifested either by percentage of all admissions or per 100,000 inhabitants per year) was highest in Switzerland (50% to 93% of all admissions) and Sweden (248 per 100,000 population per year); the lowest rates were found in Spain (1% of all admissions) and Denmark (24.4 per 100,000 population per year). Riecher-Rössler and Rössler pointed out that this difference was entirely related to different legislation and administrative regulations. For instance, the extremely high number of compulsory admissions in Switzerland was probably because of the Swiss law on "detention in the interest of the patient's welfare," which does not require danger to the self or others and broadly defines the other criteria. In Sweden the Compulsive Mental Care Act allowed commitment when a patient is "unable to take care of him or herself" or has "a lifestyle that is severely disturbing to others." Comparing these criteria with those used in the United States, where patients can be involuntarily hospitalized only when they become dangerous to themselves or others, illustrates interesting cultural differences. In the United States, the compulsive admission rate was 26% of all admissions in the year 1980, in the middle range of the rates reported from European countries.

Behind the differing criteria adopted for compulsory admission exists a basic philosophical question: How should society balance the rights of the individual with concern for the society at large? In general, individual-oriented societies place great emphasis on the benefit and protection of the individual, which leads to a focus on the human rights and individual autonomy. Collective-oriented societies focus on how best to protect and ensure the safety of the community. A Soviet psychiatrist (Yegorov, 1992), who was invited to visit the United States, commented that American people are concerned about the individual person's rights, whereas the Soviet people are more concerned about the welfare of the society at large, in fashioning and implementing civil commitments.

Even in a single society, compulsory admission may be carried out differently among different ethnic groups. In the United Kingdom, Thomas, Stone, Osborn, Thomas, and Fisher (1993) reported that in Central Manchester for the years between 1984 and 1987, for first admissions for persons aged 16- to 29-years, the proportion of Asian patients detained compulsorily (under the Mental Health Act of 1983) was similar to the proportion of European patients, but the proportion of Afro-Caribbean patients was significantly higher. However, when it came to second admissions, the situation changed. The proportion of Asian patients was high, whereas that of Afro-Caribbeans was not different from that of European patients. The authors speculated that the Asian group tended to underuse psychiatric services after their discharge and therefore needed compulsory admission when they relapsed. Similarly, Davies, Thornicroft, Leese, Higgingbotham, and Phelan (1996) examined the situation in south London and reported that among psychotic patients, nearly 50% of the European patients had been detained compulsorily, whereas 69% of African patients and 70% of Afro-Caribbean patients had been detained compulsorily, showing ethnic differences. Coid, Kahtan, Gault, and Jarman (2000) examined the admission records from 1988 to 1994 from half of England and Wales and pointed out that differences among ethnic groups in admissions to secure forensic psychiatric services could not be attributed entirely to racial bias. The difference of offense committed and the psychopathology from which patients suffered had to be included in the consideration.

Lindsey and Paul (1989) examined the situation in our society. By carefully reviewing the existing literature, they found that although other racial groups (such as Asian Americans and Native Americans) are consistently underrepresented, African Americans, compared with Caucasian Americans, are overrepresented in private inpatient and outpatient facilities. This is a well-documented and long-standing epidemiological phenomenon. Furthermore, African Americans were overrepresented compared with Caucasian Americans in involuntary commitment. There are multiple explanations for this phenomenon. African Americans, for economic reasons, may primarily have access only to the public mental health system. This may be a result of purposeful or nonpurposeful institutional racism or racial bias. Error in diagnosing, assessing, and functioning might also lead to their inappropriate voluntary or involuntary admission.

Practical issues. When a clinician decides to admit a psychiatric patient involuntarily, the clinician must make great efforts to explain to the patient the reason that he or she needs to be hospitalized against his or her will. Many people do not know the medico-legal rules governing such circumstances. Therefore, a thorough explanation should be given, even though the patient disagrees with the clinician regarding the need for hospitalization.

When the patient is a foreigner or a member of a minority ethnic group, particularly one who does not speak English, additional effort is needed to appropriately inform the patient. Explanation should cover not only the legal rules concerning civil commitment but also the possible implications of involuntary hospitalization. In many cultures there is a strong stigma attached to having a mental disorder, and there are very negative attitudes toward being admitted to a psychiatric hospital and being labeled a "mental patient." Accordingly, careful explanation, education, and involvement of the family, when appropriate, may be needed to avoid an untoward reaction.

CASE 1: ELDERLY ASIAN MAN COMMITS SUICIDE AFTER ADMISSION TO A PSYCHIATRIC HOSPITAL (JONES, 2003)

A 60-year-old male Asian patient was admitted for the first time to a psychiatric hospital for depression with thoughts of suicide.

He was very reluctant to be admitted to and treated in a mental hospital, because he held the strong view that a mental disorder was a terrible sickness and he was concerned about the reputation he would get among his friends for being treated as a psychiatric patient. He mentioned to his family that he would rather die than be put into a place full of crazy people. However, following the psychiatrist's recommendation, he was finally convinced by his family to be hospitalized and receive treatment. After admission he became even more depressed, refused to eat, and barely talked to the staff. The next morning, he was found dead in the bathroom. Apparently, at midnight he sneaked out of his room, tore his hospital clothes, made a rope, and hanged himself from the top of the bathroom door. He had reacted extremely to being hospitalized in a psychiatric ward and to the stigma of being a mental patient.

The case illustrates that patients of different cultural backgrounds hold different views about commitment and may react differently toward psychiatric hospitalization. A careful explanation is warranted to minimize fears associated with being admitted to a psychiatric hospital. This is particularly true if the patient holds a cultural view that psychiatric admission means being dumped into an institution for the rest of his or her life. In addition a close watch for suicide attempts must be ordered and carried out for cases like this depressed patient. A failure to do so may result in legal liability if the deceased patient's family files suit. In addition to the legal consequences, there are ethical issues to be considered. Arguably, the treating psychiatrist should have provided a proper explanation to the family prior to admission. Securing a family's understanding and support is often critical for civil commitment. (Regarding this point, see the section "A Spiritual Experience or Psychotic Breakdown?" in chapter 9 pp. 306–309.)

The Right to Treatment and the Right to Refuse Treatment

In contemporary societies, psychiatrists often face ethical and legal dilemmas involving the right of a person to receive treatment and the right to refuse treatment. Societies that emphasize human rights afford the patient a greater opportunity to have a say in treatment decisions. In the practice of medicine, when the patient is competent to make treatment decisions, obtaining his or her consent for treatment makes sense. However, for those psychiatric patients who are cognitively impaired and lack of insight (or awareness) into their mental disturbance, obtaining consent to treat the person's mental problems becomes a challenge.

Kullgren, Jacobsson, Lynöe, Kohn, and Levav (1996) surveyed Swedish psychiatrists regarding their attitudes toward compulsory treatment. They found that their decision-making process regarding compulsory treatment was influenced not only by the severity and dangerousness of the patient's disorder but also by family pressure. Further, female psychiatrists less often suggested the use of physical restraints and the compulsory use of electroconvulsive therapy.

PROBLEMS IN THE THERAPIST-PATIENT RELATIONSHIP

Confidentiality

In our contemporary society a therapist is ethically and legally expected to keep confidential all information obtained from the patient except under unusual circumstances. The guarantee of confidentiality encourages the patient to divulge sensitive information and is a fundamental premise of psychiatric practice and an important part of the medical culture. If confidentiality is not maintained, the therapist risks a lawsuit by the patient or the patient's family (Weinstock, Leong, & Silva, 1990). Revealing a patient's personal information to the public, although ethically and legally wrong in many instances, is permissible in others. For example, for the sake of protecting the safety of another party the law may require the therapist to break confidentiality and inform the potential victim. Therefore, clinicians must know how to deal delicately with matters of confidentiality, balancing various ethical and legal considerations. The limits on confidentiality may need to be clarified with a patient from the beginning of therapy.

To learn how psychiatrists from various cultures practice confidentiality, Ghali, Lindental, and Thomas (1991) conducted a survey of Egyptian, American, and Israeli psychiatrists by asking them to make choices based on hypothetical case vignettes presented to them. Although there was no statistically significant difference, Egyptian and Israeli psychiatrists appeared to be somewhat more inclined to break confidentiality than American psychiatrists; the subject deserves further study.

From a cultural perspective, clinicians should be aware that confidentiality is viewed differently in different cultures, and suitable adjustment may be needed for persons from different cultural backgrounds. For example, in contemporary American society, the law may require physicians to keep medical information about pregnancy, drug use, or other information about a teenage patient confidential, not even revealing it to the parents. This law has roots in the medical and cultural belief that any person over a certain age or who engages in certain behavior is mature enough to have the basic right to keep that personal information confidential. However, this concept and practice clashes with people who come from cultures that assume parents have the right to know everything about their own children—simply because children, no matter how old they become, by definition always belong to their parents. A culturally oriented physician should consider how to satisfy the parents in some measure and, at the same time, protect the child's confidentiality.

Clinicians should be aware as well that the extent to which secrecy is maintained between husband and wife varies among different cultures. In some societies honest communication is emphasized as the basis for affection between spouses and it is expected that everything should be kept transparent between spouses. However, this is not necessarily true in other cultures. For example, a spouse may keep some secret money from a spouse-partner and use it for his or her own personal reasons, such as giving it to relatives, without sharing the information with the spouse-partner. In some male-dominant societies, a husband is not expected to share anything with his wife about what happens in his work outside and may not even let his wife know how much money he makes. On the other hand, in some cases a wife may secretly take contraceptive pills, without letting her husband know. A population survey conducted in urban Zambia, in Africa ("Secrecy and Silence," 1998), found that many women who used contraceptives did so without their husbands' knowledge. In their culture, if a wife initiates a discussion of family planning, she may threaten her husband's sense of control and create discord within the family. In Muslim culture, associated with male dominance, a wife's culturally imposed duty is to bear children as often as possible. If a wife proposes family planning, she may be at risk of divorce, or she may encourage her husband to take another wife, according to the culturally permitted polygamy system. A wife may secretly use contraception but with constant fear that her husband may find out (El-Islam, 2001).

Dealing with confidentiality between a husband and wife is a delicate task for the clinician working with a couple. The therapist might have to deal with secret information about one spouse's past or current extramarital affair, without letting the other spouse know about it. The therapist might have to deal with medical information about a sexually transmitted disease (such as HIV) contracted by one spouse, without informing the other spouse. The clinician should consider what is expected from a cultural standpoint, beyond what is necessary morally and legally.

The question of whether a physician should inform a patient of his or her diagnosis raises issues of confidentiality and informed consert. In our society, ethical and legal expectations generally require the physician to inform a patient about a medical diagnosis from which the patient is suffering. The physician bears the burden of disclosure and the patient must deal with the consequences. In many other cultures, disclosure of serious or life-threatening conditions proceeds differently. When a patient is suffering from such a condition the physician will notify the family. In many cases the family does not want the patient to know the truth. The family is concerned that, knowing the actual diagnosis, particularly a serious one with a hopeless prognosis, will add stress to the patient, either worsening his or her medical condition or inducing him or her to have pessimistic thoughts, even prompting suicide. In response to this cultural belief, a physician will comply with the family's request and not inform the patient of the diagnosis. For example, in Japan a physician treating a patient with advanced stomach cancer will often give a less severe medical diagnosis, such as gastritis, in accordance with the family's wishes (Elwyn, Fetters, Sasaki, & Tsuda, 2001). Similarly, psychiatrists may diagnose neurasthenia instead of schizophrenia.

In the United States a failure to provide informed consent, including identifying the name of the illness, may result in a malpractice action or an ethical complaint against the physician. Other countries, however, may give the physician more discretion regarding what to reveal and what not to reveal. A physician treating patients from different cultural backgrounds must struggle with this issue and manage carefully from the perspective of medicine, ethics, law, and culture.

Examples of medical confidentiality issues challenging clinicians are whether to reveal genetic information to family members (Lehmann, Weeks, Klar, Biener, & Garber, 2000) or whether to reveal a serious, sex-related, contagious disease to a sexual partner. The clinician must work out the matter from moral, ethical, legal, and cultural perspectives and deal psychologically with the family or spouse in getting them to share, accept, and deal with such confidential information. Associated with technological improvements, managing medical data and records through computer systems brings new questions and problems to contemporary societies in the matter of privacy and confidentiality (Ishikawa, 2000). To what extent the medical records of a person should be kept confidential and, at the same time, meet the need for use in medical treatment and the demands from the insurance system for the regulation of medical expenses are new challenges for our time.

Problems of Professional Boundaries

Maintaining proper professional boundaries between therapist and patient is an important area of concern in our society. Proper professional boundaries are generally considered the foundation for performing appropriate and successful medical care. This is particularly true in the practice of psychiatry, especially in conducting psychotherapy. Defining and enforcing proper boundaries is important from the perspective of ethics and law.

We should keep in mind that what constitutes a proper professional boundary between therapist and patient is an issue not only of medical expectations and ethical standards but also of sociocultural definition. The proper relationship between people, whether it is ordinary interpersonal relationships in social life or a particular relationship in a professional setting, is greatly subject to social standards and practices and cultural customs, rules, and definitions.

Although many aspects of the therapeutic relationship are characterized by the influence of culture, we address only two: physical contact and gift giving. The extent of permissible physical contact between therapist and patient, whether shaking hands or hugging, will usually depend on how the society views what is normal in relationships between two people—authorities and subordinates, physicians and patients, and psychotherapists and patients. Society and culture define the ordinary and proper ways to greet each other, which depend on the nature of the relationship and the consideration of various factors, such as age difference, gender, social status and hierarchy, profession, and circumstance. The unspoken or explicit rules of how professional groups customarily handle such situations also play a role. Social standards and professional customs determine the judgment as to whether a relationship deviates from the norm and is beyond ordinary boundaries. For instance, in a society (such as Japan, for example) in which a man and woman ordinarily do not shake hands with each other, doing so would be considered out of the ordinary for a (Japanese) therapist and a patient of a different gender. In contrast, in a society (such as Hawaii) in which male and female acquaintances may hug each other in a warm greeting, it may not be wrong for a therapist to hug a patient to indicate concern and support. This is a relative issue that needs to be checked against the social norm and cultural etiquette, as well as legal and professional standards.

Giving gifts to friends to show friendship, or to a superior person to show respect, is a custom in many societies. This includes patients giving gifts to physicians to indicate appreciation or to ask for special care. Depending on social background and cultural custom, a patient may also give a gift to the psychotherapist in some cases. In deciding whether a gift is appropriate in such situations, the therapist should be concerned about the kind of gift given: whether it is too expensive, has too much personal meaning, has a special symbolic implication, or has an unusual motivation. For example, for a female patient to give a handkerchief to a male friend, colleague, superior, or therapist would be considered too personal; in the same way, giving a necktie would be interpreted as not only being too personal but also as possibly having sexual implications. In contrast, candy or chocolates (in our society) or food (in other societies) may be perceived as socially acceptable. In other words every interaction should be checked against what is proper behavior in the society and how it will be viewed in a professional setting. Confusion and problems tend to occur when the therapist and the patient belong to different cultural backgrounds and operate according to different cultural norms. Constant clarification and checking are necessary to avoid any misunderstanding and to avoid breaking professional boundaries without knowing it.

Breaking proper professional boundaries may lead to the occurrence of more serious wrongful behavior, such as sexual misconduct between the therapist and patient, a common error that occurs often in our society.

Therapist-Patient Sexual Misconduct

Sexual misconduct by professionals can occur in many kinds of relationships, such as teacher-student, supervisor-supervisee, physician-patient, clergy-church member, counselor-counselee, and so on. The feature common to these examples is a special relationship between the two parties, with a power imbalance (Bisbing, Jorgenson, & Sutherland, 1995).

Sexual misconduct between a therapist and patient occurs rather frequently in our society. The nature of psychotherapy requires that the therapist and patient maintain a close and intimate relationship throughout the process of treatment. The patient is encouraged to reveal personal information and inner feelings, to the therapist, and the therapist is expected to express concern and support to the patient. This professional interaction, occurring in a private setting over a long period of time, makes breaking the professional boundaries easy if the therapist is not able to regulate the professional relationship carefully from the beginning to the end of the therapeutic process (Stone, 1984).

Clinical experiences indicate that in our society middle-aged male therapists who are having difficulties in their own lives are at risk for perpetrating sexual misconduct. The patient may be a young female who is vulnerable and has ambivalent feelings, sometimes having borderline personality problems that are characterized by emotional instability and the seeking of emotional support from an authority figure. This has been described as a common scenario (Gutheil & Sadoff, 1992).

Examining sexual misconduct from a cultural perspective, researchers are unclear how frequently the phenomenon is seen in other cultures. In many societies, particularly developing ones, psychiatric practice is heavily oriented toward medication and there is little time for close interaction between the psychiatrist and patient. The psychiatrist deals daily with a large number of patients waiting in the clinic. Very little psychotherapy is practiced in such a situation. Even when psychotherapy takes place, the therapist-patient relationship or professional boundaries are relatively well protected by social etiquette and cultural custom. The therapist has to maintain a rather formal relationship with the patient. Besides, in the crowded clinic there is hardly an opportunity for private interaction with patients. Environmental and cultural barriers hinders the occurrence of any professional boundary breaking, the typical prelude to sexual misconduct.

Sexual misconduct between a therapist and patient, or sexual abuse by a professional, requires a fertile social setting and a cultural background to occur. In our society, where social etiquette and cultural rules have weakened over time and sexual stimulation and sexualized behavior has become more tolerated and discussed openly, a fertile environment is provided for the occurrence of sexual misconduct. Therefore, the therapist who chooses to engage a patient in intimate psychotherapeutic work over a long period of time must make extra efforts to competently maintain a proper professional relationship with the patient. Otherwise, the therapist may be unprepared to handle his or her feelings toward the patient and will be vulnerable to engaging in a sexual relationship—with problematic consequences for the patient and with the possibility of being sued or served with an ethical complaint for the psychiatrist (Stone, 1984).

ETHICAL-LEGAL ISSUES RELATING
TO MEDICAL PRACTICE

In general medical practice certain complex situations arise that involve legal issues, in addition to medical, ethnic, and cultural issues. Forensic psychiatrists may become involved in such cases to perform assessments and present professional opinions. The following are some examples of such situations.

End of Life Care

A physician at times may discontinue further treatment for a terminally ill patient. Termination of care may be based on medical futility, the family's request or the patient's own refusal of treatment, in order to end his or her life with comfort and/or dignity. The outcome of the situation will depend on the physician's medical judgment and on moral, ethical, and legal concerns. Beyond these considerations, cultural implications may be important as well.

Practices of different cultures regarding the cessation of medical care, resulting in the patient's death, differ. In a society where medical expenses must be absorbed entirely by the family, financial factors will be a major consideration. If the medical fees are taken care of by public resources, economic issues become less of a concern. The availability of medical technology and facilities also will affect the outcome. How much continued medical treatment will add to the suffering of a patient who is already very ill is often a consideration of the patient and his or her family. In each culture matters of life and death are viewed differently and attitudes toward ending life may vary.

The termination of treatment is affected by the attitudes of the medical staff. Konishi and Davis (2001) examined the perception of nurses in Japan. They distinguished between the "right to die" and the "duty to die." The right to die meant that the terminally ill person had the (human) right to refuse further treatment and end his or her life; the duty to die meant that the terminally ill person felt that he or she had no choice and had to refuse treatment out of concern for the financial burden on the family or society. In other words it was a (social) duty to end his or her life. From this survey of Japanese nurses and their counterparts in the West (mainly from North America), Konishi and Davis found that the majority of Japanese nurses and all of the Western nurses supported the concept of a right to die. However, the duty to die received weak support from the Western nurses and rather strong disagreement among the Japanese nurses.

In some cultures, such as China, ending one's life in his or her home setting, surrounded and cared for by immediate family, has traditionally been considered important. Because of this cultural attitude, Chinese people are reluctant to die in foreign places, such as in hospitals. When a Chinese patient's medical condition deteriorates such that the end of life appears near, the patient and family will ask the physician to release the patient to return home to die. This custom requires the physician to make a proper medical judgment at a critical time, to determine whether the patient is approaching a terminal stage, without further hope, and to give the patient permission to go home. When a patient with this cultural belief and custom is being cared for in a hospital by a physician who is not aware of the custom or does not know of the patient's and the family's arrangements for the last moments of life, then transcultural problems may occur that may or may not involve legal complications. Case 2 illustrates this point.

CASE 2: THE IMPORTANCE OF DYING AT HOME

Mr. Zeng was an 85-year-old, first-generation Chinese American who was admitted to a hospital for a serious medical complication.

After 2 weeks of treatment, in response to family members' inquiries, the attending (American) physician informed the patient as well as the family that all possible medical treatment had been tried and the patient failed to show any signs of improvement. The doctor observed that the patient might not live too much longer. On hearing this, Mr. Zeng and his family requested that he be discharged. The attending physician was surprised by the request, and explained to the patient and his family that removing all the life-sustaining tubes to go home would mean that the patient would surely die soon. The family explained to the physician how important it was for Mr. Zeng to die in his own home, with dignity, rather than in a strange place, such as in the hospital. After consulting with cultural experts available at the hospital, affirming that this cultural practice had been observed traditionally in China and that some elderly still considered it important to follow the old custom, the physician reluctantly allowed the patient to be discharged. The physician made sure that the patient and his family signed a release form indicating that leaving the hospital against medical advice was the wish of the patient and family. Mr. Zeng, accompanied by his family, went home to prepare for the last remaining stage of his life.

To understand the patient's and family's cultural needs is one thing. Making proper medical decisions and providing good and ethical medical care is another. The physician in this instance was able to meet the requirements of medical, ethical, and legal practice in his jurisdiction, while at the same time providing culturally sensitive care.

Legal Death of a Person

Defining death, medically and legally, has become much more complicated than in the past. Moreover, the legal definition of death becomes a more serious matter when it is associated with organ transplantation. The donor organ must be obtained from the donor quickly, while the organ is fresh and useful. Obviously, pinpointing when the person has died so that organs can be harvested becomes an important medical issue. The medical and legal definitions of death are not universal but are defined by each society, based on professional knowledge and social and legal judgments. For example, Japanese people have traditionally believed that death occurs only when the heart stops beating. Only recently was the law changed such that death is determined by when brain activity ceases, as indicated by an electroencephalogram, as is done in most European and American countries. Not only is the definition of death a matter of medical judgment but it also involves folk views and ethical concepts that are greatly influenced by culture. Consequently, the definition of death invites confusion and problems when involving medical practices on an international level.

Abortion

The practice of artificial abortion is carried out very differently across societies, because of different ethical concepts and social circumstances. In our society, because of varying religious backgrounds, moral concepts and judgments, and the legal and political atmosphere, people are polarized into either those who strongly support a woman's right to choose to have an abortion and those who are intensively against medical abortion to terminate an unwanted pregnancy. From a cultural perspective, we see that many societies (such as Catholic societies) are strongly against abortion mainly because of religious beliefs. However, attitudes vary, even among Catholic societies; some are very strict about abortion, whereas others are more liberal about it as a choice for family planning—indicating a clash between religious ideals and reality.

For practical reasons, some societies consider abortion a convenient way to control unwanted pregnancies. This is particularly true in underdeveloped or developing societies, in which raising a child is an expensive matter. In some societies, giving birth to an illegitimate child is a terribly shameful thing for the mother, and, in its extreme, the mother is saved from social shame by sacrificing the unborn, unwanted baby. If no abortion is available, infanticide becomes the last choice available for the mother in a sociocultural context (see the section "Infanticide and Filicide" in chapter 5).

At the national policy level, abortion is sometimes advocated as a means of family planning to avoid a population explosion. Since the 1970s, China has enforced the one child per couple family planning policy to control the rate of population growth. Researchers estimate that without forcefully carrying out family planning China would grow by the size of the population of the United States every decade. Compulsory artificial abortion for a couple that already has more than one child is a way that has been used to control the number of children to avoid social problems. Abortion is advocated in this different social context. Legally, it is regarded as the right thing to do whenever necessary. This is an entirely different perspective from our society, in which many childless couples work very hard to find a child to adopt.

Physician-Assisted Suicide

Whether the physician has the right to medically assist a person to end his or her own life is a controversial issue that has been debated intensely in contemporary society, not merely from a medical point of view but also from social, moral, ethical, and cultural perspectives (Boehnlein, Parker, Arnold, Bosk, & Sparr, 1995). From the standpoint of cultural anthropology, we can see that in some societies, the old and weak elderly may voluntarily choose to end their lives, so that they are not a burden to their families. Historically, for example, weak or ill elderly persons in some Eskimo tribes living in the severe cold may go out from their huts into the snow and eventually die from exposure. In a land where food is scarce during the cold winter months. Some elderly persons may commit suicide because they suffer from severe depression, often associated with a medical sickness or financial problems, or because they feel rejected by their immediate families, or they have other emotional problems. Others may seek to end their lives with the active assistance of a physician.

As we have seen, in the hospital setting many patients with a terminal illness die because of a withdrawal of care based on medical futility their own request or that of their immediate families. However, this is not assisted suicide. As observed by Becvar (2000), medical technology has succeeded in extending life in the face of what previously would have been fatal illnesses, and problems have emerged in distinguishing between a so-called natural death and a life that is artificially sustained. According to the Netherlands State Commission on Euthanasia, *euthanasia* is defined as the intentional termination of life by another party at the request of the person concerned. *Assisted suicide*, on the other hand, is defined as intentionally helping a patient terminate his or her life at his or her request. Thus, physician-assisted suicide occurs when a physician, through medical means, such as offering or injecting a toxic agent into the patient, helps the patient end his or her life in a consciously planned, medical way.

Many contemporary societies are aging, such that more than one fifth of the population will soon be beyond age 60 years, many of them beyond 80 or even 90. Many of the elderly may become physically disabled or mentally incompetent to take care of themselves and will have to rely on their middle-aged, adult children, not only for financial reasons but also for care in daily life. Thus, many societies will be forced to seriously consider how to cope with the aging population in the near future. Within this social reality, granting certain elderly persons who are ill the choice to end their own lives with dignity might become a common alternative. The attitude toward assisted death is subject to complex variables, including cultural factors. Researchers have speculated that within a society that emphasizes individualism, assisted suicide may be more easily accepted, whereas in a society characterized by the values of authoritarianism (in a group-oriented, traditional society), the assisted death (of elderly parents) may not be as welcomed (Kemmelmeier, Wiecxorkowska, Erb, & Burnstein, 2002).

We need to point out that physician-assisted suicide has serious, inherent problems, not only from an ethical or legal point of view but also from a medical, and particularly a psychiatric, perspective. Knowing whether a (elderly) person is making a sound, competent, and healthy decision to end his or her life is a medical and psychiatric challenge. Psychiatrists are familiar with the fact that many persons in a depressed state tend to lose their sound cognitive judgment. Under stress and depression, many people are overwhelmed and vulnerable and will make poor or undesirable judgments that they may regret after they have recovered from their disorder. Because it is a delicate and challenging task to assess a person's mental competence, some clinicians raise doubts as to whether psychiatrists can effectively serve as gatekeepers for physician-assisted suicide (Sullivan, Ganzini, & Youngner, 1998).

REFERENCES

Becvar, D. S. (2000). Euthanasia decisions. In F. Kaslow (Ed.), *Handbook of couple and family forensics: A sourcebook for mental health and legal professionals*. New York: John Wiley.

Bisbing, S. B., Jorgenson, L. M., & Sutherland, P. K. (1995). *Sexual abuse by professionals: A legal guide.* Charlottesville, VA: Michie Company.

Boehnlein, J. K., Parker, R. M., Arnold, R. M., Bosk, C. F., & Sparr, L. F. (1995). Medical ethics, cultural values, and physician participation in lethal injection. *Bulletin of American Academy of Psychiatry and the Law, 23*(1), 129–134.

Coid, J., Kahtan, N., Gault, S., & Jarman, B. (2000). Ethnic differences in admissions to secure forensic psychiatry services. *British Journal of Psychiatry, 177,* 241–247.

Davies, S. (1992). Assessing the "criminalization" of the mental ill in Canada. *Canadian Journal of Psychiatry, 37,* 532–538.

Davies, S., Thornicroft, G., Leese, M., Higgingbotham, A., & Phelan, M. (1996). Ethnic differences in risk of compulsory psychiatric admission among representative cases of psychosis in London. *British Medical Journal, 312*(7030), 533–537.

El-Islam, M. F. (2001). The woman with one foot in the past. In W. S. Tseng & J. Streltzer (Eds.), *Culture and psychotherapy: A guide to clinical practice.* Washington, DC: American Psychiatric Press.

Elwyn, T. S., Fetters, M. D., Sasaki, H., & Tsuda, T. (2002). Responsibility and cancer disclosure in Japan. *Social Science and Medicine, 54*(2), 281–294.

Fulop, N. J. (1995). Involuntary outpatient civil commitment: What can Britain learn from the U.S. experience? A civil liberties perspective. *International Journal of Law and Psychiatry, 18*(3), 291–303.

Ghali, A. Y., Lindental, J. J., & Thomas, C. S. (1991). The management of confidentiality in Egypt. *Medicine and Law, 10*(6), 549–554.

Griffith, E. E. (1998). Ethics in forensic psychiatry: A cultural response to stone and Appelbaum. *Journal of the American Academy of Psychiatry and the Law, 26*(2), 171–184.

Gutheil, T. G., & Sadoff, R. L. (1992). Expert opinion: A case of therapist-patient sexual misconduct. In R. I. Simon (Ed.), *Review of clinical psychiatry and the law* (Vol. 3, pp. 331–348). Washington, DC: American Psychiatric Press.

Hatling, T., Krogen, T., & Ulleberg, P. (2002). Compulsory admissions to psychiatric hospitals in Norway—International comparisons and regional variations. *Journal of Mental Health, 11,* 623–634.

Ishikawa, K. (2000). Health data use and protection policy: Based on differences by cultural and social environment. *International Journal of Medical Information, 60*(2), 119–125.

Jones, L. (2003). An elderly Asian male patient committed suicide after admission to a psychiatric hospital. In W. S. Tseng (Ed.), *Clinician's guide to cultural psychiatry* (p. 262). San Diego, CA: Academic Press.

Kemmelmeier, M., Wiecxorkowska, G., Erb, H. P., & Burnstein, E. (2002). Individualism, authoritarianism, and attitudes toward assisted death: Cross-cultural, cross-regional, and experimental evidence. *Journal of Applied Social Psychology, 32*(1), 60–85.

Konishi, E., & Davis, A. J. (2001). The right-to-die and the duty-to-die: Perceptions of nurses in the West and in Japan. *International Nursing Review, 48*(1), 17–28.

Kullgren, G., Jacobsson, L., Lynöe, N., Kohn, R., & Levav, I. (1996). Practices and attitudes among Swedish psychiatrists regarding the ethics of compulsory treatment. *Medicine and Law, 10,* 499–507.

Lehmann, L. S., Weeks, J. C., Klar, N., Biener, L., & Garber, J. E. (2000). Disclosure of familial genetic information: Perceptions of the duty to inform. *American Journal of Medicine, 109*(9), 705–711.

Lindsey, K. P., & Paul, G. L. (1989). Involuntary commitments to public mental institutions: Issues involving the overrepresentation of Blacks and assessment of relevant functioning. *Psychological Bulletin, 106*(21), 171–183.

Loue, S. (2002). The involuntary civil commitment of mentally ill persons in the United States and Romania. *Journal of Legal Medicine, 23,* 211–250.

Lyons, D., & O'Malley, L. (2002). The labeling of dissent—Politics and psychiatry behind the Great Wall. *Psychiatric Bulletin, 26,* 443–444.

Mirsky, J. (2003). China's psychiatric terror [Review of book *Dangerous minds: Political psychiatry in China today and its origins in the Mao era*]. *New York Review of Books, 50*(3).

Peszke, M. A., & Wintrob, R. M. (1974). Emergency commitment—A transcultural study. *American Journal of Psychiatry, 131*(1), 36–40.

Riecher-Rössler, A., & Rössler, W. (1993). Compulsory admission of psychiatric patients: An international comparison. *Acta Psychiatrica Scandinavica, 87,* 231–236.

Secrecy and silence: Why women hide contraceptive use. (1998). *Population Briefs, 4*(3), 3.

Singh, S. P., Croudace, T., Beck, A., & Harrison, G. (1998). Perceived ethnicity and the risk of compulsory admission. *Social Psychiatry and Psychiatric Epidemiology, 33*(1), 39–44.

Slovenko, R. (2002). *Psychiatry in law/law in psychiatry.* New York: Brunner-Routledge.

Soothill, K. L., Harding T. W., Adserballe, H., Berheim, J., Ern?, S., Magdi, S., Panpreecha, C., & Reinhold, F. (1981). Compulsory admissions to mental hospitals in six countries. *International Journal of Law and Psychiatry, 4,* 327–344.

Stone, A. A. (1984). Sexual exploitation of patients in psychiatry. In A. A. Stone, *Law, psychiatry, and morality: Essay and analysis* (pp. 191–216). Washington, DC: American Psychiatric Press.

Sullivan, M. D., Ganzini, L., & Youngner, S. J. (1998, July-August). Should psychiatrists serve as gatekeepers for physician-assisted suicide? *Hastings Center Report, 28,* 24–31.

Thomas, C. S., Stone, K., Osborn, M., Thomas, P. F., & Fisher, M. (1993). Psychiatric morbidity and compulsory admission among UK-born Europeans, Afro-Caribbeans and Asians in Central Manchester. *British Journal of Psychiatry, 163,* 91–99.

Tseng, W. S., Ebata, K., Kim, K. I., Frahl, W., Kua, E. H., Lu, Q. Y., Shen, Y. C., Tan, E. S., & Yang, M. J. (2001). Mental health in Asia: Improvements and challenges. *International Journal of Social Psychiatry, 47*(1), 8–23.

Weinstock, R., Leong, G. B., & Silva, J. A. (1990). Confidentiality and privilege. In R. I. Simon (Ed.), *Review of clinical psychiatry and the law* (Vol. 1, pp. 83–119). Washington, DC: American Psychiatric Press.

Yegorov, V. F. (1992). And how is it over there, across the ocean? *Schizophrenia Bulletin, 18*(1), 7–14.

8

Correctional Psychiatry: Culturally Relevant Care and Treatment

By the end of 1980s, the United States held nearly 1.2 million men and women in jails or prisons. Ten years later, the number substantially increased to 1.8 million (American Psychiatric Association, 2000, p. xix). Studies have consistently demonstrated that about 20% of inmates in jails and prisons have serious mental illnesses and are in need of psychiatric care (American Psychiatric Association, 2000, p. xix). Moreover, jail and prison populations include a high percentage of individuals from minority ethnic groups. Our society struggles with the question of how to provide appropriate facilities for the incarcerated, appropriate treatment for the mentally ill in prisons and jails, and culturally appropriate care when possible. The operation of a correctional system involves a broad range of personnel, including administrative, staff, correctional officers, and various professionals involved in mental health work, including general psychiatrists, clinical psychologists, and social workers, as well as specialized forensic psychiatrists or forensic psychologists. In this chapter we discuss how to promote culturally suitable care for inmates in jail and prison from the perspective of the various professionals involved, including the administrator and staff working in the institution.

GENERAL ISSUES

Offenders are committed to prison primarily for the purpose of court-imposed punishment for their wrongful behavior. Inmates are deprived of their personal liberty for a defined term, with at least the possibility of receiving rehabilitation to improve their life when and if they are released from prison. Life in prison is regulated in such a way that inmates must follow the rules and restrictions imposed on them, and they may have minimal individual freedom. They are typically confined to small cells, with iron bars, surrounded by concrete walls. They must wake up and go to bed according to a regular schedule and eat meals prepared by the institution, without choice. They may have to attend certain programs for physical exercise, recreation, and occupational rehabilitation.

Because prisons are operated by mainstream society, they are set up primarily for inmates from mainstream society. Inmates who belong to other cultures, speak other languages, and eat different kinds of folk meals will suffer more because they will be deprived of such cultural supports. The ensuing increase in the severity of punishment makes cultural consideration for this population of utmost importance when providing services.

CULTURAL CONSIDERATIONS IN PRISON CUSTODIAL CARE

Determining the extent to which cultural considerations and adjustments in the institutional environment can be made for inmates of diverse ethnic and cultural backgrounds is challenging. Many practical obstacles exist, including major economic ones. However, we discuss selected issues that may be reasonably considered from the cultural point of view, as they may significantly affect the lives of inmates.

Rooming and Living Environment

Most prisons are designed with small, simple cells, with only enough space and privacy to meet the basic, minimal requirements for living. The cells are usually built uniformly, without any individual variation. They are purposely designed in this way not only for economical reasons but also for security reasons, making it easier for a limited number of correctional officers to control a large number of inmates.

This kind of limited living environment is difficult for most ordinary people to endure. In general, life in such an environment will be particularly hard for people who like to socialize and are used to living in open spaces. From ethnic and cultural perspectives, the design causes more suffering for people who, culturally, are used to living in open areas with close social contact with others. For instance, island people in Micronesia live in thatched-roof houses with walls that can be opened up and connected to the outside in all four directions. They are used to living with a large group of people under the same roof, without being detached from others. When they come to live in a high-rise apartment in a city, they may feel so uncomfortable and unnatural that they try to tear down and remove the walls that separate the rooms, making the apartment into one large, single room. When people with this kind of background are confined to a small cell in prison, they may feel asphyxiated and hungry for space and close social contact with others. The experience will be much more difficult for them to endure than it is for inmates who are used to living in city apartments.

Even bed arrangements are extremely difficult for people of some cultural backgrounds. Because of religious beliefs or cultural custom, some people feel it is necessary to sleep with their heads facing in a certain direction. For example, Balinese people in Indonesia are accustomed to sleeping with their heads toward the north (the direction in which the holy mountain is located); Muslim people feel it is important to have their heads facing in the direction in which they believe the Holy Place, Mecca, is located; and some Asian people are very concerned with sleeping in a certain direction to meet the principle of *feng-shui* (geomancy). When those people are forced to sleep in a certain direction according to the construction of their cells, without individual choice, the experience may be quite stressful for them.

Meals

Food in prison is a potential problem for people of some ethnic groups. The meals are usually adequate from a nutritional perspective and sufficient from a caloric standpoint. However, the foods are usually prepared in a Western style, which is very different from other styles of cooking. Some people are used to eating only rice and have never eaten potatoes or other starch, whereas others have never cooked food the way it is cooked in prison. Furthermore, some people are vegetarians by habit or religious belief. They cannot eat meat, an important source of protein in prison food. Some cannot have milk or cheese, because they, biologically, lack certain enzymes to digest dairy foods. For Muslim and Jewish people, eating pork is a religious taboo. However, unless the prison system is flexible enough to make adjustments and modify food for different groups of people, those inmates who have particular preferences in food must suffer with unsuitable meals every day, in addition to not having available their usual folk foods.

Sex

Prisons are invariably unisex institutions, in which, besides many deprivations, heterosexual expression and gratification in a normal sense is extremely limited. As observed by Awofeso and Naoum (2002), this characteristic makes prison settings potentially fertile grounds for sexual aberrations. Various kinds of sexual behavior, in the form of consensual homosexuality, masturbation, prostitution, sex between prisoners and prison staff, or rape among prison inmates may take place. However, the phenomena of sexual practices in prison, although a topic of much speculation, has not generally been officially examined and managed. The ways in which inmates manage their sexual desires and expression are questions awaiting investigation and proper management.

Group Interaction

Although inmates are confined to their cells in the evening and at certain other times, time is set aside for most inmates to participate in certain activities, such as exercise, recreation, work, or, more rarely, therapeutic programs, and to interact with other inmates in a group setting. Inmates commonly tend to distinguish themselves by joining subgroups and interacting according to their particular inmate culture. For example, they may informally differentiate themselves hierarchically into subgroups according to the nature and kind of offense they committed. Those who committed murder or robbery may be considered the bravest and most manly, kidnappers or burglars are in between, and child abusers or exhibitionists may be seen as cowardly and unmanly.

Inmates also join together to form gangs, which may be based on race or culture. The interaction between individuals of different races or cultures will be colored by their gang affiliations. The prison system must carefully manage these issues because the issue of race is always potentially volatile. Dealing with problems of mistreatment or hostile relations among subgroups due to ethnic and racial differences is a complex and difficult challenge for correctional administrators and staff.

Facilities

Prisons make available various facilities for inmate recreation, exercise, or rehabilitation. However, the extent to which appropriate facilities are available for inmates of varying ethnic or cultural backgrounds deserves attention. For example, prison libraries mostly acquire books, magazines, and newspapers available in English. Very little reading material may be available in other languages, particularly the rarer ones. Inmates who cannot read English may thus have little possibility of reading in their native languages.

Rehabilitative Activities

To a limited extent, various kinds of therapeutic and rehabilitative programs may be offered to inmates. These may include individual counseling, vocational rehabilitation programs, or group therapy. On the basis of their cultural backgrounds, people may or may not be used to, or benefit from, certain therapeutic activities. For example, providing group therapy for aboriginal offenders in a Canadian forensic psychiatric facility was found to be a problematic modality not suitable for traditional aboriginal offenders and even less suitable for acculturated aboriginal offenders (Waldram & Wong, 1995).

Modifying or creating unique therapeutic and rehabilitative programs to suit inmates of various ethnic and cultural backgrounds is a difficult but potentially valuable enterprise.

CARE FOR SPECIFIC POPULATIONS

A prison operates within its own culture. Administrators and officers enforce strict rules. Intense security measures are taken to secure safety and order in the system; to avoid escapes, riots, and murders; and to ensure the safety of the inmates and the staff. Historically, brutality and unfair treatment of inmates, particularly those from certain ethnic groups, have taken place in prisons, and unfortunately may still occur to some extent in some places. Operating a prison system in a humane way for inmates of diverse ethnic and cultural backgrounds is an important social goal. Psychiatric practice for people in the general community is now expected to go beyond generally competent care and deliver special care to special populations, such as children and adolescents, the aged, women, and so forth (Tseng, 2003, pp. 353-412). This is also true in the care of inmates in closed institutional settings. We briefly touch on many special groups of inmates that need particular care.

Foreigners and new immigrants. Foreigners and new immigrants may have problems with language and differences in cultural beliefs and practices. Many will have little knowledge of and be unfamiliar with the legal system in our society. Those who come from underdeveloped or developing societies often will have less access to contact with families or friends in their home country by telephone or through other technologies. Those who originally came from autocratic societies, in which they were subject to repression by the government, will continue to be suspicious and fearful of the government and mistrustful of its agents, including their own attorneys, social workers, and others—attitudes that will require time and effort to change.

Ethnic minorities. Many minority ethnic groups face discrimination and mistreatment by the majority group, and accordingly they approach society with caution and guardedness. Native groups that have lost their lands and experienced ethnic-related trauma often harbor feelings of hatred and resentment toward the government and the majority group that they feel destroyed their culture and damaged their dignity. Extra effort is needed to establish a trusting relationship, in order to provide care for them.

Women. Although women comprise roughly half of the population, in many societies they are not treated equally to men in many circumstances. In our society, which today strongly stresses the equality of genders, the situation is much improved, but discrimination and mistreatment still occurs in public and domestic life. Biologically, women may be stronger than men in certain ways (such as having a longer life span), and have obvious physiological differences from men: menstrual cycles, the ability to bear children, and a susceptibility to certain hormonally influenced emotional disorders, such as premenstrual dysphoria or postpartum depression. Physically, women are generally less powerful than men, which can present a problem in defending themselves from aggression or violence. They may be overpowered and assaulted or raped by men.

In the prison system women require special care and attention. This care includes consideration of their biological needs and also protection from sexual attacks and abuse in prison by male correctional officers. Issues related to childbirth, breastfeeding, and access to young children should be considered as well.

Persons with different sexual orientations. Psychiatric concepts and professional attitudes have changed drastically over the past several decades toward persons with different sexual orientations. However, in the community there still exist strong biases and negative attitudes toward this population. In prison, how homosexual or lesbian inmates adjust to life in a confined setting is a question deserving more extensive study in order that better institutional care can be provided.

Adolescents and children. Children and adolescents may commit crimes and be confined to special correctional facilities established for them. Institutions need to consider various factors to accommodate this population group, particularly concerning the psychology associated with the developmental stage they are in (DePrato & Hammer, 2002). Relations with peers and with authority figures and access to close friends and family are all important issues that deserve constant consideration.

Physical handicaps, including deafness. People with physical handicaps who commit offenses and are sentenced to prison, due to limitations in their communication with other inmates, their attorneys, and correctional officers, may need special care and attention. Even though interpreters who are knowledgeable and experienced in deaf culture and sign language can be used, in reality, such personnel may be scarce, difficult to obtain, and expensive. Working with inmates who have severe problems in communication with others presents a formidable challenge.

Mentally ill inmates. Some professionals have become concerned about the trend toward "criminalization" of the mentally ill in our society. That is, instead of treating mentally disordered persons in psychiatric facilities, mental patients are charged with criminal offenses and put into prison when they commit unlawful behavior because of their disturbed mental conditions (Davis, 1992). Researchers have expressed particular concern that the criminalization of the mentally ill is partly due to racial factors (Grekin, Jemelka, & Trupin, 1994; Kaplan & Busner, 1992).

Whatever the reasons and mechanisms behind the phenomenon, a considerable number of inmates suffer from various mental illnesses (Hartwell, 2001; Jordon, Schlenger, Fairbank, & Caddell, 1996) that deserve professional attention. If an inmate has a major mental disorder, manifested as an acute and severe psychotic condition, commonly he or she will receive prompt professional attention and possibly will be transferred to an appropriate psychiatric facility or specialized unit for proper care. However, if the mental disorder is minor, such as anxiety, mild depression, obsessive-compulsive disorder, phobia, and so on, the inmate may not receive proper attention and needed psychiatric care. If the inmate is from an ethnic minority, is a foreigner and faces language difficulties, or is not used to expressing psychiatric complaints, his or her mental health problems will probably not receive needed attention. Sympton manifestation may be different from that of the majority group and the inmate's problems may worsen if not given professional attention.

Drug therapy for mental illnesses deserves special consideration regarding the inmate's ethnic or racial background. Psychiatrists have increasingly become aware that people of different ethnic groups react differently to drugs for the treatment of mental disorders, demonstrating a difference in the severity of side effects and the therapeutic doses needed. For example, persons from Asian backgrounds may require much lower doses of many medications to obtain a therapeutic effect. If given the dose recommended for Caucasians, Asian people may develop more severe side effects and may require a significant downward adjustment in dosage. Professionals should be aware of information about the effects of race or ethnicity on the metabolism of medicines when treating persons of different backgrounds (Tseng, 2003, pp. 343–352).

COUNSELING AND PSYCHOTHERAPY FOR OFFENDERS

General Issues About Counseling Offenders in Prison

Depending on the case and the situation, some offenders will be offered counseling or psychotherapy while they are in prison. Counseling for inmates in prison is rather different from counseling ordinary people on the outside at a mental health clinic in the community, for example. First, because the inmates are confined in prison when the counseling takes place, there will be less opportunity for them to apply what they have learned in counseling to actual life in the community. This is particularly true for offenders who are sentenced to prison for life without parole. The effects of counseling are expected to occur mainly at the mental level (intrapsychically), with some at the interpersonal level, involving peer inmates or officers in prison. There is little opportunity to observe the effects at the interpersonal level, with family members or others in the community. For example, for sexual offenders, there is no chance to see how they are going to adjust their psychosexual behavior with people in the outside community.

The motivation for inmates to seek counseling is often different as well. Some inmates may be motivated out of the desire to establish a favorable profile when applying for parole. Others may hope to be given psychotropic medications that will give them a high or an altered sense of reality. Some may be ordered to receive counseling because of poor adjustment to prison. There is a lack of genuine motivation to receive counseling in such situations, at least in the initial stage. Only some inmates seek counseling because they are suffering from psychological problems and looking for solutions to their emotional pain. Therefore, the starting points for counseling different inmates may be quite different. This point needs to be kept in mind by the counselor from the start in order to deal skillfully with the situation.

Besides the possible personal differences that may exist between inmates and counselors, such as age, gender, educational background, or socioeconomic status, there are usually significant differences in past personal life experiences. That is, the inmates may have participated extensively in criminal behavior, and many have grown up in an environment of people exhibiting antisocial behavior, whereas the counselors seldom have similar life experiences. There is a significant enough gap in life experiences between them that it may be difficult for the counselor to develop an empathic relationship with the inmate.

The gap between the counselor and inmates can be much wider when their ethnic and cultural backgrounds are significantly different. There may be communication problems between them due to the lack of a common language. Such counseling across cultures and knowledge.

Basic Problems and Tasks Related to Intercultural Psychotherapy

Intercultural psychotherapy refers to therapy that is delivered to patients with ethnic or cultural backgrounds that are considerably different from that of the therapist. With significant differences between the cultures of the therapist and the patient, the bidirectional interaction of cultural components is, consciously or unconsciously, heavily involved in and significantly influences the process of psychotherapy. Intercultural therapy (Hsu & Tseng, 1972; Tseng, 2003, pp. 291–309) is in contrast to intracultural therapy, which takes place between a therapist and patient with basically the same cultural backgrounds. As there is a need to transcend cultural barriers between the therapist and the patient, intercultural psychotherapy is also called transcultural psychotherapy.

Closely related to the emerging human rights movement in the United States, as well as the increased migration of non-European minority groups into European countries, was increased concern in the 1970s and 1980s with how to deliver mental health services for minorities, migrants, refugees, and foreign students.

Many technical issues have been described in the clinical practice of intercultural psychotherapy. These include examining the congruence and incongruence of cultural backgrounds between therapist and patient; communicating with patients on verbal as well as nonverbal levels; learning how racism may affect interracial counseling; working with the problem of ethnic or cultural identification with the therapist; managing cultural transference and countertransference; dealing with a therapist's cultural rigidity or cultural blindness; and providing therapy that is culture fair, matched, sensitive, relevant, or reactive (Tseng & Streltzer, 2001).

There are some basic problems generally inherent in interethnic, interracial, or intercultural counseling that the counselor must be aware of and that deserve careful management. We elaborate some of them next.

Familiarity with counseling. The first concern in the practice of intercultural psychotherapy is the matter of the patient's familiarity with psychotherapy and his or her expectations of it. This is particularly true if the client comes from a culture or subculture where psychotherapy is not a common professional practice, or if there are certain biases against it as a healing practice. In many societies, people value medically oriented service and see medical practices as effective and valuable. In contrast, many people regard "talking" therapy as nothing more than talk, which they believe will be unhelpful in solving their problems. The therapist must first explain the nature of therapy, to orient and prepare the client for it, and not assume that he or she is familiar with its procedures. This step, while generally important, is particularly crucial in situations of intercultural therapy where clients are not familiar with psychotherapy.

Communication problems. Communication between therapist and client is considered by psychotherapists to be a core element of therapy. Achieving informative, comprehensive, meaningful, and therapeutic communication is necessary for effective results. In intercultural psychotherapy there are many issues in the area of communication that need attention. If the therapist and the client do not share a common language, an interpreter is needed for communication. We have elaborated previously on the art of using an interpreter and the potential obstacles and pitfalls (see the section "Transcultural Assessments Using Interpreters: Overcoming Language Barriers" in chapter 2).

Even when the therapist and the client share a common language, caution is still needed to grasp on a cultural level the

meaning of the words expressed explicitly, subtly, or symboli-
cally. Transculturally, comprehending the subtle or symbolic
meaning of words is difficult. Meanings must be understood
in a cultural context and with cultural knowledge. From a cultural point of view, there are numerous words, phrases, or
idioms commonly used by certain cultural groups to convey
specific, but subtle, meanings. For example, if someone says,
"My house is far away," he or she may mean that you are not
welcome to visit his or her house. Someone asking you if you
have already eaten may not be an expression of concern about
whether you have had a meal or would like a meal. Instead, it
may be simply a form of social greeting, like asking, "How are
you?"

As a related matter, both clinicians and patients may use psychiatric terms in their communication, such as "depression"
and "hysterical," which deserve careful discussion and clarification of their actual meanings. Even when a patient reveals a
wish to kill him or herself, the clinician should not merely take
it literally but also form a clinical judgment about the patient,
his or her psychopathology, and his or her possible motivation
for such a revelation. In addition, it is necessary to understand
the general custom in the patient's culture of revealing a wish
to end one's life, its common implication, and the possible message that the patient wants to communicate. For example, if a
Muslim person, whose faith forbids self-killing, says that he or
she wishes he or she were dead, the clinician must interpret this
potentially suicidal idea and react to in an especially careful
manner.

Beyond the words and language used for communication,
cultural factors influence how a person communicates with others, which has an impact on the clinical setting. For example,
the Japanese tend to respond by saying, "*Hai! Hai!*" when someone speaks with them. Although *hai* in Japanese literally means
"yes," in this context saying it does not mean that the person
is saying "yes" or responding affirmatively to whatever has
been said. It simply indicates that the person is listening to
what is being said (and may or may not agree with it). The therapist needs to be aware of this to avoid any misunderstandings.

Difficulties occur in the area of nonverbal communication as
well, including facial expressions, gestures, or behavior. Even
though human beings share certain universal nonverbal communication, such as nodding their heads to indicate affirmation,

shaking their heads to express denial or disagreement, and using certain facial expressions to demonstrate emotions of pleasure and displeasure, certain nonverbal communication is culture patterned in specific ways. Without knowing this, a person's message may be missed or misunderstood.

Pattern of problem presentation. It is important that clinicians, and especially psychotherapists, recognize that there are culturally molded styles of problem presentation. A good example is that a patient may present a somatic complaint, not because he or she actually suffers from a somatic problem but simply because it is a culture-patterned behavior to present somatic problems (initially) to a physician, or even to a counselor. After proper inquiry or guidance, the patient will more easily reveal emotional problems that he or she may have. In contrast, a patient may present a psychologized complaint, such as how much he or she hates his or her father, a trauma the patient encountered in early childhood, and so on, at the first session with the therapist, as if the patient were psychologically minded and aware of his or her psychological problems. However, as the therapy goes on it becomes clear the patient learned to present such psychodynamic material from the media or from friends, without actually having insight into his or her own psychological problems.

Disclosure of private matters. In general, a therapist prefers that a client disclose as much personal information as possible, so that an in-depth understanding of the client can be achieved. However, culture may dictate how much private information a person should reveal to an outsider and what issues are considered taboo.

For instance, in Micronesia it is taboo to mention the death of an ancestor. Even a physician, as an outsider, should not ask a patient about how his or her parents or grandparents died, although physicians need to know the medical history of the family. The physician may hint to the patient that it is important to know the family's medical history, so that a proper diagnosis can be made of the patient's present illness. Nevertheless, the physician should not blatantly ask "When did your father die?" or "What was the cause of your grandmother's death?" It is culturally forbidden for the patient to reply to these questions, and the physician would be asking the patient to break the culture's taboos.

In a less serious way, people from many Asian cultures do not feel comfortable revealing certain family secrets. Revealing that a family member suffered from tuberculosis, indulged in gambling, had an extramarital affair, and so on is considered shameful. Taking proper personal and family histories and dealing with cultural resistance to information needed for case formulation become challenging matters in intercultural therapy.

The use of an interpreter. When there are language barriers between the counselor and the client, an interpreter must be used. The interpreter should be professionally trained and able to translate accurately, relevantly, and meaningfully for clinical purposes. There are three ways for an interpreter to function in a clinical situation: simple translation, cultural interpretation, or adjunct therapy (Westermeyer, 1990).

Among the numerous factors that need consideration is whether to use an interpreter from the same ethnic group as the client (in-group) or someone outside the client's ethnic group (out-group). Normally an in-group interpreter will possess more knowledge of the client's culture and greater language efficiency, which will increase the cultural accuracy of the interpretation. However, clinical experience has shown that potential problems exist in using interpreters from the same ethnic group as the client. The interpreter may explicitly or implicitly identify with a client of his or her own ethnic group. The interpreter may feel ashamed to reveal the culturally negative information about a person who shares his or her ethnicity, or the interpreter may project his or her own ethnic views and feelings in the process of interpreting. Furthermore, the client may hesitate to reveal his or her personal life to the therapist through an interpreter of the same ethnicity, with the concern, or even fear, that his or her secrets may become known to other members of the local ethnic community.

Therapist-client relationship. The therapist-client relationship usually plays a significant role in the process of counseling and therefore is often closely examined and regulated by the therapist. As clinicians know, the nature of the therapist-client relationship may vary according to the personalities, genders, and ages of the therapist and client; the nature of the psychopathology; and the process of therapy. Beyond these factors, the therapist should comprehend and manage the aspects of the therapist-client relationship that are culturally influenced. Attitudes toward and relationships with authority vary widely across cultural groups. Clients who come from backgrounds where authority tends to be autocratic will expect the therapist to be active, instructive, and responsible while the client plays a submissive role and hesitates to make any responses that may be considered disobedient. In contrast, clients who are used to relating to authority in a more democratic way will prefer a more egalitarian relationship.

The relationship between the client and therapist will be affected by the culture's view of male-female relations. A strong cultural view about the role and status of men and women, such as the man's superiority and the woman's inferiority, can become problematic if a male client is counseled by a female therapist.

Ethnic and cultural transference and countertransference deserve special attention. Ethnic or cultural transference refers to the situation in which a client develops a certain relationship, feeling, or attitude toward the therapist because of the ethnic or cultural background of the therapist. Ethnic or cultural countertransference is the reverse phenomenon, when a therapist develops a certain relationship with the client mainly because of the client's ethnic or cultural background. Ethnocultural transference may be manifested as denial of ethnicity and culture; mistrust, suspicion, and hostility; ambivalence toward the therapist; or overcompliance and friendliness. Likewise, countertransference can be shown as denying ethnocultural differences; being overly curious about the patient's ethnocultural background and developing a "clinical anthropological syndrome"; or demonstrating excessive feelings of guilt, anger, or ambivalence toward the patient (Comas-Díaz & Jacobsen, 1991).

Therapeutic interpretation and advice. A therapist needs to know how to provide interpretation or advice at the proper time in a suitable way. This is a matter of clinical judgment, depending on the therapeutic process and numerous other factors, including the patient's psychopathological condition, ego strength, readiness for explanation, level of psychological sophistication, and so on. Intercultural psychotherapy needs to consider further how to make interpretations that are culturally suitable, proper, meaningful, and effective. The best language and concepts are those familiar to the client, so that the client can receive the explanations with ease and find them meaningful.

Contemporary Western psychotherapists are sometimes trained not to offer any advice to their patients, particularly regarding major life matters, such as decisions about adoption, separation, divorce, or remarriage. This approach is based on the belief that clients should be respected for making their own decisions, which reflects a cultural emphasis on basic human rights and a professional orientation rooted in the psychoanalytic approach. However, no matter how much the therapist pretends he or she is not making any decisions for the client, the client is always looking for clues given by the therapist and the therapist does send messages to the client regarding choices that the client should make, with or without knowing that he or she is doing so through verbal or nonverbal communication.

Many clients seek guidance from counselors for dilemmas that they encounter in their daily lives. Common psychological problems encountered by clients include parental authority; the proper role of a wife; whether to act for the sake of oneself or for one's family; issues surrounding sexual relations, an abortion, or an extramarital affair; or how to make the proper choice regarding separation, divorce, remarriage, or continuing in the present unhappy marriage. The choices are subject to personal as well as cultural considerations. Offering advice on these daily life matters is a challenge for the therapist, one that cannot be avoided in intercultural psychotherapy. A culturally relevant therapist should actively explore the implications of each choice available to the client and review the implications of different decisions the client may make, from the different levels of personal self, the family, the group, and social and cultural perspectives.

Special Cultural Considerations in Counseling for Offenders

As we discussed previously, counseling offenders is different from ordinary counseling in the community because of the nature of the client, the circumstances of counseling, and the goals of counseling. Therefore, some special considerations are necessary. Following are some considerations, particularly from a cultural perspective.

Confidentiality. In prison revealing private matters and handling confidentiality are very delicate, but important, issues. Therapists should be aware that confidentiality is dealt with differently in different cultures. If, in the client's original social setting, the rights of the individual are more or less emphasized and personal boundaries are relatively well established, confidentiality can be observed and maintained in the clinical situation. However, in a society where the rights of group (or family) is emphasized more than are rights of the individual, and the boundaries between individual members are not especially stressed, the therapist may need to make appropriate adjustments. For example, a conversation with an adolescent child is expected to be shared with his or her parents in a society where parents are in a strong position of authority. If a therapist refuses to share information about adolescent children with the parents, under the concept of confidentially as conceived by the therapist according to the professional culture, the parents may interpret the therapist's behavior as offending parental authority. A similar situation may occur in a society where a husband's status is superior to his wife's. The husband may become angry if he finds that the therapist is withholding information about his wife. Thus, confidentiality needs to be handled sensitively and with due consideration of the client's cultural background, or it may cause unexpected trouble.

In the prison setting confidentially may be rather limited. If an inmate reveals certain information to the counselor, such as an intention to escape, to harm other inmates, to kill him- or herself, and so on, the counselor must reveal the information to the appropriate persons involved. If the inmate reveals certain secrets about the crime that he or she committed, the counselor has to make a relevant judgment regarding how to deal with the information. The rules dealing with confidentiality need to be explored, discussed, and clarified from the very beginning, before counseling takes place. This is particularly important when the client has a different understanding about confidentiality because of his or her cultural background.

Impact of racism on counseling. The potentially negative impact on psychotherapy of race-related issues has attracted a great deal of attention in our society. Negative, or even hostile, relations that preexist between the two racial groups concerned will likely be an issue for therapy. For example, individual contact between a White therapist and a Black client may be influenced by the overall relationship between Blacks and Whites in the society, and these elements may severely affect the therapeutic relationship. The Black client may have difficulty trusting the White therapist, while the therapist may have difficulty handling the Black client's anger and hatred toward Whites in general, which may be projected onto the therapist.

The psychotherapy of an Arab client by a Jewish therapist is another example of how religious and racial factors may intrude on interracial psychotherapy and interfere with the therapist-patient relationship. Being open with patients at an early stage of therapy about the possible effects of race and ethnic differences on therapy is encouraged, and working on a suitable therapeutic relationship is suggested to minimize the ill effects that are associated with negative interracial relations. The impact of racism on counseling is more prominent in the prison setting, and it needs a special effort to be dealt with in the process of counseling.

Goals of counseling. The final issue that needs attention in counseling for inmates concerns the ultimate goals of therapy. The definition of a normal, healthy, or mature person is subject to cultural influence. The route that should be taken to resolve problems and the coping mechanisms that should be used are subject to cultural determination. The final goals of counseling for inmates who are going to stay in prison for many years or even the rest of their lives are not only clinical questions but also philosophical challenges. What counseling can offer and what inmates can expect from counseling when they are going to face the death penalty or life in prison without parole are all important questions to be answered.

Cultural and religious backgrounds will influence a person's philosophical views and attitudes toward life. Some believe that life is for achievement, enjoyment, and success, whereas others view life as suffering, enduring, and accepting. Using a client's philosophical views to work on their ultimate goals in life is a challenge for counseling in general, and particularly for counseling inmates who are confined in prison for many years.

Clinical competence is clearly a fundamental requirement for a therapist. This competence includes being sensitive, caring, equipped with clinical knowledge and theories of human behavior, and experienced in clinical work. To be successful in conducting culturally relevant clinical work, particularly for intercultural psychotherapy, the therapist may need additional qualities, such as cultural sensitivity, knowledge, empathy, the ability to establish proper interaction and relations between the therapist and patient, and the ability to offer relevant cultural guidance to the patient (Tseng, 2003, pp. 219–225). Providing counseling for inmates in prison brings another requirement: being fully aware of the reality of the setting, the circumstances associated with the prison system, and the goals that can be expected and accomplished in the correctional system.

REFERENCES

American Psychiatric Association. (2000). *Psychiatric services in jails and prisons: A task force report of the American Psychiatric Association.* Washington, DC.

Awofeso, N., & Naoum, R. (2002). Sex in prisons: A management guide. *Australian Health Review, 25*(4), 149–158.

Comas-Díaz, L., & Jacobsen, F. M. (1991). Ethnocultural transference and countertransference in the therapeutic dyad. *American Journal of Orthopsychiatry, 61*, 392–402.

Davis, S. (1992). Assessing the "criminalization" of the mental ill in Canada. *Canadian Journal of Psychiatry, 37*, 532–538.

DePrato, D. K., & Hammer, J. H. (2002). Assessment and treatment of juvenile offenders. In D. H. Shetky & E. P. Benedek (Eds.), *Principles and practice of child and adolescent forensic psychiatry* (pp. 267–278). Washington, DC: American Psychiatric Publishing.

Grekin, P. M., Jemelka, R., & Trupin, E. W. (1994). Racial differences in the criminalization of the mentally ill. *Bulletin of American Academy of Psychiatry and the Law, 22*(3), 411–420.

Hartwell, S. (2001). An examination of racial differences among mentally ill offenders in Massachusetts. *Psychiatric Services, 52*(2), 234–236.

Hsu, J., & Tseng, W. S. (1972). Intercultural psychotherapy. *Archives of General Psychiatry, 27*, 700–705.

Jordon, B. K., Schlenger, W. E., Fairbank, J. A., & Caddell, J. M. (1996). Prevalence of psychiatric disorders among incarcerated women. II: Convicted felons entering prison. *Archives of General Psychiatry, 53*(6), 513–519.

Kaplan, S. L., & Busner, J. (1992). A note on racial bias in the admission of children and adolescents to state mental health facilities versus correctional facilities in New York. *American Journal of Psychiatry, 149*(6), 768–772.

Tseng, W. S. (2003). *Clinican's guide to cultural psychiatry.* San Diego, CA: Academic Press.

Tseng, W. S., & Streltzer, J. (Eds.). (2001). *Culture and psychotherapy: A guide to clinical practice.* Washington, DC: American Psychiatric Press.

Waldram, J. B., & Wong, S. (1995). Group therapy of aboriginal offenders in a Canadian forensic psychiatric facility. *American Indian Alaska Native Mental Health Research, 6*(2), 34–56.

Westermeyer, J. (1990). Working with an interpreter in psychiatric assessment and treatment. *Journal of Nervous and Mental Disease, 178*, 745–749.

9

Cultural Analysis of Forensic Psychiatric Cases

Following on the elaboration of cultural considerations in various stages of the legal process, and in various types of forensic psychiatric assessments (see chapter 6), we present in this chapter case materials for discussion and illustration regarding how cultural issues may be incorporated when working on forensic cases. We selected illustrative cases, many of them landmark cases in mental health law, for examination from a cultural perspective. After discussing these cases we comment on the cultural aspects of cases in which defendants attempted to use a cultural defense in court. Finally, we present forensic cases that have involved the collaboration of a cultural psychiatrist or cultural expert. The latter group of cases illustrates how cultural issues have been played out within the legal process and demonstrates how suitable cultural experts can provide useful information. In discussing the cases selected in this chapter, we have not attempted to review or reexamine them with regard to their legal aspects but rather have used them as a fabric to analyze and elaborate how to deal with and understand the cultural information they contain. Even though detailed information about these cases is already available in various legal documents, in this chapter we minimized the personal information to the extent possible out of respect for confidentiality.

CULTURAL EXAMINATION OF SELECTED LANDMARK CASES

INDIAN MAN KILLS HIS "UNFAITHFUL" AMERICAN GIRLFRIEND: A CASE OF CULTURAL CLASH AND CONFUSION

Case Material (Tarasoff v. Regents, 1976)

Mr. Poddar, a graduate student from India who was studying at the University of California, Berkeley, began to date a Caucasian student, Ms. Tarasoff. Mr. Poddar was completely unfamiliar with the nature of male-female relationships in American culture and had never had a date before, even when he lived in India. He kissed Ms. Tarasoff a few times and thus felt he had a "special relationship" with her, believing that she would become his wife in the future. He felt betrayed when Ms. Tarasoff later flaunted her relationships with other men.

Depressed, he went to see a psychologist at the University Mental Health Service, where he revealed his intention to get a gun and shoot Ms. Tarasoff. The psychologist sent the campus police a letter requesting that they take Mr. Poddar to a psychiatric hospital. The campus police interviewed Mr. Poddar, but he convinced them that he was not dangerous. The campus police then released him, with his promise that he would stay away from Ms. Tarasoff.

Mr. Poddar moved in with Ms. Tarasoff's brother over the summer, while Ms. Tarasoff was visiting her aunt in Brazil. When Ms. Tarasoff returned, Mr. Poddar, believing that she had been unfaithful to him while she was in Brazil, stalked her and stabbed her to death.

Further Information (Blum, 1986)

Mr. Poddar was a 23-year-old Hindu youth who was born a member of the "untouchable" caste in India, an outcaste group whose members are not permitted to marry persons of other, higher caste groups. Like most unmarried Indian men his age, Mr. Poddar was an innocent when it came to women. Not only did he come from a culture that enforced strict separation between the sexes, he also had grown up in an all-boy household. There had been only two times in his youth when he had had private conversations with girls. Because of his intelligence, he was able to pursue academic studies at one of the top universities in the United States, majoring in architectural engineering.

Ms. Tarasoff was a 19-year-old Caucasian freshman. To her dismay, she was still living at home with her parents. Most of her girlfriends had their own apartments, but her father was old-fashioned and refused to even consider letting her move out. Her father accused her of chasing after anything in pants, but in reality she was shy and naive. Awkward around boys, she always assumed they would not like her.

Mr. Poddar was attracted to Ms. Tarasoff, whom he encountered accidentally one day when they were skating, and he invited her out to see a movie. Ms. Tarasoff never allowed Mr. Poddar to accompany her home or to meet her parents, and she always suggested they meet someplace else, such as in front of a theater. Mr. Poddar failed to pick up the subtle message this conveyed, probably because of his cultural ignorance.

Mr. Poddar fell madly in love with Ms. Tarasoff, but he was annoyed that she did not hesitate to let him know that there were other men interested in her. Mr. Poddar did not understand that, in the United States girls like to be popular with boys, and that, before having a fixed relationship with a man, it was culturally permissible to meet and go out with many boys. According to his Indian cultural beliefs, Mr. Poddar thought that a girl should be faithful to one man, once they started going out together.

Their relationship was up and down, until one day Ms. Tarasoff allowed Mr. Poddar to kiss her. He interpreted this as an indication that she would marry him, because in India if a woman allowed a man to become physically intimate with her this would be the case. With the conviction that Ms. Tarasoff would wed him in the future, he gave her a fine silk sari as a gift, which in India was considered a special gift from a groom-to-be to a bride-to-be. Ms. Tarasoff was delighted with the gift, but she never considered that it might have a special cultural implication. Ms. Tarasoff knew that the Taj Mahal and the *Kama Sutra* were Indian, but she knew little else about Indian culture.

Cultural Discussion and Comment

This case clearly demonstrates a severe gap in cultural knowledge and understanding between two people. Mr. Poddar viewed Ms. Tarasoff's actions from the perspective of his own culture, without learning the norms of the host society. He assumed that if a woman allowed a man to kiss her, she indicated a promise to become betrothed to him. Mr. Poddar responded appropriately according to his own culture and gave a sari to Ms. Tarasoff, believing that it confirmed their future marriage but without properly explaining the significance of the special gift to her. Ms. Tarasoff, without knowing or trying to find out the meaning of this particular gift, received it as if it was simply an ordinary gift. In other words both of them related to the other based entirely on their own cultures, without any awareness that a major cultural gap existed between them. The woman continued to openly meet with other men, flaunting her relationships, and Mr. Poddar became jealous and furious enough to eventually murder her.

At the individual level, it is not clear to what extent of Mr. Poddar's ethnic background, as a member of the untouchable caste in India, made him susceptible to feelings of inferiority and resentfulness in his interpersonal relationships, particularly when he was mistreated or rejected. Whether he was suffering from schizophrenic paranoia, as diagnosed by his therapist, or merely from an obsession with Ms. Tarasoff remains a clinical question. It is equally unclear how Ms. Tarasoff's own personality and family background, such as having an extremely conservative, strict father, might have influenced her relations with men: being interested in a man with a foreign background of a different race, and dating many men, unable or unwilling to devote herself to one. However, such personal factors are not of concern here, because they go beyond cultural issues.

It is important to point out that in India, as in many cultures in the world, if a woman is found to be unfaithful to her future husband, he has the right to become extremely angry and even physically punish her. However, there is no custom in India that grants a future husband the right to murder his unfaithful future wife. If this happened, he would be considered guilty of criminal behavior and most likely would be sentenced to prison (I. Ahmed, personal communication, 2003).

Furthermore, as we noted previously, in India a person from the untouchable caste is not permitted to marry someone from another caste. This is still true today; if a man tries to marry into a higher caste, not only he but also his family may be subject to severe punishment. Several years ago, a local newspaper reported an incident that occurred in a remote rural area of India. A young man from a lower caste tried to elope with a girl from an upper caste. When the girl's father found out, he became very angry, went to the young man's house, and raped the young man's mother in the street as punishment for the young man's misbehavior, while the villagers watched. Mr. Poddar, falling in love with and believing that he was going to marry an American Caucasian girl, was breaking his own country's taboo against crossing caste boundaries.

Legal Outcome (Blum, 1986, pp. 303–304; Tarasoff v. Regents, 1976)

Mr. Poddar was charged with first-degree murder, because he had brought a gun with him intending to kill Ms. Tarasoff. He employed a psychiatric defense. During his trial extensive testimony was introduced in support of the contention that, because of his cultural background, he had been tormented by the situation to the point of becoming so mentally ill that he had suffered diminished capacity and could not have harbored malice aforethought at the time of the killing. He was found guilty of second-degree murder and was sentenced to 5 years to life in prison. Mr. Poddar appealed, and 4 years later the California Supreme Court overturned his conviction on the grounds that the trial judge had not given adequate instructions to the jury about the meaning of diminished capacity. A new trial was ordered. The trial judge agreed to a compromise: Mr. Poddar's release in return for his deportation to India.

Follow-Up and Final Comments

Mr. Poddar returned to India, where his father arranged a marriage for him. Two years later, he received a scholarship to resume his study of naval architecture at a prestigious institute in Germany. It was last heard that he was happily married and leading a normal life with his wife and daughter.

This case gave rise to the legal concept of the duty to protect third parties from a dangerous patient. The first decision in this case, handed down in 1974, is known as the *Tarasoff I* decision. It was later modified in 1976 in a second decision, known as *Tarasoff II* (American Academy of Psychiatry and the Law, 2003).

This case became a landmark case in the history of American mental health law, but, from a cultural point of view, it provides an example of how a cultural gap in understanding between individuals can lead to tragedy. Most important, it illustrates that ethnic or cultural excuses can be used in court and be potentially misused, resulting in what many would consider an unfair legal outcome.

Case Information Available (Application of the President and Directors of Georgetown College, 1964)

Mrs. Jones, a 25-year-old mother of a young child, had acute gastrointestinal bleeding. It was estimated that she had lost about two thirds of her total blood volume. The surgeon recommended an operation for her ulcer but felt it would be too risky to perform surgery without giving her a blood transfusion. However, because the patient and her husband were Jehovah's Witnesses, they refused to consent to a blood transfusion.

When death was imminent, the hospital staff consulted their attorney, who applied to the district court for a court order permitting a transfusion. The district court judge refused to grant the petition. The petition was then brought to the appellate court for a single justice ruling aimed at setting aside the lower court's ruling. The presiding judge, Judge Wright, came to the hospital and spoke to Mrs. Jones's husband, who refused to permit the transfusion on religious grounds. Judge Wright was able to get the husband to admit that if a transfusion were judicially ordered, it would not be the husband's responsibility. The husband gave permission for Judge Wright to talk to the patient.

In his interview, when the judge urged Mrs. Jones to consent to the transfusion, she only said, "Against my will." The judge asked her whether she would oppose a transfusion if he ordered one; she responded that it would then not be her responsibility. After deciding that the patient was not competent to decide the issue, the judge ordered the transfusion. The patient recovered after the operation.

Cultural Discussion

The interesting point about this case is that the judge took action and visited the patient's husband as well as the patient to investigate the situation and determine the nature of their beliefs and attitudes about refusing blood transfusions. Instead of trying to reason with them or persuade them to change their minds, from a psychological perspective, the judge dealt with the situation through legal means.

The judge discovered that if the legal system took the responsibility for ordering a transfusion, thereby taking away responsibility from the patient and her spouse, they would not oppose it. On the basis of these findings, the judge successfully handled the problem. This case illustrates that the judge was culturally oriented and, at the same time, wise enough to know how to deal with the patient and her husband by shifting the locus of responsibility. His actions saved the woman's life, helping the hospital to accomplish its medical mission without contravening the moral standards of the patient and her husband. If the judge had tried to change the minds of the couple, hoping for a cultural change within a limited time frame, his attempts would most likely have ended in failure.

Actual Legal Outcome

After the operation the patient recovered and left the hospital. She and her husband apparently did not find the judge's order to be entirely satisfactory, and they filed an appeal for an en banc (whole bench instead of a single justice) rehearing (Application of President and Directors of Georgetown College, 1964). Perhaps the petitioners had changed their minds about the transfusion, or perhaps the appellate judge was mistaken in his assessment. In any event, the appeal was denied.

MORMON POLYGAMIST WHO MARRIES HIS UNDERAGE NIECE:
A CASE OF INCEST?

Case Information Available (Religion News Blog, 2003)

Mr. David Ortell Kingston was a polygamist and member of the Church of Jesus Christ of Latter-Day Saints, one of Utah's most secretive polygamous sects. The sect is believed to have about 1,000 members who practice polygamy, including the marriage of half-sisters, first cousins, nieces, and aunts, as a part of their religious beliefs. Mr. Kingston, following the church's religious customs, married his brother's 16-year-old daughter as his 15th wife. His brother and niece also belonged to this group. According to Mr. Kingston, the two were wed in a spiritual ceremony only after the girl and her entire family agreed to it. He was subsequently arrested and charged with committing incest with his niece, although he denied having had sex with her. His niece testified that she was forced to become his 15th wife.

Actual Legal Outcome

In 1999 Mr. Kingston was convicted of third-degree felony incest and unlawful sexual contact with a minor and was sentenced to two consecutive prison terms of up to 5 years. After serving 4 years of a potential 10-year sentence the Board of Pardons and Parole for the State of Utah opted to terminate his sentence and released him in 2003. Because he was released from prison without parole, the state has no responsibility to follow up on him.

Cultural Comments

Polygamy (one man having more than one wife) is a practice with deep historical roots that is still observed among various societies, including some Muslim countries and some societies in Africa. Most contemporary societies legally proscribe this marital arrangement. In our society monogamy has long been the only acceptable arrangement, although small groups of people, many of them followers of branch sects of the Church of Jesus Christ of Latter-Day Saints (Mormons), still practice polygamy. State law, and the main branch of the Mormon Church, have banned polygamy since 1890, yet an estimated 20,000 to 30,000 polygamists still reside in Utah (Yotnotisian, 2003). The state has long been tolerant of polygamy, although in this case they were willing to prosecute incest.

Polygamist sects often are ruled over by authoritarian prophets who essentially speak for God. Plural marriage is interpreted as the way to heaven and failure to submit to such practices potentially places that person in outer darkness for eternity (Ross, 2003). The religious leader often commands young girls to marry an older man who could be her father's age. Thus, polygamist practices are founded on religious belief and custom.

Mr. Kingston's case is exceptional in that, after taking more than a dozen wives without encountering any legal problems, his 15th wife was an underage niece. He claimed in court that he did not have sexual relations with his young niece although she was his wife. Later, before the board of parole, he admitted that he did have sex with her. Surprising to many people was that the sentence was terminated so early, after only 4 years, and with no parole. Some have speculated this may be because of the fact that Mr. Kingston's brother is the leader of the church, which is also a business empire with assets and influence.

Recent news reports indicate that legislation under consideration in Utah would make marrying a second wife who is a minor a second-degree felony, with a possible 15-year prison term (Ross, 2003). This action suggests that the state is trying to actively deal with the issue of polygamy, but the results remain to be seen.

Both this case and the preceding case ("A Jehovah's Witness Who Refused Needed Blood Transfusions for an Operation") illustrate that culture-related legal problems exist not only for ethnic immigrants or minorities but also among the majority. Religion-related subcultural differences demonstrate some of the variations of cultural beliefs that exist in the majority society (of Caucasian background) that require an understanding of the relationship between culture and the law.

TREATING A PSYCHOTIC DEFENDANT IN ORDER TO EXECUTE HIM: A REFLECTION OF THE SPIRIT AND CULTURE OF THE LAW

Legal Information Relating to the Case (State v. Perry, 1992)

Mr. Perry was convicted of murdering his mother, father, nephew, and two cousins with firearms in 1983 and was sentenced to death. At the age of 16 years, his mental condition was diagnosed as schizophrenia. Whenever his mental condition deteriorated, he was brought by his parents to see a psychiatrist, and he was committed to psychiatric hospitals several times.

Medical experts reported that while awaiting execution, "Perry suffered from an incurable schizoaffective disorder that caused his days to be a series of hallucinations, delusions, disordered thinking, incoherent speech, and manic behavior." Symptoms could be diminished with antipsychotic drugs. The experts said that Mr. Perry could be made competent for execution only while he was being maintained on antipsychotic medication.

The trial court found Mr. Perry to be incompetent to be executed, but it ordered the medical staff of the Louisiana Department of Corrections to administer medication forcibly to make him competent to be executed.

On appeal, the U.S. Supreme Court remanded the case back to the trial court for reconsideration. After considering the Supreme Court's remand, the trial court reinstated its forcible medication order. The Louisiana Supreme Court issued a stay order to prevent forcible medication until it reviewed the case. The Louisiana Supreme Court affirmed the trial court's determination that Perry was not competent for execution without the administration of antipsychotic drugs. However, the trial court's order requiring the state to medicate Perry against his will was reversed. The court ruled that the state could apply to the Louisiana Supreme Court for a modification of the stay of execution if Perry ever regained his sanity, without antipsychotic drugs.

Cultural Discussion

We present this case for discussion not, primarily, because of the specific facts of the case itself but rather to comment on the legal decision and the debates that have occurred subsequently surrounding the case, particularly relating to the order to involuntarily medicate a psychotic patient in order for him to regain his mental competency so that he could be executed. Clearly, forcibly treating a psychiatric patient with medication to help him become sane enough to face his own execution is discordant with the goals and ethics of medicine, as the World Psychiatric Association in its Declaration of Madrid (World Psychiatric Association, 2002) and among other groups around the world, have found. However, the court issued the order based solely on the spirit of U.S. law, which asserts that a person receiving legal punishment should be consciously aware of it and be able to recognize why he or she is being punished.

Often, it takes an outsider to see inconsistencies in our practices. This is particularly true regarding cultural patterns. If we asked people from a variety of other cultures whether it made sense to them to treat a person in order to kill him or her, it is likely that many of them would say no. They would probably look puzzled and ask what the purpose would be. This case stimulates us to realize how even a complex, highly evolved legal system such as ours can be trapped in a cultural system of beliefs that may not make sense when viewed from other perspectives.

ANALYSIS OF CASES THAT USED A CULTURAL DEFENSE

Japanese American Mother Drowns Her Two Children

Case Information Available (People v. Kimura, 1985; modified from Magnarella, 1991; Woo, 1989)

Mrs. Kimura, a Japanese American woman in her 30s who was a wife and the mother of two children, waded into the sea on a California beach one day with her 4-year-old son and 6-month-old daughter with the intention of committing parent-child suicide (*oyako-shinju* in Japanese). This occurred several days after she learned that her Japanese American husband had been secretly keeping a mistress for many years. She reacted to this with emotional turmoil, and she thought of returning to Japan with her two children. She called her sister in Japan, informing her of her plan to return to Japan and stay at an expensive hotel. Her sister sensed something strange and informed their mother, who prepared to rush to California to see what was happening to her daughter. Mrs. Kimura actually visited an airline office to seek a return ticket to Japan, but she cancelled her plans when she learned that the travel expenses would exceed the limit on her charge card. Subsequently, Mrs. Kimura took a long bus ride to the beach with her two children. She pushed the children into the water and they drowned. She then tried to drown herself, but she was rescued by passersby.

Actual Legal Outcome

Mrs. Kimura was arrested, and the prosecutor charged her with the first-degree murder of her two children. Interestingly enough, on hearing the news the local Japanese American community reacted very strongly. Thousands of people signed a petition requesting the court to reduce the charge, emphasizing that parent-child suicide was a Japanese cultural behavior. They claimed it was "the root of her Japanese culture" that directed her to act and that her behavior should be judged with reference to a Japanese standard, which provides more sympathetic treatment.

Six psychiatrists, including three board-certified forensic psychiatrists, were asked to examine Mrs. Kimura. Among them, three concurred that Mrs. Kimura was legally suffering from temporary insanity at the time of the drowning. One of the psychiatrists diagnosed a "brief reactive psychosis." As a result of this strongly supportive psychiatric testimony and the community's reaction, the charge of double homicide was reduced through plea bargaining to voluntary manslaughter. Finally, the defendant was sentenced to 1 year in custody, which was satisfied by the time she had already served, and 5 years probation. Psychiatric counseling also was advised.

Cultural Comments

Family suicide and parent-child suicide in Japan. Japanese psychiatrists (Ohara, 1963; Yoshimatsu, 1992) and cultural psychiatrists (Tseng, 2001, pp. 387-388) pointed out not only that suicide is prevalent in Japan but also that various types of suicide occur that are recognized by specific terminology. For instance, *ika-shinju* (family suicide) means both parents commit suicide together with their children, whereas *oyako-shinju* (parent-child suicide) refers to one parent committing suicide after killing his or her child (or children) first. As pointed out by Ohara (1963) there are various ways in which the parents and children may die together, such as driving a car with everyone inside into the sea from a cliff or having all family members take poison together. In most cases the parents kill their children first and then commit suicide. Therefore, more strictly speaking, it is a combination of child murder followed by parental suicide.

Whether it is family suicide or parent-child suicide, several motives may underlie this great tragedy. In Japanese culture death is viewed as one way to resolve problems in life. If people are willing to take their own life, all the debts or problems that they leave behind will be resolved—their responsibility is carried no further. Furthermore, it is a cultural belief that "blood is thicker than water." It is assumed that no one will care for the children when they become orphans after their parents commit suicide. Family suicide thus occurs in a society that greatly values the ties between parents and their own children; it is believed that it is better to die together as a family than to leave behind a member of a broken family. Sometimes parent-child suicides occur out of revenge against the other parent (mostly out of anger toward an unfaithful partner), but recently it has been reported to happen when a parent suffers from some kind of mental or emotional problem.

Legally, family suicide has been forbidden in Japan for more than a century, since the end of the Meiji era, but the practice is still observed. It has been estimated that, nationwide, about 70 to 100 episodes of family suicide are reported in the news media yearly. Japanese society reacts to family suicide or parent-child suicide with sympathy rather than condemnation. Clearly, this form of suicide is closely related to key cultural beliefs and attitudes. In a sense it could be considered a culture-related, specific phenomenon based on culturally patterned stress-coping reactions. However, most important, parents in Japan who attempt to murder or murder their children, if they survive themselves, will receive legal punishment.

Legal decision in a Japanese case. For the sake of comparison, we present information about the sentence given in an actual parent-child suicide case that occurred in Japan (Heisei 14, 2002; provided by Keisuke Ebata, personal communication, 2003) that has been translated from the original Japanese.

The offense. Mrs. Yamamoto (a pseudonym), age 30, was divorced and had a daughter. After the divorce, and without financial support from her ex-husband, Mrs. Yamamoto suffered from monetary difficulties and became pessimistic about the future. She attempted parent-child suicide by strangling her 7-year-old daughter while she slept. She then attempted to kill herself, but she failed. She was arrested and prosecuted for murdering her daughter.

Sentence. Five years of "labor work" in prison.

Considerations of the judge in passing sentence. Even though the defendant had parents and an elder sister, from whom she could potentially have sought help, she chose to commit parent-child suicide to resolve her difficulties. Culturally, her strangling her young, defenseless daughter and being able to witness her daughter's suffering was considered cruel, criminal, and irresponsible. The victim was a first-grade student who was deprived of her potential future by the most trusted person in her life. The mother's behavior was extremely unfortunate. Therefore, she deserved to be found severely culpable.

Despite the potential help available from her immediate family, the defendant's pride made her want to cope with her difficult situation alone. Not wanting to leave her beloved daughter behind in the world by herself, she committed child homicide before trying to kill herself. Thus, what she did was not merely an act of attempted suicide; it was the result of not being able to face the hardships in her life.

Furthermore, there was no sign in the past that she had, in any way, abused her daughter. The defendant had no history of antisocial, violent, or impulsive behavior. She showed deep regret for what she had done. It was considered that a severe sentence would be more meaningful to her and would help her repair her guilty mind.

This case illustrates that in Japan, when a parent who intends parent-child suicide is charged with homicide, even though some reduction in sentence for culpability is usually considered, the punishment is still more severe (5 years of labor in prison) than the case sentenced in our society for Mrs. Kimura (1 year in custody and 5 years probation). In our society a judge gave a Japanese woman who killed her children a rather liberal sentence, on the basis of cultural considerations and temporary insanity.

Problems arising from translation. This case illustrates another issue: the problem of translating foreign languages. Several cultural and legal issues related to language were encountered and debated during the course of the legal action in this case. Even though the defendant had been living in the United States for 14 years, she had a limited knowledge of English. Legal complications occurred because of problems with language. For example, the defense attorney argued that the confession obtained by the police officer at the time of arrest was improperly obtained, because there had been no appropriate translation informing the defendant of her Miranda rights. During the court hearing, before an audience packed with Japanese Americans, the defense strongly objected that the Japanese-English translation was not properly performed by the interpreters, who were Japanese-speaking Korean interpreters for the prosecution and the defense.

For example, the English terms for being "crazy," "insane," "mentally ill," or "psychotic" have different implications depending on the context in which they are used. Similarly, the equivalent Japanese words have different connotations depending on the context. Without properly explaining the context, the word may be misused and wrongly interpreted during the translation process. Furthermore, a word in one language is not necessarily equivalent to a similar word in another language, even when it is properly translated. For instance, the word *kill* has different connotations even in the same language. For example, it can mean to murder someone (with premeditated intention and planning) or to accidentally injure someone, resulting in death. However, those meanings are associated with quite different legal implications and require very careful translation and explanation, a challenge that the court must face, particularly in dealing with foreigners who do not share our language.

CHINESE AMERICAN HUSBAND KILLS HIS UNFAITHFUL WIFE

Case Information Available (People v. Chen, 1989; based and modified from Volpp, 1994; Woo, 1989)

In 1987 Mr. Chen, a 49-year-old immigrant from China, used a claw hammer to smash the skull of his 40-year-old wife, believing her to have been unfaithful to him.

His personal history revealed that Mr. Chen was born in China, worked as a farmer after he left school, and married his wife, who was 9 years younger than he was, in an arranged marriage in 1963. They had three children. It also was discovered that in 1968, when Mr. Chen was 30 years old and still living in China, he believed that he heard voices around him, and local Chinese doctors told him then that there was something wrong with his mind.

In 1986, at age 48, Mr. Chen migrated with his wife and three children from China to the United States. His oldest child was already 18 years old and the youngest was 12. Initially, Mr. Chen found a job as a dishwasher in Maryland, while Mrs. Chen and their three children stayed in New York. Mr. Chen occasionally returned to New York to visit his family, but during one visit, his wife, according to Mr. Chen, refused to have sex with him and became abusive to him. Mr. Chen became suspicious that she was having an affair with another man. He returned to Maryland, burdened with the stress of his wife's assumed infidelity. He developed difficulties in sleeping, suffered from heart palpitations, and began to hear the voice of his wife's unidentified lover planning to hurt him.

Finally, in 1987 Mr. Chen moved to New York to join his family. One evening several months later, he rushed into his wife's bedroom and grabbed her breasts and vaginal area. To him, his wife's private areas seemed more developed, which he "took as a sign" that she was having affairs. The next day he confronted her and said he wanted to have sex. He reported that she said, "I won't let you hold me, because I have other guys who will do this." His head felt dizzy, and he pressed her down and asked her for how long this had been going on. She responded, "For three months." Mr. Chen, feeling confused and dizzy, picked up a claw hammer and hit his wife repeatedly on the head. He then passed out.

Actual Legal Outcome

The prosecutor charged Mr. Chen with murder. After spending a year and a half in jail, he faced a nonjury trial. At trial, the defense attorney argued that cultural pressure had provoked Mr. Chen into a state of diminished mental capacity, rendering him incapable of forming the requisite intent for premeditated murder. The attorney provided a cultural defense, asking an anthropologist to serve as a cultural expert to testify for the defendant. The American anthropolgist explained that in traditional Chinese culture a wife's adultery evidences her husband's weak character. He testified that it would not be unusual for a normal Chinese husband to react very violently in such a situation. He explained that under such conditions divorce would cast great shame on his ancestors and make him undesirable to other women. The expert maintained that although adultery rarely results in a wife's homicide, it does make a Chinese man prone to violence.

The judge, listening to the cultural defense, concluded that traditional Chinese values about adultery and loss of manhood drove Mr. Chen to kill his wife. The judge found Mr. Chen guilty of the lesser crime of second-degree manslaughter, which carried a maximum sentence of 5 to 15 years in prison and a minimum sentence of probation. Some observers were surprised when the judge sentenced Mr. Chen to 5 years probation.

Cultural Discussion and Clinical Comments

Cultural view of wife's infidelity and husband's usual reaction. Several things need first to be clarified from the perspective of Chinese culture. Traditionally, marriage is considered a lifetime contract that is not to be broken. Certain circumstances, such as that in which a husband has another woman besides his wife, although not desirable, are relatively tolerated by the family, particularly if the husband is affluent or in a powerful position.

In contrast, it is absolutely not permitted for a wife to have affairs with other men. For a woman to do so is considered unvirtuous behavior. The husband whose wife has another man is considered by others to be very shamed. Therefore, the expert was correct that it was highly stressful for a Chinese man to discover that his wife was unfaithful to him and that many husbands could potentially become violent and physically abusive toward their wives. However, no husband is allowed to murder his wife, even when he is in such a furious state. It has been considered a severely criminal act in the past as well as in the present. Mr. Chen committed a major offense judged by Chinese standards, and he would have received a severe sentence if he committed the crime in China. According to the experiences of Chinese forensic psychiatrists, such an offense would result in a prison sentence of perhaps 10 years (Li Congpei & Fang Ming-zhao, personal communication, 2003). Chinese people would be very surprised that an American judge gave such a remarkably light sentence to Mr. Chen.

Misrepresentation and overgeneralization by experts? Another surprising aspect to this case is that the cultural expert's testimony about many issues was based on an overgeneralization or a stereotyping of culture in China. Although he had been in China twice (for an unknown length of time), he was not necessarily familiar with the entire political and legal situation there, particularly at present. What he described was an idealized, stereotypical, traditional culture, not the actual culture that exists today. Even though he admitted that during his stay in China as an anthropologist he could not recall a single instance of a man killing his wife and had never heard of such an event, he suggested that a husband murdering his wife was accepted in China. The so-called cultural expert's description of Chinese society was not substantiated by objective evidence. It was, in fact, his own American fantasy or misrepresentation (Volpp, 1994, p. 70) that was used by the defense attorney to influence the judge's decision.

There was no one other than the defendant to explain why the couple chose to live separately after migrating to the United States. Was it because Mr. Chen had problems finding a job close to home, or was it because of relational problems between husband and wife? Why would the wife physically abuse her husband, which is rather unusual behavior for a Chinese wife?

Defense counsel presented all the statements made by the defendant as true, without checking carefully into whether and to what degree they might have been products of his own suspicions or possible delusions. Perhaps Mr. Chen was suffering from a delusional disorder—jealous type—with the delusion that his wife was unfaithful to him.

Neglected mental disorder? Based on the material available, there is no indication that a psychiatric expert was involved in the case. However, it is interesting to note that the judge opined that Mr. Chen's behavioral problems constituted mitigating circumstances, such as those caused by premenstrual syndrome or post-traumatic stress disorder. That is, he equated the cultural stress he believed Mr. Chen encountered as a psychological factor, similar to certain kinds of mental disorders.

If we focus more carefully on mental disorders, however, we encounter the issue of whether Mr. Chen might have been suffering from a delusional disorder. Reviewing the available history, we notice that the defendant started suffering from auditory hallucinations at the age of 30, the most common age for developing a delusional disorder, and his symptoms had been diagnosed by physicians in China as a mental disorder. He suffered from visual or auditory hallucinations that his wife's lover was going to harm him. He touched his wife's private parts and concluded that she was having an affair with another man. All this information leads us to suspect that Mr. Chen might have been suffering from a chronic delusional disorder and that his conviction that his wife was having an extramarital affair might have been delusional in nature. Unfortunately, a psychiatric assessment was not pursued in this case; instead, cultural issues inappropriately dominated the evidence brought forward at trial.

Consideration for Being a Recent Immigrant

From a cultural perspective, one aspect of this case was handled correctly. The judge showed sensitivity to cultural considerations in noting that Mr. Chen, as a new immigrant from a foreign county who could not communicate well in English, had been beaten by other inmates while he served 1 and a half years in jail awaiting trial. It was not clear whether his language difficulties, his minority ethnic status, or his possible mental disorder contributed to abuse by other inmates. However non-English-speaking immigrants kept in jail face added stress levels in confinement because of language and cultural problems. (We discussed this issue further in chapter 8.)

CASES THAT PROCEEDED WITH INPUT ON CULTURAL ISSUES

CHINESE STUDENT SUSPECTS HIS KOREAN PROFESSOR OF PERSECUTING HIM

Case Information (Indiana v. Yin, 2002; Matthews, Martell, & Tseng, 2002)

Mr. Yin was a 28-year-old, married Chinese national who was charged with murder in connection with the deaths of two Korean women. Mr. Yin was born in China. As he grew up, he tended to avoid social settings involving groups, except in relationships with some of his closest friends. He excelled in his academic work and eventually entered medical school.

After completing his internship, because he preferred research work to patient care, he applied for an opportunity to study in the United States. He was offered a position as a graduate student in a state university and after 1 year was transferred to another university to work with a Korean American professor of neuroscience on a subject related to genetics. He worked very hard, and his professor described him as "one of the most advanced, most motivated, and most talented students" he had ever taught.

Mr. Yin returned to China shortly thereafter to marry his wife, whom he had known since high school. He returned to the United States with his new wife, who took a position as a teaching assistant at the same university.

Mr. Yin had no past psychiatric history, but his family history revealed that Mr. Yin's grandmother had suffered from an episodic paranoid state with emotional outbursts since age 60, and recently, in her 80s, she had become mentally demented and was being cared for in a nursing home. Besides this, three of Mr. Yin's relatives had committed suicide in the past.

Police Reports

The local police found the bodies of two women, Korean American sisters living together in an apartment near the university campus. Both women were lying in pools of blood, with blankets over their bodies. A bloody paring knife was also found in the apartment. No wallets were found belonging to the victims. Autopsies revealed that both victims suffered incision wounds to their throats and had multiple blunt-force trauma wounds to their heads.

Because one of the victims was a graduate student in the same department as Mr. Yin, the police interviewed him on the evening the bodies were found. Mr. Yin admitted knowing the graduate student, but he denied knowledge of the murders. After this police interview, Mr. Yin urged his wife to take a long ride to another state to visit one of his old schoolmates from China. Without saying anything, he later tried to cross the border into Canada.

While they were on their way to the Canadian border, Mr. Yin confessed to his wife that he was responsible for the deaths of two women and asked her for forgiveness. Mrs. Yin immediately contacted the police department and urged Mr. Yin to turn himself in to the police.

Mr. Yin told police officers that he had been depressed recently because of financial losses in the stock market and was under pressure from the failure of a laboratory experiment. At noon on the day of the murder, he was riding his bicycle when an Asian female driving a vehicle, one of the victims, almost hit him. Mr. Yin reported that he became angry and followed her into her apartment building. When she entered her apartment, he took a hammer out of his backpack and followed her in. He began striking her on the head with the hammer. When she began making noises after falling, he took a knife from the kitchen and stabbed her in the neck.

While cleaning up, the other victim opened the door and entered the apartment. Mr. Yin picked up the hammer and approached her, at which point he recognized her as his fellow graduate student, working in the same department. Seeing no other choice, he hit her head with the hammer and stabbed her in the throat as well, this time with a bigger knife.

Realizing what he had done, he took the victims' car keys and wallets. He left the apartment, bought a new shirt and socks, which he changed into, and threw the bloody clothing and hammer into the river.

Initial Forensic Assessment

A Caucasian forensic psychiatrist was assigned to the case and interviewed Mr. Yin. The psychiatrist was impressed that

Mr. Yin was very slow in answering questions, as if he were searching for the "best" answer for himself. Initially, Mr. Yin put forward the same account that he had presented to the police. However, confronted by the forensic psychiatrist with the lack of plausibility of his story, he provided a new account, which remained quite consistent throughout later retellings.

According to Mr. Yin, his recent financial losses affected his emotional condition. He became anxious and depressed, and he was unable to concentrate fully on his research work. His Korean American professor expected him to finish his research project and complete his reports for publication within several months, but he found that he was not able to make any progress in his work. Another Korean American instructor and, recently, a Korean American female graduate student (who became one of the victims) had recently joined them under the leadership of the Korean American professor, and they all worked together in the same laboratory.

Mr. Yin's research involved the microscopic examination of tiny fruit flies known as drosophila. He reported that while working on his experiments, he developed the view that people he had known had become fruit flies and were showing up under the microscope he was using.

He began to believe that the Korean American people he worked with were jealous of his research and were conspiring to foil it. He even came to believe that the female Korean American graduate student, who had recently joined the laboratory, was assigned to monitor the course of his work more closely. Mr. Yin stopped keeping records of his experiments out of the fear that they would steal his findings. Later, he came to believe that his Korean American professor and his Korean American colleagues were controlling all the operations of the city and that it was the professor who changed people into fruit flies. Mr. Yin began to carry a hammer in his backpack to protect himself from being attacked by the group that was plotting to steal his research data. He believed that the hammer was the best weapon with which to kill his not fully human persecutors.

Under this persecutory delusion, Mr. Yin finally decided that it would be better to take matters into his own hands to eliminate the "enemy." He initially thought about killing the professor, but, fearing that the leader was too powerful for him to attack, he decided instead to first kill the most vulnerable enemy, the female graduate student.

He approached her apartment. When the door opened, a female was standing there; without thinking, he attacked and killed her. When he realized that the person he had killed was not the graduate student, but her sister, he waited until the graduate student returned to the apartment and attacked and killed her as well. After committing these acts and considering what he had done, he began to think about how to escape capture.

Although Mr. Yin seemed to be presenting a true story of what had happened and what he had experienced, and considering he may have been psychotic when he committed the crime, the forensic psychiatrist was unsure to what extent the defendant was telling the truth. His doubt was based not only on the way the defendant described what had happened but also on the fact that he had changed his story quite substantially from what he had said when arrested. Furthermore, a psychologist, who had performed nearly two dozen psychological tests to assess Mr. Yin's neuropsychological function, personality, and psychopathology, reported that the defendant's response to the testing was doubtful. However, the results were difficult for the psychologist to interpret, because the defendant's responses tended to overly pathologize his problems.

Further Assessment with Cultural Considerations

Although Mr. Yin, as a college graduate student, spoke English reasonably well, to ensure that issues of language and culture were appropriately considered in assessing competency issues and mental state at the time of the offense, the forensic mental health team was later joined by a Chinese cultural psychiatrist who was fluent in Mandarin, Mr. Yin's primary language.

At the same time, Mr. Yin, feeling frustrated for not telling the truth and for changing his story, and realizing the difficulties in communicating in detail what actually had happened and what he had experienced in his mind, spent a week writing a 12-page statement in Chinese. He hoped through this statement someone knowledgeable in his mother language could really understand the internal mental experience through which he had gone and the process of committing the offense.

The cultural psychiatrist examined the Chinese statement written by Mr. Yin and found that it was a very rich and informative document. In the statement, Mr. Yin described clearly that in his psychotic condition, he experienced the visual hallucinations of seeing eyelids on the fruit flies under the microscope winking at him, making him believe that those fruit flies were all his friends or classmates who had been transformed by his professor. He also experienced seeing his professor appearing in the TV, making signs to him and warning him to behave. This statement was translated into English for the team as well as for the court.

Subsequently, the Chinese cultural psychiatrist interviewed Mr. Yin, who was quite relieved that he could now communicate with the examiner and present his story in his own language. He soon began to develop trust in the examiner, and he started to communicate without hesitation. Several key issues were clarified and some obstacles encountered in the examination process were removed.

Ruling out the possibility of malingering. The first thing the examining team had to rule out was the possibility that the defendant was making up his psychosis. This question was raised not only because he changed his story but also because he had been medically trained and might have sufficient psychiatric knowledge to malinger psychosis. After careful inquiry the team found that in medical school in China Mr. Yin had received only a minimal education in psychiatry. He had read only a simple, 100-page psychiatric text, had one or two hours of lectures, and had never had any clinical experience with actual psychiatric patients. This information was confirmed as reliable by the cultural psychiatrist, who had been in China for many years and knew that local medical schools at the time provided a very limited psychiatric education. Psychiatry was not considered an important subject, and little effort was made to educate medical students about it.

Clarifying possible ethnic conflict or love affair. Another question raised was whether the defendant committed the offense because of ethnic conflict between Chinese and Koreans. This issue was resolved immediately, after asking several students and faculty about the general situation on the university campus. The existence of any ethnic conflict among students or faculty was denied. Mr. Yin admitted that even in his deluded state, he suspected that the Korean American professor was the leader of a plot trying to persecute him. Nevertheless, he always respected the professor as a competent teacher who had appreciated him as a graduate student from the very beginning. Mr. Yin described the female Korean American graduate student as a charming, friendly person. He had no bad personal feelings toward her, even though she acted as one of the "enemies" who was to watch his behavior and steal his research data. Mr. Yin denied having an affair with her and there was no evidence of one.

Communicating with family and clarifying family history. Another finding in the case supporting the notion that Mr. Yin committed the offense in a psychotic state was his positive family psychiatric history. With Mr. Yin's permission, his parents in China were contacted by letter and on the telephone. His mother was later interviewed when she came to visit Mr. Yin at the presentencing stage. Through letters and telephone interviews, Mr. Yin's family revealed that Mr. Yin's grandmother had suffered from a delusional disorder at an elderly age. The family also revealed that three relatives, one from Mr. Yin's paternal side and two from his maternal side, had committed suicide.

During the Cultural Revolution in China, many people committed suicide because of political pressures and fights, and it was not clear whether this was the case with the three relatives who had committed suicide. No clear answer was obtained from communication by letter. However, when the mother was interviewed face-to-face, she revealed, after some hesitation, that two of the relatives had committed suicide because of personal matters. One uncle committed suicide after being accused of having an affair with his daughter-in-law, and one aunt killed herself when she found out that her ex-boyfriend was going to leave town and desert her. Only one person, an elderly uncle, might have chosen to end his life because of the repeated political struggles he had encountered.

Thus, Mr. Yin's detailed family information supported his having a strong family history of mental illness, and the team felt it was very plausible that he had suffered from a psychotic episode during the period when he committed his offense.

Psychological testing response. As we mentioned previously, Mr. Yin's initial psychological test results were equivocal. During the interview, the cultural psychiatrist explained to Mr. Yin that in American culture honesty is considered very important, not only in society in general but also in court in particular. The cultural psychiatrist explained to Mr. Yin the nature of psychological testing, urging him to give responses honestly according to what was true for him. A fairly extensive battery of tests was administered to the defendant again, and this time the results were considered reliable for interpretation. The test results revealed that the defendant was a very intelligent person, with situational anxiety and depression, as well as underlying evidence of paranoia consistent with a psychotic illness.

The test and interview results led the team to formulate an opinion that the defendant was suffering from a psychotic condition, a major depressive disorder with delusional features, at the time of the offense but was in substantial remission at the time of the assessment.

Legal Outcome

The defendant entered a plea of guilty and the prosecution declined to seek the death penalty because of Mr. Yin's mental disorder. The judge sentenced the defendant to life in prison without parole.

Final Comments

Adding a cultural psychiatrist to the investigating team helped the process of assessment not only by overcoming some of the language barriers encountered but also, most importantly, by ensuring the establishment of trust with the defendant because they came from the same ethnic background. Based on this trusting relationship, more reliable and meaningful information become obtainable, and the defendant's behavior and statements could be more accurately interpreted and comprehended, ensuring a more detailed and comprehensive final formulation and opinion.

There was a minor difference in diagnostic opinion between the investigating team's forensic psychiatrist and the cultural psychiatrist. The American forensic psychiatrist preferred to use the American diagnostic classification system and give a diagnosis of "major depressive disorder" to the American court; the cultural psychiatrist was more in favor of using diagnostic criteria from China for the Chinese patient, giving a diagnosis of "acute delusional disorder." However, it was merely a minor difference of psychiatric views, which did not affect the overall opinion that the defendant was suffering from a psychotic illness at the time the offense was committed and there was significant impairment of mental capacity, although not rising to the level of legal insanity.

A Spiritual Experience or Psychotic Breakdown? (Tina R. Melendrez-Chu, M.D., & Malina Kaulukukui, LSW)

Clinical Case Information (Tina R. Melendrez-Chu, M.D.)

Mr. Kealoha is a 30-year-old, full-blooded Hawaiian male who was brought by his wife to the emergency room. The patient had not eaten or slept for 3 days. His wife was very concerned and urged him to visit the emergency room.

According to his wife, the patient's behavior had begun to change approximately a month before, when he had taken a camping trip as a counselor for Hawaiian youth. During the trip, he had exerted himself physically by hiking, planting taro, and paddling; had slept very little; and had eaten at irregular times. He and the young people also had visited an ancient battleground where the patient's ancestors had fought. According to Mr. Kealoha, he was the descendent of King Kamehameha, the great king who united all the Hawaiian Islands into one kingdom. During the visit to the battleground, he began hearing the voices of his *kupuna* (ancestors). Mr. Kealoha became elated at hearing the voices, believing he had been touched by the ancient chiefs and chosen for a great mission. Subsequently, following Hawaiian tradition, he began to fast to attain spiritual clarity.

After returning home, Mr. Kealoha continued to refuse to eat or sleep. He reverted to speaking only in Hawaiian, and he began to tell his wife that he had an important mission. He became unable to work and showed some unusual behaviors, such as wanting to get in his car and drive in the middle of the night to places considered holy by Native Hawaiians that were a great distance from where he lived. One evening, while naked, he tried to go hiking on a mountain with a waterfall. It was this behavior that prompted his wife to urge him to visit the emergency room, where the patient was noted to be very distrustful of the staff. He would speak only single syllables in Hawaiian to his wife and would not make eye contact with the doctors who tried to examine him. He was severely dehydrated, and blood tests showed that he suffered from an electrolyte imbalance. He looked very angry with his wife and appeared to be in an almost catatonic state. The psychiatrist in the emergency room felt that the patient needed hospitalization, but the patient refused. The psychiatrist considered civil commitment, but, fortunately, the wife was able to persuade the patient at the last moment to agree to voluntary admission. Once the patient was hospitalized, the attending psychiatrist tried to medicate him with a neuroleptic. However, the patient refused to take any medication and also refused food.

Two days after admission, a family meeting was called, and several of the patient's relatives came to the hospital. Upon seeing Mr. Kealoha in his semicatatonic state, the family became very upset with the medical staff. According to Mr. Kealoha's mother, he was receiving communications from his *kupuna*, who would reveal their plans to him. The family agreed with the patient's fasting and with his decision not to be medicated. The patient's mother angrily complained that the attending psychiatrist (who was Caucasian) did not understand local Hawaiian culture, and she accused the staff of interfering with her son's spiritual mission by attempting to medicate him. The patient's whole family, except his wife, believed that Mr. Kealoha was experiencing a blessed gift from his ancestors, who were communicating their wishes to him.

The patient deteriorated mentally more and more, until finally his wife stated that she did not believe any divine spirit would incapacitate her husband to such an extent. The wife told him that as a Hawaiian herself, she believed what he was experiencing was the result of a mental illness and not divine in nature. The wife informed him that if he did not take medicine, he would not be welcome in their home with her anymore. In Hawaiian culture the wife has rather strong powers to influence family affairs. Mr. Kealoha began to take medication and eat his meals, and his psychotic condition subsequently resolved. The patient left the hospital still believing that there was nothing wrong with him, however, he agreed to take his medicines only to save his marriage.

Consultation with a Cultural Expert for Clarification

An aftermath consultation was made with a Hawaiian cultural expert, an experienced Hawaiian female mental health social worker. The consultant (Malina Kaulukukui, LSW) agreed that the question of whether Mr. Kealoha's episode was a spiritual experience or a psychotic breakdown was an interesting one. She commented that one could certainly understand Mr. Kealoha's experience to be culturally consonant because his mental symptoms were noticed shortly after what sounded like a meaningful cultural immersion experience. She pointed out that being a full-blooded Hawaiian has special meaning. Most of the native Hawaiians have intermarried and are only part Hawaiian. The people who are still pure Hawaiian, becoming fewer in number in the community, have a certain pride. Furthermore, believing that he was the descendant of the famous King Kamehameha made it more probable that Mr. Kealoha believed he had been chosen by his Hawaiian ancestors to carry out a special mission.

However, it was further clarified that, as explained in the often quoted text of Hawaiian culture, *Nana I Ke Kumu* (Look to the Source) (Pukui, Haerting, & Lee, 1975), although `ulaleo (hearing supernatural voices or sounds) has traditionally been part of the Hawaiian experience, these voices (and to a larger extent, visions) are for specific purposes (p. 11). They are usually warnings and dispensings of guidance. Also, as a rule, they are meant to bring comfort and solace, and most often they are experiences shared by a group. It was pointed out that those two features distinguished a mental illness from a culturally congruent, special experience. If the voices resulted in harm to the person, it was not a "true" `ulaleo. Mr. Kealoha's experience of trying to hike naked at night, then, was not a culturally congruent, spiritual experience. It also should be noted that fasting is not a traditional Hawaiian activity but rather a Christian import. Eventually, Mrs. Kealoha's remark that no divine spirit would incapacitate her husband demonstrated her understanding of the phenomenon.

We comment that it was important to the family that the phenomenon be tested and their beliefs respected. A critical task of the psychiatric treatment team, then, is to integrate a culture-rooted explanation of behaviors with a psychiatric formal, clinical diagnosis and to form a therapeutic alliance with the family to advance the notion that medication might be a useful intervention.

Further Comments

It is fortunate that the patient's wife happened to be Hawaiian and a professional person of some occupational achievement who had good commonsense knowledge and judgment. She was willing to stand up to her mother-in-law and other family members to insist that her husband was suffering from a psychotic condition and to be supportive of psychiatric treatment. Otherwise, it would have been necessary to hospitalize the patient involuntarily, making it very difficult to treat him, because of the issue of forcing treatment without his consent. In the worst scenario, a professional may have to face a legal battle over the involuntary commitment of a person who claimed to be having a spiritual experience (as did the patient, his mother, and other relatives) and not suffering from a psychotic condition (as diagnosed by clinicians).

FINAL DISCUSSION AND COMMENTS

In the following we make several comments regarding the presentation, discussion, and analysis of the preceding cases.

Cultural ignorance and overuse of cultural excuses. Culture can be entirely ignored or overplayed in court, depending on the understanding of ethnic and cultural issues by the attorneys and the judge and their strategy of either avoiding or emphasizing them; in a similar way the status of a foreigner can be used intensively (as in Mr. Poddar's case), or the differences between American culture and other cultures can be extremely magnified for the benefit of the defendant (as in Mrs. Kimura's case).

Cultural stereotyping and overgeneralization. Similarly, the matter of culture can be examined from different levels (refer to the section "What Is Culture?" in chapter 1). In court the characteristics of a particular culture can be presented by an expert, without consideration of whether the culture was presented as an ideal, an ongoing way of life, or a stereotype. As we have seen, presentations of traditional or ideal culture have been used in court as though they actually represented the current cultural situation (as in Mr. Chen's case).

Every person deserves cultural consideration. It is a fundamental conceptual error to assume that only minority ethnic groups or foreigners have culture, while most people in a society, including the majority ethnic group, do not have their own culture. It is important to recognize that within a society of even the same ethnic background, there are usually many subcultures based on economic, occupational, religious, or geographic factors. Some people lead lives that are very different from others, because of a unique lifestyle with certain beliefs and value systems (as in the Jones case). In other words every person in a society needs cultural consideration if indicated, whether or not they belong to the majority or a minority ethnic or racial group. On the other hand, cultural issues should not be raised simply because people are of a minority ethnic or racial group or are foreigners unless there is substantial evidence to indicate a need to focus on cultural issues.

Cultural considerations during the entire legal process. Another important issue is that cultural consideration is needed during the entire forensic process, starting with the selection of the examiners and experts, through the process of assessment and testing, when interpreting and integrating all the information gathered, and in presenting findings to attorneys and the court. (This is well illustrated in Mr. Yin's case.)

Cultural experts' need for legal orientation and medical knowledge. These cases illustrate that cultural experts may have cultural knowledge but be naive about the law, and they may testify without being fully aware of the legal implications of their testimony. In other words cultural experts involved in litigation need forensic training. Otherwise, their testimony may mislead the jury, and the attorneys may lead them into inaccurate opinions (as in Mr. Chen's case). On the other hand, when cultural experts have full knowledge of mental health issues and are experienced in forensic issues, consulting with them can be very beneficial (as in Mr. Kealoha's case).

Legal professionals' need for cultural training and competency. Of equal importance is the need for legal professionals to receive training in cultural sensitivity, knowledge, and experience to know how to use cultural information in processing the cases legally (such as the judge in the Jones case). Otherwise, legal personnel may end up understanding and using cultural excuses in inappropriate ways (as in Mr. Chen's case).

Forensic psychiatrists' need for cultural consultation and collaboration. Finally, forensic psychiatrists and cultural psychiatrists should learn how to work together as a team. Experts need professional skill and experience collaborating with colleagues from other disciplines, working out minor differences that may occur among them, in order for the collaboration or consultation to result in a fruitful outcome (as illustrated in Mr. Yin's case and in Mr. Kealoha's case).

We elaborate on these issues in further detail in chapter 10, in which we present suggestions for future enhancement of cultural competence in forensic psychiatry.

REFERENCES

American Academy of Psychiatry and the Law. (1993). *Landmark cases* (Vol. 2, pp. 617–645). Bloomfield, CT: Author.

American Academy of Psychiatry and the Law. (2003). *Forensic psychiatry review course.* Bloomfield, CT: Author.

Application of the President and Directors of Georgetown College, 331 F.2d 1000, (CADC), rehearing en banc denied, 331 F.2d 1010, 118 U.S.App.D.C. 90, cert. denied, 377 U.S. 978 (1964).

Blum, D. (1986). *Bad karma: A true story of obsession and murder.* New York: Jove Books (Berkley Publishing Group).

Heisei 14, Wa-No. 30, Aomori Local Court, Japan (2002).

Indiana v. Yin, No. 79D01-0108-CF-77, Tippecanoe Super. Ct. (2002).

Magnarella, P. J. (1991). Justice in a culturally pluralistic society: The cultural defense on trial. *Journal of Ethnic Studies, 19*(3), 65–84.

Matthews, D. B., Martell, D. A., & Tseng, W. S. (2002). *Defendant's pre-sentence investigation.* Re : *Indiana v. Yin.* No. 79D01-0108-CF-77.

Ohara, K. (1963). Characteristics of suicide in Japan, especially of parent-child double suicide. *American Journal of Psychiatry, 120*(4), 382–385.

People v. Chen, No. 87-7774, N.Y. Super. Ct. (1989).

People v. Kimura, No. A-091133, La. Super. Ct. (1985).

Pukui, M. K., Haerting, E. W., & Lee, C. A. (1975). *Nana I Ke Kumu* [Look to the source] (Vol. I). Honolulu, HI: Queen Lili'uokalani Children's Center.

Religion News Blog. (2003). *Polygamist with secretive Mormon sect released from Utah prison.* Retrieved November 21, 2003, from http://www.religionnews-blog/archives/00003469.html

Ross, R. (2003). *Utah moves to outlaw child brides for polygamists.* Cult News.com. Retrieved November 21, 2003, from http:/www.cultnes.com/archives/000052.html

State v. Perry, 610 S.2d 746 (1992).

Tarasoff v. Regents, Univ. of Cal., 551 P.2d 334 (Cal. 1976).

Tseng, W. S. (2001). *Handbook of cultural psychiatry.* San Diego, CA: Academic Press.

Volpp, L. (1994). (Mis)identifying culture: Asian women and the "culture defense." *Harvard Women's Law Journal, 17,* 57–101.

Woo, D. (1989). The People v. Fumiko Kimura: But which people? *International Journal of the Sociology of Law, 17,* 403–428.

World Psychiatric Association. (2002). Declaration of Madrid. Retrieved April 30, 2004, from http://www.wplanet.org/generalinfo/ethic1.html

Yoshimatsu, K. (1992). Suicidal behavior in Japan. In L. P. Kok & W. S. Tseng (Eds.), *Suicidal behavior in the Asia-Pacific region.* Singapore: Singapore University Press.

Yotnotsian, T. (2003). *Polygamy and incest in Utah.* Summer Sundial Online. Retrieved November 21, 2003, from http:/sundial.csu.edu/sun/summer03/opinion/06/23/ utah.yotnotsian.html

10

Closure: Review, Comments, and Suggestions

In this closing chapter we briefly review the status of forensic psychiatry in our society, as well as in other societies, with particular emphasis on its cultural aspects. We then make general comments about culture and the law, and we suggest how the legal system might further adapt to meet the needs of people living in a culturally diverse, contemporary society, while retaining the fundamental spirit of the law. Finally, we offer suggestions on how forensic psychiatrists can improve their cultural competence and how legal personnel can increase their cultural sensitivity. We discuss the importance of cultural sensitivity in the court system for all persons involved in legal proceedings.

REVIEW OF THE PRESENT SITUATION

Forensic Psychiatry in the United States: A Cultural Perspective

Weller, Martin, and Lederach (2001) observed that practitioners in the justice system of the United States have worked very hard, especially over the past few decades, to ensure that the courts do not discriminate against individuals because of their ethnicity, race, or cultural background. However, the premise that equal treatment brings equal justice may not hold in the case of some litigants, because the courts and the justice system embody values and expectations that largely reflect the long-dominant views of Anglo-European culture. The United States is becoming a more diversified ethnic society, and the population has seen a particular increase in the number of persons with Latin American or Asian roots. One challenge for the courts will be dealing fairly and effectively with litigants from different ethnic, racial, and cultural backgrounds.

As we discussed in the beginning of this book (see the section "Incorporation of Cultural Considerations in Legal Systems"), contemporary society has already seen a number of cases in which the legal system of a country has explicitly recognized the need to consider cultural factors in executing the law. For instance, when Micronesia became a Trust Territory of the United States in 1945, the law explicitly provided that "the customs of the inhabitants of the Trust Territory, not in conflict with the (overall) laws of the Trust Territory, shall be preserved" (Bloom & Bloom, 1982). In Alaska, after a conference regarding legal matters was held in 1974, the difficulties experienced by the local people were described as follows: "The village people do not generally understand the State justice system and the State justice system does not generally understand the village people. . . . It was suggested that village life should be governed by village law and customs as much as possible" (Bloom, 1975). Both Alaska and Micronesia are geographically and historically detached from the mainland United States and are inhabited by native peoples who are quite different from the majority of people on the mainland proper. A legal system rooted in cultural traditions may be easier for them to understand and accept than one imposed on them.

On the United States mainland, as pointed out by Levesque (2000), American society did not begin to show concern for the culture of ethnic minority groups until the 1990s. The Indian Child Welfare Act, enacted by the federal government in 1994, protects Native American populations against unnecessary removal of Indian children from their families and tribes. In 1996, in the multiethnic state of California, the law concerning child maltreatment was changed and began to require authorities to pay attention to "cultural and religious childrearing practices and beliefs." The law states that "such practices shall not in themselves create a need for child welfare services to intervene unless the practices present a specific danger to the safety of the child." In a similar way, the child abuse laws of Colorado in 1997 began requiring investigators to take into account accepted child-rearing practices in the parents' culture. Since 1996 New Mexico's statute has required authorities "to provide for a culturally appropriate treatment plan, access to cultural practices and traditional treatment for an Indian child."

Thus, we have begun to see that, here and there, the various states in the United States have begun to require the consideration of ethnic and cultural dimensions to accommodate the needs and rights of people of diverse cultural backgrounds, particularly those from minority ethnic groups. Perhaps in the future we will see the development of a system that considers the culture of every person, regardless of whether his or her ethnic background is minority or majority. Such a system might better ensure that all persons are treated in courts that pay due regard to cultural factors.

Forensic Psychiatry in Various Societies: International Review

Looking beyond our own borders to see how forensic psychiatry is practiced in other societies around the world is both worthwhile and necessary. Through examining how forensic matters are handled in other societies we learn more about cultural and legal differences between our systems. Further, by acquiring an international perspective, we can obtain insight into our own situation and enrich our understanding about where we might aim for future improvement.

At present great variations exist internationally in the level and quality of forensic psychiatry ic services. Societies differ greatly in terms of how the service is valued, the level of sophistication reached, and the volume of service provided (Durst, Jabotinsky-Rubin, & Ginath, 1993; Gonçalves, 1997; Gordon, 1996; Murad, 1999). These differences are associated with various factors, including the level of socioeconomic development of the society, psychiatric sophistication, attitudes toward mental illness, the society's past history, and the culture that is valued in the society.

Indonesia, for example, is a country inhabited by 234 million people, making it the world's fourth most populated society. According to Soejoenoes (1982), the people are divided into about

300 different ethnic groups, speaking approximately 365 languages and dialects and living on an archipelago of 12,000 islands. The culture of the country was originally Malay-Polynesian; however, a strong Islamic influence came later, and now some 95% of the people are Muslim. Three and a half centuries of Dutch colonization profoundly affected day-to-day secular affairs. The new constitution provides that the existing law continues in force, except when it conflicts with a constitutional provision. Thus, the Dutch penal and civil codes continue to operate, which, for psychiatrists and the judiciary, means that the mentally impaired may not be held responsible for their criminal actions. According to Soejoenoes's description, in 1982 there were only about 150 psychiatrists and 7,000 beds for the mentally impaired, about 100 times less than what public mental health officials calculate is needed for the total population. Over the previous 5 years, the courts had requested a psychiatric evaluation of an accused person on only two or three occasions per hospital. Thus, as a developing society of limited economic resources, with interisland transportation difficulties and an extreme shortage of psychiatrists, forensic psychiatric service is very minimal.

In China the development of mental health resources since the beginning of the 20th century, such as the development of medicine generally, has been delayed by the repeated mass destruction in the country associated with civil and international wars, in addition to the decade-long (1966–1976) Cultural Revolution. Forensic psychiatry is in its early stages of development, but the demand for forensic psychiatric services, as might be expected for a country embracing one fifth of the world's population, is very great. According to Li (2000, p. 5), the number of forensic cases reported in the first national forensic psychiatric conference in the year 1987 alone exceeded 10,000, a huge number for the limited number of experienced forensic psychiatrists to handle. Most forensic psychiatric work has been done clinically, without reference to objective measurement instruments, by a small number of forensic psychiatrists. As long as a severe mental disorder is established clinically, the mentally ill offender will not be held legally responsible.

Li (2000, pp. 103–104) asserted that in more than 20% of the cases in which a defendant underwent a forensic psychiatric evaluation, the judge ordered a second assessment by another forensic psychiatrist. The incongruence of opinion among different psychiatrists reached 75%, indicating that even among experts, opinions can be quite different. Psychiatrists may arrive at different opinions about clinical diagnoses.

Japan, which is considered to be a developed society because of its remarkable industrial and economic achievements, has yet to reach desirable levels of psychiatric services. Only a few university-affiliated psychiatric institutions perhaps provide forensic training and services. The forensic psychiatrists available are relatively experienced, but their numbers are not enough to meet the service demands. The legal system in Japan is modeled after the German system: legal decisions are made by judges, and there is no jury system. According to Satsumi and Oda (1995), the judicial system and the process of forensic examination are virtually uniform throughout Japan. Competence to stand trial is rarely assessed in Japan, and plea bargaining is not used. The public prosecutor generally refers mentally ill offenders (who have been acquitted through a verdict of not guilty by reason of insanity) to the prefectural governor for involuntary admission to a psychiatric hospital in accordance with the Mental Health Law enacted in 1988.

The most interesting situation is found in Muslim societies that operate under Islamic jurisprudence. According to Chaleby (1996, 2001), Islam is a monotheistic religion perceived by its followers to involve all aspects of human life, spiritual and environmental, including the laws of society. Islamic jurisprudence, referred to as *Sharia*, has its roots in the scripture (the Koran), which is the word of God, and in the *Hadith*, which contains the sayings of the Prophet Mohammed. Both sources are regarded as so divine that they never have been or ever will be affected by whatever changes occur in the universe at large. However, as new lifestyles and social settings evolve, the need for new laws to deal with new problems becomes inevitable. With the advent of technology and the scientific revolution, a new kind of study, called *Fiqh Al-Nawazel* (namely, the *Fiqh* that deals with new events) was developed and has addressed such issues as brain death, organ transplants, autopsies, and the like.

An Islamic court will not qualify a witness to testify against a Muslim defendant unless the witness is of the same religion. This principle is not limited to criminal cases, but involves civil matters, as well. In other words, only a Muslim can testify in court against a Muslim defendant. As pointed out by Chaleby (1996), the psychiatrist must be a Muslim to present an expert opinion about a Muslim patient.

Regarding criminal responsibility, Islamic law protects mentally incompetent individuals, termed *Majnoun*, and views them as not responsible for their actions. Finding relevance between the nature of the mental illness and the crime committed is not deemed necessary. In other words the law is not concerned with the mental condition of the accused at the time of the crime, as long as the individual already has been proved to have a mental disorder.

Appelbaum's (2002) comments reviewing forensic psychiatry under Islamic jurisprudence (Chaleby, 2001) are particularly insightful from a cultural perspective. That is, American forensic psychiatrists, who are faced with a plethora of jurisdictions in this country, have enough to do just keeping up with developments in the United States, without exploring the approaches taken in the rest of the world. Understandable and practical as this solipsism may be, it tends to blind us to the reality that there are other—sometimes better, or at least different—ways of responding to the issues that form the core of forensic practice, in addition to those that we use every day.

It is clear that the level of forensic psychiatric services, like the different degrees of concern with cultural competence, varies greatly among different societies. This difference can be attributed to many factors, such as socioeconomic development, the political and religious systems, the level of psychiatric development, the historical background of the society, and the cultural system in operation.

To develop cultural competence in forensic mental health, practitioners involved in the legal system would benefit from the knowledge and experience derived from various cultures at the international level. After all, cultural issues are best examined, compared, and comprehended with reference to very diversified cultural examples. In this way, cultural dimensions, like sociopolitical dimensions, can be properly explored, and cultural insight can be obtained through such cross-cultural comparative study.

OVERALL CULTURAL COMMENTS

Individual Versus Society

While proper consideration of the cultural dimensions of each person is important, what is good for the society at large must also be considered. After all, the purpose of enforcing the law is to protect and keep safe the people in the society. When the cultural beliefs and practices of an individual collide with the rules of the society, appropriate protection be given to the society. Traditionally, tension between an individual or small group and the larger society is resolved hierarchically, particularly where society's rules are fair and reasonable (such as, for example, laws against killing others or requiring every citizen to produce identification upon the request of the authorities) and not unreasonably ethnocentric, discriminatory, or displaying ethnocentrism against the minority. Immigrant peoples must learn the rules observed in the host society, and minority people (because of ethnicity, religion, or other factors) need to respect the basic rules followed by others in the society. Resolving these issues will be a delicate and challenging matter. Philosophical and professional judgment requires seeking a proper balance between them.

Absolute Dichotomization Versus Relative Grading

As an extension of this idea, we must recognize that not everything in the world can necessarily be dichotomized with absolute definition. Things cannot always be categorized into black and white, good and bad, or right and wrong. We pass through a developmental stage early in life in which, cognitively, we view the world in dichotomous terms. This is followed by a later stage in which we realize that there is always a gray area between black and white, and many areas in between can be found even for good and bad or right and wrong. Although things are often not simply and absolutely divided into two groups in life, in law making the distinction between right and wrong is fundamentally important (Slovenko, 2002). However, it is equally critical to recognize that between the polarized extremes there is room for various gradations. It is not easy for the law to make all-or-none culpability decisions; it is much easier to use a schema of grading (Finkel & Slobogin, 1995).

This is particularly important when the law decides the degree of severity that should be meted out to offenders at the sentencing stage. Individual factors, such as the nature of the motivation, the severity of the offense, and the mental condition of the defendant at the time of the offense are all factors that are usually considered. There is room to consider an additional factor; namely, culture. In practice, considering culture means comprehending the meaning of the offense to the individual from a cultural perspective, and possibly making adjustments to culpability based on the individual's cultural views, thoughts, beliefs, and values relative to the unlawful behavior (Neapolitan, 2001). This is applicable particularly to the argument for diminished responsibility (Diamond, 1978).

Appropriate Application of Cultural Knowledge and Insight

Whether society accepts cultural relativism or obeys the spirit of universality, legal personnel and related experts should gain knowledge and familiarity with the ethnic and cultural backgrounds of the persons involved in proceedings. This may help them develop a better understanding of the issues involved and make more culturally appropriate and competent assessments and judgments. Not only is cultural knowledge necessary but, more important, the law should be applied with appropriate cultural empathy and insight. We must focus not only on the individual offenders; we should also give attention and consideration to the family, friends, colleagues, and neighbors of the accused for a more comprehensive understanding of his or her life. That person's culpability can be assessed based on a systematic review of the situation and the life of the offender (Regan & Alderson, 2002). This is a basic, cultural approach.

Just as it would be a mistake if our basic approach ignored relevant ethnic or cultural factors, it would be equally wrong to overuse ethnic or cultural excuses in the legal system. Cultural explanations must be used only when they are relevant and there is sufficient reason to do so. The culturally competent practice of forensic psychiatry requires distinguishing when cultural issues are appropriate, relevant, and suitable for application to the legal setting.

Cultural Consideration for Every Person

We should emphasize that not all offenders who are ethnic minorities will automatically require cultural considerations in court. Moreover, even offenders from the ethnic majority will at times deserve cultural considerations in the legal process when there is sufficient reason to believe that the offenders' cultural beliefs have a significant impact on the wrongful behavior committed. The idea is that every person, regardless of whether he or she is from a minority or a majority ethnic group, is influenced by his or her own culture in his or her mind, behavior, and, in particular, concepts of right and wrong. This may affect the person's criminal intent (*mens rea*) for the incident offense. People in the majority group, in particular, often have distinguishable subcultural differences from the so-called ordinary people of the majority, in terms of socioeconomic level, religious beliefs, historical roots, or other factors. Each person should have his or her cultural factors taken into account, when necessary, in assessing the wrongful act and criminal intent. Legal punishment may then need to be adjusted accordingly.

Input Throughout the Legal Process: From Assessment to Sentencing

Finally, we emphasize that culture should not be considered only at the sentencing stage of a case but also must extend through the entire judicial process, from beginning to end. Attention should be paid to cultural issues starting from the initial assessment stage, when approaching the parties in the suit, in deciding how to evaluate them, in determining how to formulate a professional opinion about the wrongful behavior at issue, in deciding how to communicate and emphasize one's expert opinion in court during the trial, at the sentencing stage, and during the postsentencing care of the offender. Cultural issues should be considered from the very beginning and continue throughout the entire process (for details see the section "Cultural Input in Various Phases of the Legal Process" in chapter 6).

SUGGESTIONS FOR THE FUTURE

Cultural Competence Training

Requirements for training. In response to our society becoming more ethnically diverse and emphasizing human rights to a greater degree, there is an increased need to provide culturally competent medical and psychiatric care for its people. Offering cultural training has become an official requirement in the formal curriculum of programs training future physicians and psychiatrists. Extending this to the field of forensics, we suggest that forensic psychiatrists also undergo cultural training, as part of their mandatory continuing-education requirements, to fulfill the urgent need for professionals with such knowledge and experience.

Consultation to cultural experts. Whenever forensic psychiatrists or psychologists encounter forensic cases that deserve cultural consideration, they should seek professional consultation from cultural experts. Experts such as cultural anthropologists, cross-cultural psychologists, or cultural psychiatrists can assist them in clarifying the relevant cultural matters, particularly if these matters extend beyond their professional knowledge and experience. Not every culturally focused behavioral scientist will possess the needed knowledge and information about the particular ethnic or cultural group related to the case. Therefore, a suitable expert must be researched, selected, and approached. In general, cultural anthropologists will have more anthropological knowledge and a better understanding of general concepts. If chosen correctly, they will have more information about the particular culture concerned. However, they may not be familiar with clinical issues, particularly those related to psychiatric matters. In contrast, cultural psychiatrists may have enough knowledge regarding the cultural aspects of psychiatric matters, but they may not have the depth of information needed about the cultural behavior of a particular ethnic group. The strengths and shortcomings of the cultural experts of various professional disciplines, as well as the competencies and experiences of individual practitioners, need to be recognized and approached accordingly.

Collaboration between cultural psychiatry and forensic psychiatry. We strongly encourage forensic psychiatrists to work collaboratively with cultural psychiatrists on these cases. In general, forensic psychiatrists are relatively knowledgeable regarding legal issues but have less familiarity with cultural matters. The reverse is usually also true, that cultural psychiatrists are familiar with culture, at least at a conceptual level, but often are unfamiliar with legal matters. By working together they can compensate for their respective shortcomings and become a much stronger professional team. Deficiencies will be minimized through combining their professional knowledge and experiences.

Increased Cultural Awareness and Sensitivity for Legal Professionals

Attorneys and judges should become informed about and sensitive to cultural issues, so that a more culturally relevant legal process can be conducted. Through exposure to cases that raise culturally related issues, legal professionals may be able to enhance their understanding of cultural matters and develop the necessary cultural awareness, sensitivity, and knowledge.

Furthermore, attorneys and judges may find it useful to participate in formal seminars that address specifically the cultural aspects of forensic psychiatry and legal issues, through either professional conventions or specially held conferences that grant continuing legal education credits. Such educational programs are not widely in operation at present, but special efforts should be made to make them available to legal professionals. Such seminars should allow for mutual discussion and exchanges of opinions by participants from multiple disciplines, including legal professionals, cultural anthropologists, sociologists, social workers, cross-cultural psychologists, and cultural psychiatrists, as well as forensic psychiatrists and psychologists.

Culture, Court, and Legal Systems

As we have stated from the beginning of this book (see the section "Effects of Culture in Court" in chapter 1), many professional groups operate within their inherited professional cultures. The legal system is no exception; it operates and functions within a legal culture. For instance, the law, unlike science, requires a yes or no answer in making a final decision (Slovenko, 2002, p. xxiii). Psychiatrists, as practitioners of applied behavioral science, conceptually regard mental disorders as occurring along a continuum of imperceptible gradations from mild to extreme pathology, whereas criminal law allows for no gradations. For the purposes of conviction there is no twilight zone between abnormality and insanity. In the legal system, an offender must be wholly sane or wholly insane.

The law focuses primarily on the individual who commits unlawful behavior. There is often less concern about the extent to which the individual is affected by the people around him or her, including the environment or the culture, in undertaking the wrongful behavior and to what extent the family or people surrounding him or her deserve to share culpability (Regan & Alderson, 2002). Individualism versus collectivism is a basic difference in professional culture for the law and for culture-focused behavior science and psychiatry.

Beyond this inherited legal culture, there is also the culture of the legal personnel involved in the case. This includes attorneys, jurors, and, of course, the judge. They are all human beings and they all have unique personalities as well as unique sets of cultural beliefs, values, and attitudes beyond their professional knowledge and experiences, which, either directly or indirectly, will affect their functioning in the legal process.

The court is a legal institution affected by the factors mentioned previously, plus social, administrative, and various logistical matters. It is often operated in a certain way that may or may not be suitable for people of diverse ethnic or cultural backgrounds. As a result, it has recently been advocated that when clients seek help from the court, particularly for mitigation of conflicts or disputes, the service to be provided by the court must be suitable for the ethnic-cultural background of the clients to be served.

For instance, Weller and colleagues (2001) suggested that when offering services to Latino groups for family dispute resolution, the court must provide services that are different from those offered to Anglo-European groups. For example, with court-attached family mediation for litigants, the mediator must recognize the importance of the extended family for Latino people and may want to gather perspectives from extended family members, including grandparents or godparents, rather than focus on the litigants individually (as is done customarily for Anglo-European litigants). From the standpoint of procedure, the mediator may want to allow the litigants to take time to vent, perhaps even about things other than the dispute before the court. It may be time-consuming and not appear to be functional, but it may be important in moving the parties to agreement. During the negotiation, the mediators may have to be more direct, because the parties may want to have their say to someone in authority who will provide some direction. Latino parties may want someone to help them get through the system. That is, the mediator may have to become involved with the parties after an agreement has been reached, to enforce the agreement and help them tie into other social agencies in the community.

In summary, there is a great deal of room for future improvement in the courts to meet the needs of people from various
ethnic and cultural backgrounds. Within the constraints of reality, there is still a great need for concern, attention, and effort
to provide courts that are culturally relevant, responsive, meaningful, and effective for the culturally diverse people in our
society.

REFERENCES

Appelbaum, P. S. (2002). Review of book: Forensic psychiatry in Islamic
jurisprudence, by K. S. Chaleby (2001). *Journal of the American Academy of
Psychiatry and the Law, 30*(3), 462–463.

Bloom, J. D. (1975). Cross-cultural forensic psychiatry in Alaska. *Bulletin of the
American Academy of Psychiatry and the Law, 3*(4), 252–256.

Bloom, J. D., & Bloom, J. L. (1982). An examination of the use of transcultural
data in the courtroom. *Bulletin of the American Academy of Psychiatry and the
Law, 10*(2), 89–95.

Chaleby, K. S. (1996). Issues in forensic psychiatry in Islamic jurisprudence.
Bulletin of the American Academy of Psychiatry and the Law, 24(1), 117–124.

Chaleby, K. S. (2001). *Forensic psychiatry in Islamic jurisprudence.* Herndon, VA:
International Institute of Islamic Thought.

Diamond, B. L. (1978). Social and cultural factors as a diminished capacity
defense in criminal law. *Bulletin of the American Academy of Psychiatry and
the Law, 6*(2), 195–208.

Durst, R., Jabotinsky-Rubin, K., & Ginath, Y. (1993). A look at court appointed
psychiatric evaluations in Israel with special reference to criminal liability.
Medicine and Law, 12, 153–163.

Finkel, N. J., & Slobogin, C. (1995). Insanity, justification, and culpability
toward a unifying schema. *Law and Human Behavior, 19*(5), 447–464.

Gonçalves, R. A. (1997). Criminological and legal psychology in Portugal:
Past, present and future. In S. Redondo, V. Garrido, J. Péres, & R. Barberet
(Eds.), *Advances in psychology and law: International contributions* (pp. 34–42).
Berlin: de Gruyter.

Gordon, H. (1996). Forensic psychiatry in Israel and Britain: Some developing
links. *Israel Journal of Psychiatry Related Sciences, 33*(3), 194–195.

Levesque, R. J. R. (2000). Cultural evidence, child maltreatment, and the law.
Child Maltreatment, 5(2), 146–160.

Li, C. P. (2000). *Practice and theory of forensic psychiatric assessment: Including
analysis and discussion of 97 forensic cases.* Beijing, China: Beijing Medical
University Publisher. (In Chinese).

Murad, I. J. (1999). Psychiatry in the Palestine authority: Legal, ethical and
forensic issues. *Israel Journal of Psychiatry Related Sciences, 36*(1), 65–74.

Neapolitan, J. L. (2001). An examination of cross-national variations in punitiveness. *International Journal of Offender Therapy and Comparative Criminology, 45*(6), 691–710.

Regan, J., & Alderson, A. (2002, August). Criminal responsibility or lack of cultural awareness? The Andrea Yates story. *Tennessee Medicine, 337–339* .

Satsumi, Y., & Oda, S. (1995). Mentally ill offenders referred for psychiatric examination in Japan: Descriptive statistics of a university unit of forensic assessment. *International Journal of Law and Psychiatry, 18*(3), 323–331.

Slovenko, R. (2002). *Psychiatry in law/law in psychiatry.* New York: Brunner-Routledge.

Soejoenoes, H. R. M. (1982). Forensic psychiatric services in Indonesia. *International Journal of Law and Psychiatry, 5,* 439–440.

Weller, S., Martin, J. A., & Lederach, J. P. (2001). Fostering culturally responsive courts: The case of family dispute resolution for Latinos. *Family Court Review, 39*(2), 185–202.

INDEX

CPSIA information can be obtained
at www.ICGtesting.com
Printed in the USA
FFHW011814060319
50860896-56271FF